W9-AZD-594

Study Guide to Accompany
ORGANIZATIONAL BEHAVIOR
SIXTH EDITION

Don Hellriegel
Texas A & M University

John W. Slocum, Jr.
Southern Methodist University

Richard W. Woodman
Texas A & M University

Prepared by
Roger D. Roderick
California State University-Long Beach

Ariel M. Castillo
Center of Management Innovation

WEST PUBLISHING COMPANY

St. Paul   New York   Los Angeles   San Francisco

WEST'S COMMITMENT TO THE ENVIRONMENT

In 1906, West Publishing Company began recycling materials left over from the production of books. This began a tradition of efficient and responsible use of resources. Today, up to 95% of our legal books and 70% of our college texts are printed on recycled, acid-free stock. West also recycles nearly 22 million pounds of scrap paper annually—the equivalent of 181,717 trees. Since the 1960s, West has devised ways to capture and recycle waste inks, solvents, oils, and vapors created in the printing process. We also recycle plastics of all kinds, wood, glass, corrugated cardboard, and batteries, and have eliminated the use of styrofoam book packaging. We at West are proud of the longevity and the scope of our commitment to our environment.

Production, Prepress, Printing and Binding by West Publishing Company.

CONTENTS

CONTENTS

TO THE STUDENTS

SOME NOTES ON HOW TO USE THIS STUDY GUIDE

This study guide is intended for your <u>active</u> use. Use it actively! It will help you to learn the material (and to do well on your exams). Use it as an initial learning aid after reading each chapter, and then again as a review mechanism when studying for quizzes and exams.

There are five parts to each chapter in the Guide:

1. A list of the authors' "Learning Objectives," to <u>jog your memory</u>;

2. A "Chapter Outline" of the material contained in text, to help you <u>highlight</u> and <u>organize</u> the material;

3. A set of "Directed Questions," to help you <u>recognize</u> concepts, principles, and terms;

4. A set of "Applied Questions," to help you <u>understand</u> the important ideas set forth by the authors; and

5. A "Programmed Study Supplement," to give you a final <u>summary</u> of the chapter by guiding you once more through what the authors have identified as the "Key Words and Concepts" of the chapter.

Be sure to <u>think</u> about the **LEARNING OBJECTIVES** before continuing on through the rest of the chapter. They are the <u>behavioral</u> objectives. You should be able to <u>do</u> those activities itemized for each chapter. If you cannot, stop and ask yourself: Is it because I do not <u>recall</u> the points the authors have made? Or, is it because I do not <u>understand</u> the meaning of what the authors have said? Once you have determined what you need to work on--continue.

The **CHAPTER OUTLINES** cover the main concepts, definitions, explanations, and, in many cases, examples. The material is categorized in a way that is intended to help you best organize it for studying. The principal parts of the chapters are outlined and you are asked to provide the details. This exercise is structured in such a way that you will familiarize yourself with the key points made by the authors. Understand, however, that this is <u>not a substitute for reading the text</u>, but instead should be done <u>after</u> you have read the text.

The wording of the **DIRECTED QUESTIONS** comes almost directly out of the text. The questions are designed to assist you in <u>recognizing</u> the principal ideas contained in the chapters. They are organized according to the major headings of the chapter outline in the text. Go back into the text and read the material surrounding any questions that may cause you trouble.

The **APPLIED QUESTIONS** are intended to help you <u>understand</u> the meaning of the principal ideas in the chapters. They test your understanding in some cases simply by expressing the ideas somewhat differently than did the authors, requiring that you apply the material to examples of life and/or work situations by answering direct questions or by solving brief problem scenarios. These questions are grouped either by chapter outline headings or by learning objectives.

Finally, the **PROGRAMMED STUDY SUPPLEMENT** closes each set of exercises by using the authors' list of "Key Words and Concepts" to give you a <u>summary</u> of what they consider most important in the chapter. By the time you get to this section, these words and concepts should stand out in your mind. But, if not, open the text to the list provided near the end of the chapter in question. Before going on to the next chapter, be sure you have mastered these words and concepts well enough to enable you to go through these questions quickly and without error.

You will notice that the answers are provided in the right margins for each of the different types of exercises. This allows you to check your own answers quickly, without leafing through either this study guide or the text. Cover these answers with a sheet of paper, revealing each only after you have selected your own answer. Hopefully, you will find the exercises both easy to use and helpful.

Good luck!!

CHAPTER 1

MANAGERS AND ORGANIZATIONAL BEHAVIOR

LEARNING OBJECTIVES

When you read and when you review Chapter 1, keep in mind the learning objectives which have been established by the authors. Look them over first as a guide to picking out the most important parts of the chapter, and then think about them as you are going through the chapter. When you have finished the chapter, ask yourself whether you have met the objectives.

The authors intend that when you have finished studying this chapter you should be able to:

* Discuss how the changing demographics of the work force and changes in organizations will affect employees.
* State how managers spend their time during a day.
* Describe the roles that managers play.
* Define three approaches to studying organizational behavior.
* Explain how using contingency concepts in studying organizational behavior will help you as a manager.

CHAPTER OUTLINE

After you have read the chapter, complete the following outline.

I.   SOME INITIAL DEFINITIONS.

    A.   Organizational iceberg:

    B.   Organizational behavior:

II.   CHANGING WORLD OF WORK.

    A.   Work Force Issues.

        1.

        2.

        3.

        4.

        5.

    B.   Revolutionary Changes in Organizations.

        1.

        2.

        3.

        4.

    C.   The challenge that the changing world of work holds for managers is:

III. BASIC CHARACTERISTICS OF MANAGERIAL WORK.

    A.

    B.

C.

D.

E.

IV. MINTZBERG'S MANAGERIAL ROLES.

A. Interpersonal Roles.

1.

2.

3.

B. Informational Roles.

1.

2.

3.

C. Decisional Roles.

1.

2.

3.

4.

V. APPROACHES TO ORGANIZATIONAL BEHAVIOR.

A. Traditional Approach.

1. Frederick W. Taylor's approach was

2. Mayo & Roethlesberger's approach was

3.   McGregor's approach was

B.   Systems Approach.

1.   The systems approach assures that

2.   The systems approach emphasizes

3.   Basic elements of the systems approach.

a.

b.

c.

C.   Contingency Approach

1.   The basis of the contingency approach is that

2.   The primary advantage of the contingency approach is that

VI.   FUNDAMENTAL CONCEPTS OF ORGANIZATIONAL BEHAVIOR.

A.   The basics of human behavior include

B.   A situational perspective of human behavior means

1.   The components of a specific situation are

a.

b.

c.

d.

e.

C. Organizations are social systems in which people:

1. Have what kinds of needs

a.

b.

2. Are influenced by

D. Organizations require interaction between

1. _____, which is

2. _____, which is

VII. ORGANIZATIONAL BEHAVIOR: A FRAMEWORK

A. The basic components of organizational behavior are

1.

2.

3.

4.

B. Individual Processes include

1.

2.

3.

4.

5.

6.

7.

C.   Interpersonal and group processes include

1.

2.

3.

4.

5.

D.   Organizational processes include

1.

2.

3.

4.

5.

E.   Individual and organizational change processes include

1.

2.

3.

DIRECTED QUESTIONS

I.   What Do Managers Do?

  1.   "Fragmentation," as a characteristic of managerial
       work, means that:
       a)   Most managerial actions take a relatively short
            time;
       b)   A manager typically works undisturbed for only   b
            short periods of time;
       c)   A manager works at a large number of things each
            day;
       d)   None of the above.
  2.   Regarding communication, most managers:
       a)   Prefer written communication over oral
            communication;
       b)   Use written communication to transmit and   d
            receive "live" information;
       c)   Use oral communication for events involving
            large numbers of people;
       d)   Prefer oral communication over written
            communication.
  3.   Managers tend to:
       a)   Work in a stimulus-response environment;
       b)   Respond to immediate situations;
       c)   Use unscheduled and informal meetings as   d
            important sources of information;
       d)   All of the above;
       e)   None of the above.
  4.   Which of the following is characteristic of
       managers' involvement in communication networks:
       a)   They spend more time with subordinates than
            with superiors;
       b)   Their communication with superiors is usually
            informal;   a
       c)   They are usually on the outer edges of
            communication networks that include
            subordinates, peers, and superiors.
  5.   Regarding managers' rights and duties:
       a)   Managers make the decisions that initially
            define their long-term commitments;
       b)   Managers are generally restricted to the   a
            information channels established for them;
       c)   Managers need to avoid obligations such as
            speeches whenever possible;
       d)   All of the above.
  6.   Which of the following is a true statement:
       a)   The importance of "hot" information decreases as
            the managerial level increases;

b) The frequency of interaction with others is   b
    different at different managerial levels;
c) Managers spend most of their time reading or
    preparing written communication;
d) All of the above.

II. Changing World of Work.

1. Which of the following types of managerial skills
    is <u>not</u> in increasing demand?
    a) Specialization;
    b) Conceptual;   a
    c) Communication;
    d) Interpersonal.
2. Gender related issues include:
    a) Promotion;
    b) Glass ceiling;   d
    c) Growing part of the work force;
    d) All of the above.
3. Race/ethnicity issues include:
    a) Promotion;
    b) Glass ceiling;
    c) Growing part of the work force;   d
    d) All of the above.
4. Today's "organizational revolution" includes:
    a) Expanding organizational size;
    b) Shrinking service sector;
    c) Increasing globalization;   c
    d) All of the above.

III. The Roles Managers Play.

1. Ceremonial duties that are important to an
    organization's success are part of the:
    a) Disturbance handler role;
    b) Company spokesperson role;   c
    c) Figurehead role;
    d) Disseminator role.
2. Entrepreneurship, disturbance handling, and
    resource allocation are types of:
    a) Interpersonal roles;
    b) Informational roles;   c
    c) Decisional roles.
3. A manager seeking to improve an organization by
    initiating new projects is playing a(n):
    a) Leadership role;
    b) Entrepreneurship role;   b
    c) Resource allocator role;
    d) Disseminator role.

4. The responsibility for directing and coordinating the activities of subordinates is found in the:
    a) Monitor role;
    b) Leadership role;   b
    c) Liaison role;
    d) Figurehead role.
5. The responsibility for dealing with people other than subordinates or supervisors is found in the:
    a) Figurehead role;
    b) Spokesperson role;   d
    c) Leadership role;
    d) Liaison role.
6. Regarding the ten managerial roles:
    a) No one manager can perform all ten;
    b) Managers need to be able to perform all ten   c
        roles equally well;
    c) Personal style and managerial level affect a
        manager's relative emphasis of the ten roles;
    d) None of the above.

IV. Approaches to Organizational Behavior.

1. The systems approach:
    a) Is represented by the works of Taylor, Mayo,
        and McGregor;
    b) Stems from the belief that no one set of rules   d
        can apply to all situations;
    c) Assumes that people do what they do for simple,
        uncomplicated reasons;
    d) None of the above.
2. "Universal principles" were the basis for:
    a) The traditional approach;   a
    b) The systems approach;
    c) The contingency approach.
3. The contingency approach:
    a) Does not consider "principles" of behavior;
    b) Assumes all workers want challenging jobs;
    c) Emphasizes the interrelatedness of the   d
        various parts of an organization;
    d) Looks at the characteristics of each situation
        and derives managerial recommendations
        accordingly.
4. Which approach assumes multiple causation and a
    complex interrelationship of forces:
    a) The traditional approach;   b
    b) The systems approach;
    c) The contingency approach.

V.   Basic Concepts of the Contingency Approach.

    1.   Advantages of using the contingency approach
          include:
          a)   It requires managers to diagnose situations
                correctly;
          b)   It pushes organizations toward adapting to   d
                different situations;
          c)   It pushes managers to adapt to internal and
                external change;
          d)   All of the above.
    2.   The contingency approach deals with:
          a)   Problems confronting the organization;
          b)   Opportunities available to the organization;   d
          c)   Changing environments;
          d)   All of the above.

APPLIED QUESTIONS

I.   Changing World of Work.

    1.   Which of the following changes require increased
          interpersonal skills among managers?
          a)   Glass ceiling;
          b)   More women in the workforce;   d
          c)   Greater race/ethnic diversity;
          d)   All of the above.
    2.   Which of the following is likely to present the
          greatest barrier to solving the glass ceiling
          problem?
          a)   Expanding service organizations;
          b)   Downsizing;   b
          c)   Globalization;
          d)   None of the above related to the problem.

II.   What Do Managers Do?

    1.   A manager arrives at work at 8:00 a.m., and
          immediately engages in the following: five
          telephone calls of approximately 5 minutes each;
          one 3-minute trip to his assistant's office;
          signing of six letters; and touching base with
          his boss about a meeting scheduled for the next
          day. This is an example of which characteristics
          of managerial activity:
          a)   Brevity;   a
          b)   Preference for non-routine tasks;
          c)   Face-to-face communication.

2. A manager makes the decision to pursue a goal of a 10% increase in market penetration by 1988. Having done this, he must then do all those things that are necessary to support that pursuit. This best   d
exemplifies which characteristic of managerial work:
   a) Hard work in a variety of activities;
   b) Preference for non-routine tasks;
   c) Involvement in communication networks;
   d) Blend of rights and duties.

3. An employee was recently promoted to a managerial position as a reward for highly positive performance ratings in the past. His strongest point has been his diligence in following tasks through to their completion and making certain all details are wrapped up. Which of the following characteristics of managerial work may cause him most trouble: a
   a) Hard work in a variety of activities;
   b) Preference for non-routine tasks;
   c) Involvement in communication networks;
   d) Blend of rights and duties.

4. The inclusion of an "executive summary" at the front of a detailed statistical report reflects an understanding of which of the following characteristics of managerial work:
   a) The frequency of interaction with others varies by level of management;   d
   b) The importance of "grapevine" information increases with the level of manager;
   c) Managers have a preference for written communication;
   d) Managers work hard on a variety of activities.

III. The Roles Managers Play.

1. A company is surprised by the union's decision to walk out on strike. The Industrial Relations Manager temporarily stops all other activities in which he is involved and devotes full attention to the strike. Which of the following roles is he laying:
   a) Figurehead;   c
   b) Disseminator;
   c) Disturbance handler;
   d) Resource allocator.

2. From time to time during the strike the Industrial Relations Manager issued news releases to all supervisors in the plant, filling them in on the progress of things. Which role is involved in this activity:

      a) Figurehead;

      b) Leadership;

      c) Disseminator;

      d) Monitor.

    c

3. A manager calls her employees together to explain the importance of getting a particular job done on time, and assures them that they will be rewarded if the goal is met. She is serving in a:

      a) Monitor role;

      b) Spokesperson role;

      c) Liaison role;

      d) Leadership role.

    d

4. The Vice President meets briefly with each new college graduate being interviewed for a job, just prior to the candidate's departure from the plant. Which role is involved in this activity:

      a) Figurehead;

      b) Leadership;

      c) Negotiator;

      d) Disturbance handler.

    a

IV. Approaches to Organizational Behavior.

1. A manager whose behavior is premised on the assumption that it is his role to coerce and control employees is using which of the following approaches to organizational behavior;

      a) Systems approach;

      b) Contingency approach;

      c) Theory Y approach;

      d) None of the above.

    d

2. A consultant, using records of results that have occurred elsewhere, convinces top management at a small Tennessee manufacturing facility that job enrichment will solve the productivity problems that exist there. First line supervisors argue that some of their workers may not react well to such a program. These supervisors are arguing for which approach to organizational behavior:

      a) Systems approach;

      b) Contingency approach;

      c) Traditional approach;

      d) None of the above.

    b

3. A manager who accepts the explanation that "pay" is the sole cause of turnover in his organization might well need a better understanding of which approach to organizational behavior:

      a) Systems approach;

      b) Interpersonal approach;

    a

c) Traditional approach;
d) Theory X approach.
4. Which of the following approaches to organizational behavior is most useful to an organization needing to take into consideration the constantly changing nature of the environment in which it operates:
a) Systems approach;   b
b) Contingency approach;
c) Traditional approach;
d) Theory Y approach.
5. In which of the following approaches to organizational behavior is it the case that the key to becoming a successful manager is the ability to diagnose situations correctly:
a) Systems approach;   b
b) Contingency approach;
c) Theory X approach;
d) Scientific Management approach.

PROGRAMMED STUDY SUPPLEMENT

1.	The inability of a manager to see beyond the results of a performance to the behavioral aspects of that performance is known as _____.	organizational iceberg
2.	The study of _____ provides a systematic way to attempt to understand the behavior of people in organizations.	organizational behavior
3.	A _____ is an organized set of behaviors.	role
4.	The _____ include such sub-roles as disturbance handling and resource allocation.	decisional roles
5.	"Monitor," "disseminator," and "spokesperson" are _____	informational roles
6.	"Figurehead," "leadership," and "liaison" are _____.	interpersonal roles

7.   The _____ to organizational behavior emphasizes principles that were applicable to all organizations and tasks.

traditional approach

---

8.   The _____ to organizational behavior emphasizes the interrelatedness of the various parts of an organization.

systems approach

---

9.   The basis of the _____ to organizational behavior is the belief that no one set of rules can be applied to all situations.

contingency approach

---

10. _____ refers to how people are grouped within an organization.

structure

---

11. _____ refers to how the sequence of activities in an organization are carried out.

process

---

12. The _____ represent a systematic body of knowledge drawn from sociology, psychology, and anthropology for the purpose of helping us understand why and how people behave as they do.

behavioral sciences

---

13. _____ implies an autocratic approach to managing people, while _____ implies a humanistic and supportive approach.

Theory X;

Theory Y

---

14. The _____ role includes the handling of symbolic and ceremonial tasks.

figurehead

---

15. The _____ role involves responsibility for directing and coordinating the tasks of subordinates in order to accomplish organizational goals.

leadership

---

16. The _____ role pertains to the development of information sources both inside and outside of the organization.

liaison

17. The _____ role involves the manager seeking and receiving information.

monitor

---

18. In the _____ role, the manager shares and distributes information to other members of the organization.

disseminator

---

19. In the _____ role, the manager seeks to improve the department and organization by initiating new projects or identifying changes needed in the organization.

entrepreneur

---

20. In the _____ role, managers resolve conflicts between subordinates or departments.

disturbance handler

---

21. In the _____ role, a manager is responsible for deciding who will get which resources and how much they will get.

resource allocator

---

22. In the _____ role, a manager bargains with others to represent the organization.

negotiator

---

23. An individual's ability to apply specific methods, procedures, and techniques to a problem refers to his/her _____.

technical skills

---

24. _____ refer to the individual's ability to send and receive information, thoughts, feelings, and attitudes.

communication skills

---

25. An individual's ability to understand how his/her organization is affected by competitors refer to his/her _____.

conceptual skills

---

26. _____ include the ability to lead, motivate, manage conflict, and work with others.

interpersonal skills

27. The _____ is a transparent barrier   glass
     that is so strong that it prevents women   ceiling
     and minorities from moving up management
     ranks.

---

28. _____ is the process of terminating   downsizing
     people in order to improve efficiency.

---

29. _____ uses text editing to transmit   electronic
     written information quickly, inexpensively,   mail
     and efficiently.

---

30. In the _____, the manager makes   spokesperson
     official statements to outsiders on behalf   role
     of the organization.

---

31. The _____ is the technology   transforma-
     that the organization uses to transform   tion
     _____ into _____.   process;
                                                             inputs;
                                                             outputs

---

32. _____ is knowledge of results.   feedback

CHAPTER 2

LEARNING ABOUT ORGANIZATIONAL BEHAVIOR

LEARNING OBJECTIVES

When you read and when you review Chapter 2, keep in mind the learning objectives which have been established by the authors. Look them over first as a guide to picking out the most important parts of the chapter, and then think about them as you are going through the chapter. When you have finished the chapter, ask yourself whether you have met the objectives.

The authors intend that when you have finished studying this chapter you should be able to:

* State the three steps in the scientific approach.
* Give the conditions for well and poorly designed research projects.
* Describe the four research designs commonly used in organizational research.
* Describe the ways that individuals can gather data for a research project.
* State three ethical dilemmas that individuals could face when carrying out their research in organizations.

CHAPTER OUTLINE

After you have read the chapter, complete the following outline.

I.   THE SCIENTIFIC APPROACH.

    A.   The scientific approach is

    B.   The three basic steps of the scientific approach are

        1.

        2.

        3.

II.   PREPARATION OF RESEARCH DESIGNS.

    A.   A research design is

        1.   The plan is

        2.   The structure is

        3.   The strategy is

    B.   The major purposes of research designs are

        1.

        2.

    C.   The fundamental components of research designs are

        1.   _____, which is

        2.   _____, which is

Also, with regard to research designs, define:

1. Independent variable:

2. Dependent variable:

3. Experimental group:

4. Central group:

5. Random selection:

6. Matching:

III. TYPES OF RESEARCH DESIGNS.

    A. Describe the most common types of research designs.

        1.

        2.

        3.

        4.

    B. Major relationships between types of research designs.

        1.

        2.

        3.

    C. Case Studies.

        1. Three distinctive features are

            a.

            b.

            c.

    2. Principal limitations of case studies include

       a.

       b.

D. Field Survey.

    1. The intent of the field survey is

    2. Principal limitations of the field survey are

       a.

       b.

E. Laboratory Experiments.

    1. The purpose of the laboratory experiment is

    2. The principal disadvantages of the laboratory experiments are

       a.

       b.

F. Field Experiments.

    1. A field experiment is

    2. A limitation of the field experiment is

G. Compare the types of research designs according to

    1. Realism

    2. Scope

    3. Precision

      4.   Control

      5.   Cost

IV.   DATA COLLECTION METHODS.

    A.   The major data collection methods are

        1.

        2.

        3.

        4.

        5.

    B.   Interviews.

        1.   The quality of an interview depends on

        2.   Major limitations of the interview are

           a.

           b.

           c.

           d.

    C.   Questionnaires.

        1.   Questionnaires are used to measure such variables as

        2.   Advantages of using questionnaires are

           a.

           b.

c.

d.

e.

3.   Disadvantages of using questionnaires are

a.

b.

c.

d.

D.   Observations.

1.   A major advantage of the observation method is

2.   A major disadvantage of the observation method is

E.   Nonreactive Measures.

1.   The advantage in using nonreactive measures is

F.   Qualitative Measures.

1.   Qualitative measures are

G.   Criteria for Data Collection.

1.   Reliability is

2.   Validity is

3.   Practicality is

V.   ETHICS IN RESEARCH.

     A.   Three types of ethical issues facing managers and researchers are

         1.

         2.

         3.

DIRECTED QUESTIONS

I.   Research Design.

     1.   Research design includes all but one of the following parts of the investigation:
         a)   Plan;
         b)   Structure;   d
         c)   Strategy;
         d)   Outcome.

     2.   Anything the researcher has little control over is considered a:
         a)   Dependent variable;
         b)   Independent variable;   c
         c)   Nonrelevant effect;
         d)   Relevant effect.

     3.   An experimental group is one that is:
         a)   Exposed to treatment;
         b)   Selected randomly;   a
         c)   Not exposed to treatment;
         d)   Unaware of the experience.

     4.   A design method in which a researcher seeks detailed information through records, interviews, questionnaires, and observation is:
         a)   Field survey;
         b)   Field experiment;   d
         c)   Laboratory experiment;
         d)   Case study.

     5.   An attempt to apply the laboratory method to ongoing real-life situations is:
         a)   Field survey;
         b)   Field experiment;   b
         c)   Laboratory experiment;
         d)   Case study.

6. Research designs can be compared according to:
    a) Realism;
    b) Precision;
    c) Duration;   d
    d) a and b;
    e) b and c.

II. Data Collection Methods.

1. Among the advantages of questionnaires is:
    a) Can be administered by relatively unskilled
        people;
    b) Low response rates do not cause problems;   a
    c) Give respondent greater flexibility;
    d) All of the above.
2. A major disadvantage of observation is:
    a) Observers are free to make their own
        inferences;
    b) Observers can operate in all work situations;   c
    c) Focuses attention on behavior of individuals;
    d) All of the above.
3. A major shortcoming of interviews is:
    a) Interviews can build trust;
    b) People may not open up in a face-to-face
        situation;   e
    c) Take a lot of time;
    d) a and b;
    e) b and c.
4. Measures used by investigators to describe and
    clarify the meaning of naturally occurring events
    are:
    a) Nonreactive;
    b) Qualitative;   b
    c) Quantitative;
    d) None of the above.
5. Ethnography is which kind of measure?
    a) Nonreactive;
    b) Qualitative;   b
    c) Quantitative;
    d) None of the above.
6. Criteria for data collection include:
    a) Reliability;
    b) Validity;
    c) Practicality;   d
    d) All of the above;
    e) a and b.

III. Ethics in Research.

    1. Computer monitoring is:
        a) Making certain computers are used for the
            right work;
        b) Determining whether computer results are
            correct;   d
        c) Determining when computers need repair;
        d) Conducting surveillance of employees.
    2. Typical ethical issues facing managers regarding
        research:
        a) Correct design;
        b) Value and goal conflict;
        c) Data misuse;   e
        d) All of the above;
        e) b and c.
    3. Luring an individual into committing a prohibited
        act is:
        a) Entrapment;
        b) Whistle-blowing;   a
        c) Misuse of data;
        d) Value conflict.

APPLIED QUESTIONS

I.   Research Design.

    1. "If the quality and the quantity of the employee's
        work increase, then the employee will earn more
        money." The dependent variable is:
        a) The entire statement;
        b) The quality of work;   d
        c) The quantity of work;
        d) Increased earnings.
    2. In question number 1, the independent variable is:
        a) The employee himself/herself;
        b) The quality of work;   e
        c) The quantity of work;
        d) Increased earnings;
        e) b and c.
    3. In question number 1, the hypothesis is:
        a) The entire statement;
        b) The quality of work;   a
        c) The quantity of work;
        d) Increased earnings.
    4. All senior managers with production experience
        were given a series of labor relations problems
        and instructed to develop solutions. Their
        results were compared with results developed by

another group of managers who had been picked by drawing their names out of a hat. Which concepts exist there:
  a) Random selection;
  b) Matching;
  c) Experimental group;
  d) Central group;
  e) All of the above.

                            e

5. We want to study how a number of firms conduct performance appraisals and determine a set of "best practices" in handling performance appraisal. Which type of design would be best?
  a) Case study;
  b) Laboratory experiment;
  c) Field experiment;
  d) One is as good as the other.

                            a

6. We want an independent neutral study of what people think of the new bill we wish to propose to the legislative. Which type of design would be best?
  a) Field survey;
  b) Laboratory experiment;
  c) Case study;
  d) Field experiment.

                            a

II. Data Collection.

1. We are conducting a study of what people actually do in their jobs. One set of jobs is unique. They are new; none of us has ever hold those jobs or supervised people doing those jobs. What data collection method should we be sure to include?
  a) Questionnaire;
  b) Interview;
  c) Observation.

                            c

2. Most of the people we have collecting information for us have little training or experience in doing this. What is probably the best method of data collection?
  a) Questionnaire;
  b) Interview;
  c) Observation.

                            a

3. We need to probe for details and in-depth information. What is probably the best method of data collection?
  a) Questionnaire;

                            b

   b)   Interview;
   c)   Observation.
4. We want to find out how well a piece work
   incentive plan worked when we used it in the
   plant 5 years ago. Which of the following
   should be used:
   a)   Nonreactive measures;   a
   b)   Interviews;
   c)   Observation;
   d)   Qualitative measures.
5. We want to find our how people feel about the
   new flextime program. Which of the following
   should be used:
   a)   Nonreactive measures;
   b)   Quantitative measures;   c
   c)   Qualitative measures.
6. We have used a questionnaire several times, and
   although we have controlled the situation
   carefully, we continue to get different sorts
   of results from the same questionnaire. What
   seems to be the problem:
   a)   Validity;
   b)   Practicality;   c
   c)   Reliability;
   d)   Scope.

III. Ethics in Research.

1. After analyzing the data, the researcher reports
   a set of conclusions. No one believes that these
   conclusions represent the true situation. If they
   are correct, this suggests a problem of:
   a)   Misrepresentation;   a
   b)   Value and goal conflicts;
   c)   Manipulation.
2. A worker has been fired because he refused to send
   a bus on the road with a faulty set of tires. He
   has asked the state public utility commission,
   which licenses the buses, to look into the
   situation. He has engaged in:
   a)   Unethical behavior;   c
   b)   Entrapment;
   c)   Whistle blowing;
   d)   Manipulation.
3. A boss has tried to get rid of a problem employee
   for a long time. Today, the boss left a valuable
   tool near the worker's car, hoping she would steal
   it. The boss may be guilty of:

   a) Unethical behavior;   c
   b) Entrapment;
   c) Whistle blowing;
   d) Manipulation.

PROGRAMMED STUDY SUPPLEMENT

1. The _____ is a method for seeking and analyzing information in a systematic and unbiased manner.
         scientific method

---

2. A _____ is a plan, structure, and strategy of investigation developed to obtain answers to one or more questions.
         research design

---

3. A_____ is anything that the researcher has little control over but that could affect the results.
         nonrelevant effect

---

4. A _____ is a statement about the relationship between two or more variables.
         hypothesis

---

5. A particular characteristic or occurrence of a(n) _____ determines the characteristic of a(n) _____ .
         independent variable; dependent variable

---

6. In an experiment, the _____ is exposed to the treatment in question while the _____ is not.
         experimental group; control group

---

7. _____ is a method of selecting people who are equal in all respects to participate in an experiment, while in _____ everyone has an equal chance of being selected.
         matching; random selection

8. In a _____, a researcher looks for information through a review of records, interviews, questionnaires, and observations.

case study

9. In a _____, data are collected through interviews or a questionnaire from a representative sample of the population under study.

field survey

10. _____ is sexually related behaviors that are annoying and unwelcome.

sexual harassment

11. _____ do not require the cooperation of the person being measured.

nonreactive measures

12. Interpretative, non-quantitative methods to describe and clarify the meaning of naturally occurring events in organizations are _____.

qualitative methods

13. Consistency of results is known as _____, while _____ is the extent to which a measure actually measures which it claims to measure.

reliability; validity

14. _____ is the extent to which a method is acceptable to all parties in a research design.

practicality

15. _____ refers to the collection of minute-to-minute information through computer surveillance.

computer monitoring

16. The process of luring an individual into performing an illegal act is _____.

entrapment

17. _____ is the act of turning in the organization for wrong-doing.

whistle blowing

18. The data collection method whereby the investigator becomes a participant observer is _____.

    ethnography

---

19. A _____ manipulates independent variables to observe the effects on one or more dependent variables.

    laboratory experiment

---

20. A _____ is an attempt to apply the laboratory method to ongoing real-life situations.

    field experiment

CHAPTER 3:

PERSONALITY AND ATTITUDES

LEARNING OBJECTIVES

When you read and when you review Chapter 3, keep in mind the learning objectives which have been established by the authors. Look them over first as a guide to picking out the most important parts of the chapter, and then think about them as you are going through the chapter. When you have finished the chapter, ask yourself whether you have met the objectives.

The authors intend that when you have finished studying this chapter you should be able to:

* Define personality and describe the basic sources of personality differences.
* Provide some examples of personality dimensions that influence individual behavior.
* Explain the concept of attitudes and describe their components.
* Describe the general relationship between attitudes and behavior.
* Define job satisfaction and explain why it is important.

32   **PERSONALITY AND ATTITUDES**

<u>**CHAPTER OUTLINE**</u>

After you have read the chapter, complete the following outline.

I.   PERSONALITY.

   A.   Personality theory is *stable disposition to behavor consistenly in different situations)*

II.   SOURCES OF PERSONALITY DIFFERENCE.

   A.   Major sources of personality differences are

   1. *heredity*

   2. *Culture*

   3. *family*

   4. *group membership - playmates, schoolmaes, co-workers*

   5. *life experiences)*

   B.   The current thinking with regard to the nature-nurture controversy is that *Extreme nature→personality is inherit*
        Extreme nurture→pers. attributes are not inherit but rather determ. by person Experi.8m

   1. *degree to which personality is genetically or environmentally determined varies great deal from one personality charact. to another*

   2. *Must Examine the interaction btwn heredity & environment*

   3. *heredity sets limits on the range of development of characteristic; w/in this range, characteristics are determined by environmental forces*

   C.   Culture is *the distinctive ways that different populations or societies of humans organize their lives; it defines how the different roles necessary to life in that society are to be preformed.*

   D.   Parents influence their children's development by

   1. *thru their own behaviors, they present situations that bring out certain behaviors in children.*

   2. *they serve as a role models w/ children often strongly identified*

   3. *they selectively reward a punish certain behaviors*

   -family situations (socio-econ level, birth order...)
   important source of person. diff. btwn people

III. PERSONALITY AND BEHAVIOR.

    A. Self esteem is *the evaluation an individual makes of him/herself.* *Self esteem is related to a number of important social and work behaviors.*

        1. Self esteem is positively related to *attempts to achieve or a willingness to expend effort to accomplish tasks. ie: lowest → low goals; high → higher goals.*

    B. Locus of control is *the extent to which individuals believe that they can control events affecting them.*

        1. High internals believe *that events in their lives are primarily the result of their own behavior and actions. They see themselves as controlling their environment, making things happen rather than letting things happen to them.*

work is central life interest, high need for autonomy

        2. High externals believe *that events in their lives are determined by chance, fate or other people; controlled by environment low need for autonomy or responsibility work is not a central interest.*

    C. Introversion/Extraversion.

        1. Introversion is *a tendency of the mind to be directed inward and have a greater sensitivity to abstract ideas and personal feelings*

        2. Extraversion is *an orientation of the mind toward other people, events, and objects.*

    D. Authoritarianism and Dogmatism.

        1. Authoritarianism is *one who rigidly adheres to conventional values, readily obeys recognized authority, exhibits a negative view of mankind, is concerned w/power & toughness, & opposes the use of subjective feelings.*

        2. Dogmatism is *the rigidity of a person's beliefs. High Dogmatic (HD) person sees the world as threatening place, regards legit. authority as absolute accepts/rejects people on basis of agreement & disagree w/accepted doctrine/auth. HD person is close-minded; Low Dogm. person is open-minded.*

IV. THE PERSON AND THE SITUATION.

    A. The interactionist perspective on understanding behavior is *examination of both the person and the situation in which the person is behaving in order to fully understand & explain the individual's behavior.*

V. ATTITUDES.

    A. Attitudes are *relatively lasting feelings, beliefs, & behavioral tendency directed towards specific persons, groups, ideas, issues or objects.*
- another form of individual difference.
- result of the person's background & various life experience.

B.   Components of attitudes. *Attitudes are learned & can Δ over time.*

1.   The affective component is *the feelings, sentiments, moods, & emotions about person, idea, event etc.*

2.   The cognitive component is *the beliefs, opinions, knowledge or info. held by the individual*

3.   The behavior component is *the intention & predisposition to act.*

VI.   ATTITUDES AND BEHAVIOR.

A.   Principles to observe in trying to predict behavior from attitudes:

1. *general attitudes best predict general behaviors*

2. *general attitudes best predict specific behaviors*

3. *The less the time that elapses btwn attitude measurement & behaviors, the more consistent will be the relationship btwn attitude & behavior.*

B.   The behavioral intentions model focuses on *a person's specific intentions to behave in a certain way rather than solely on his/her attitudes toward that behavior. Intentions depends on both attitudes & norms regard behavior.*

1.   The behavioral intentions model explains *why the relationship btwn attitudes & behaviors can be strong & weak at different times.*

VII. WORK ATTITUDES: JOB SATISFACTION.

A.   Job satisfaction is ~~appraisable~~ *positive emotional state resulting from apprasial of one's job. Positive assessment occurs when work is in harmony w/ individual needs & values*

B.   Work factors affecting job satisfaction include

1. *Work itself: challenge, physical demands, personal interest*

2. *Reward structure - provides feedback for performance*

3. *Working conditions: physical, goal attainment*

4. *Self - high self-esteem conducive to job sat.*

5. *Others in org.*

6. *Organization & management - policies /procedures develop. to attain rewards*

7. *Fringe benefits*

C. Job satisfaction is important because
1. *satisf. represents an outcome of work experience, high level of dissatisfact. provide diagnostic tool for mngt. identify aspect of org. need attention*
2. *dissat. link to absenteeism, turnover, physical & mental health problems.*

D. Cognitive moral development refers to *an individual's level of moral judgement.*

DIRECTED QUESTIONS

I.   The Meaning of Personality.

   1. Personality is:
       a) Constantly changing, so that understanding
           behavior requires continuous communication
           with individuals;
       b) The basis of the fact that every person is a   d
           unique individual, totally unlike any other;
       c) The one aspect of a person's psychological
           makeup that remains constant over time;
       d) A stable set of characteristics determining
           individual commonalities and differences.
   2. Personality development:
       a) Occurs at increasingly greater rates after we
           reach adulthood and maturity develops;
       b) Generally occurs suddenly and dramatically;
       c) Is evidence that personality is not stable   d
           over time;
       d) Occurs throughout life, but most rapidly
           during early childhood.

II. Basic Sources of Personality Differences.

   1. Regarding the "nature-nurture" debate:
       a) There is no consensus as to which has the
           stronger influence on personality;
       b) "Nurture" means that personality attributes
           are inherited;   c

    c)   Nature sets the outer limits of personality, while nurture influences its development within those limits;

    d)   The effect of heredity is constant across individuals, while that of environment varies from person to person.

2.   Culture affects personality formation by:
   a)   Prescribing the behavioral responses that are to be reinforced;
   b)   Ensuring that there are responses to norms and values are alike;
   c)   Expecting the same responses from all members of society;
   d)   All of the above.

a

3.   The various sources of personality differences:
   a)   Relate to inherited traits rather than to life experiences;
   b)   Act independently of each other;
   c)   Are interdependent;
   d)   Relate to life experiences rather than to inherited traits.

c

4.   Group membership beyond the family:
   a)   Has little influence on the personality because family influences almost totally shape the personality;
   b)   Has a major impact on personality because of the variety of roles and experiences that come from membership in a variety of groups;
   c)   Are more important than the family in shaping the personality;
   d)   Determine the role that life experiences will play in affecting personality.

b

III.   The Relationship Between Personality and Behavior.

1.   "Locus of control" refers to:
   a)   Which part of an individual's brain controls his/her behavior;
   b)   The extent to which people try to control the events in their lives;
   c)   The extent to which people believe they are in control of the events in their lives;
   d)   The extent to which people actually are in control of the events in their lives.

c

2.   "Internals":
   a)   Believe they are in control, and so engage in less social interaction and are less active in seeking out information than are "externals";
   b)   Are more likely to be introverted than are "externals";

c

   c) Are more likely to attempt to influence or persuade others than are "externals";

   d) Are more likely to prefer a structured environment than are "externals."

3. Extraversion:

   a) Is in the conscious mind, while introversion is in the unconscious;

   b) Is found in about the same proportions within individuals across society;

   c) Is the tendency to have a strong sensitivity to personal feelings;

   d) Is believed to be necessary in some measure to handle managerial roles successfully.

d

4. Dogmatism:

   a) Refers to the rigidity of one's belief system;

   b) Is an orientation toward the inner, subjective, world;

   c) Contributes to a tendency to be dependent upon authority figures;

   d) Is associated with a strong reliance on subjective feelings.

a

5. Self-esteem:

   a) Is affected by situations and events;

   b) Is stable enough to be regarded as a basic personality dimension;

   c) Is positively associated with the willingness to take risks;

   d) All of the above.

d

6. The situation within which behavior occurs:

   a) Is less important than the personal determinants of behavior;

   b) May sometimes be more important than individual differences in determining behavior;

   c) Is independent of the personal determinants of behavior;

   d) Is less important than the events surrounding the behavior.

b

IV. The Meaning of Attitudes.

1. The beliefs, opinions, knowledge, or information that accompany an attitude are the attitude's:

   a) Affective component;

   b) Cognitive component;

   c) Behavioral component;

   d) Interaction component;

b

2. Attitudes:

   a) Are helpful in analyzing behavior because of the clear-cut simple relationships between attitudes and behavior;

        b)   Are independent of a person's background and   c
life experience;
        c)   Represent an interaction of a person's
emotions, cognitions, and behavioral
tendencies.

V.   The Relationship Between Attitudes and Behavior.

   1.   Regarding the ability to predict behavior from
measurements of attitudes:
        a)   General attitudes predict specific behavior;
        b)   The longer the period between measurement and   c
behavior the better the predictive capacity,
since attitudes need time to develop;
        c)   The shorter the period between measurement
and behavior the better the predictive capacity, since attitudes can change over time.
   2.   The Behavioral Intentions Model of attitudes says
that:
        a)   Intentions depend on both attitudes and norms
regarding the behavior;
        b)   The affective, cognitive, and behavioral
components of attitudes play little or no role   a
in determining behavior;
        c)   Intentions are beliefs regarding the outcomes
of behaviors;
        d)   All of the above.

VI.   The Meaning of "Job Satisfaction."

   1.   Job satisfaction:
        a)   Does not lead to good performance;
        b)   Has been shown to be linked to certain employee
behaviors other than performance;   b
        c)   Is such a vague concept that its measures are
not very useful to employers;
        d)   Stems from a set of sources common within
all employees.
   2.   Measures of overall job satisfaction:
        a)   Are not very useful in predicting job
performance because overall job satisfaction is
"general" and job performance is "specific";
        b)   Are more useful than are measures of any single
component of job satisfaction;   a
        c)   Measure an individual's intentions to engage
in certain behavior;
        d)   Are relied upon because measures of specific
attitudes have not yet been developed.

VII. Individual Differences and Ethical Behavior.

    1. Regarding cognitive moral development:
      a) People with high external locus of control tend to exhibit more ethical behavior when making organizational decisions than do those with high internal locus of control;
      b) People with high cognitive moral development are most likely to behave ethically;   b
      c) With psychological maturity, one becomes more dependent upon outside influences;
      d) All of the above.
    2. Which of the following means an indifference to moral issues?
      a) Immoral management;
      b) Moral management;   c
      c) Amoral management.

APPLIED QUESTIONS

1. A supervisor reprimands two employees. One ("A") gets defensive; then hostile, and quits. The other ("B") takes steps to correct the behavior that prompted the reprimand and in doing so becomes a much more productive employee. Which of the following is likely to best explain the difference between the two workers:
    a) "A" has tendencies toward extraversion;
    b) "A" is a "high dogmatic" individual;   d
    c) Situational rather than personal determinants influenced "A"'s behavior;
    d) "A" has been influenced by different family, group, and life experience characteristics than has "B."
2. An individual with an internal locus of control orientation would:
    a) Feel more at home than would an "external" in an organization with a lengthy and detailed set of work rules;
    b) Be better suited to an assembly line job than to a "trouble shooter" job;   c
    c) Likely be more satisfied with a job as a lobbyist than would an "external";
    d) Work better under close supervision than would an "external."
3. Regarding introversion and extraversion:
    a) Because they spend their time socializing, extroverts are less well-suited to working around numbers of people than are introverts;

    b)   Introverts are more suited to managerial occupations than are extraverts;

    c)   A problem stemming from introversion could be that a manager would make decisions without involving enough people and without obtaining all the facts;

    d)   The extreme introvert might work better than the extrovert in a noisy crowded office environment because of the ability to shut out other people and objects.

                                                          c

4.   Regarding authoritarianism and dogmatism:

    a)   HD's (high dogmatics) would likely work better in stable organizations than in new ventures;

    b)   LD's (low dogmatics) are less likely than HD's to be receptive to new ideas and fluid relationships;

    c)   An individual with an authoritarian personality would probably have a difficult time working for another authoritarian;

    d)   Authoritarians would make good labor relations people because they are comfortable using power and toughness.

                                                           a

5.   Low self-esteem would be most likely to explain which of the following work-related behaviors:

    a)   High amounts of social interaction at work;

    b)   The search for high-status occupations;

    c)   In general, being a hard worker;

    d)   Being more easily influenced by peer group pressure.

                                                           d

6.   "Your supervisor asks you to do something which you hold to be unethical. You immediately report her to her supervisor." Which of the components that make up one's attitudes is more likely to have caused you to do this:

    a)   The affective component;

    b)   The cognitive component;

    c)   The behavioral component;

    d)   None of the above.

                                                           a

7.   Which of the following would be most helpful in predicting a group of workers' behavioral intentions regarding voting in favor of having the "ABC" union represent them:

    a)   Knowing their attitudes toward labor unions;

    b)   Knowing their attitudes toward the "ABC" union;

    c)   Knowing whether the employees felt they could find other jobs if they lost their current jobs.

                                                           b

8.   There is to be an election to determine whether the workers want the "ABC" union to represent them. Employee "X" does not believe in unions, but he feels pressure from co-workers to vote union. Which of the following is most likely to occur:

    a)   The intention to vote in favor of the union will be high;

b) If attitudes are stronger than norms, "X" will
    vote union;   c

c) If norms are stronger than attitudes, "X" will
    vote union;

d) The employee will vote union.

9. Job satisfaction measures:

a) Are useful in predicting performance;

b) Have never been refined enough to really identify
    "satisfaction";   d

c) Have been found to show that a person either is or
    is not satisfied with a job;

d) Have been found to be related to some forms of work
    behavior other than performance.

10. Which of the following is the best explanation of why
    an employee might turndown an opportunity for a
    promotion:

a) Having low self-esteem;

b) Being an LD (low dogmatic);   a

c) Being an extravert;

d) Having low job satisfaction.

11. "I am concerned with whether or not this is the right
    decision, but I'm not going to spend a lot of time
    on it because whatever is going to happen is going
    to happen." This person is exhibiting:

a) Low cognitive moral development;

b) Typical unethical behavior associated with high   d
    internal locus of control;

c) Behavior typical of a strong "internal";

d) None of the above.

PROGRAMMED STUDY SUPPLEMENT

1. The _____ refers to whether
    individuals believe that events which occur   locus of
    in their lives result from their own behavior   control
    behavior or from external forces.

---

2. Personality theory is a _____ in that   general
    it is an attempt to understand or describe the   theory of
    behavior of all people, all of the time.   behavior

---

3. Heredity, culture, family, group membership,   individ-
    and life experiences help to explain   ual dif-
    _____.   ferences

4.	The debate over the extent to which personality is influenced by genetics is known as the _____.	nature-nurture contro-versy
5.	An orientation of the mind toward other people, events, and objects is known as _____.	extraver-sion
6.	_____ represents the personal characteristics that account for consistent patterns of behavior.	personal-ity
7.	The concept which refers to the rigidity of a person's belief is known as _____.	dogmatism
8.	A general assessment of one's own worthiness develops the amount of _____ which an individual has.	self-esteem
9.	_____ have an affective component, a cognitive component, and a behavioral component.	attitudes
10.	One who rigidly adheres to conventional values and is concerned with toughness and power is said to have a(n) _____ personality.	authori-tarian
11.	_____ is a collection of related job attitudes about a variety of the aspects of a job.	job satis-faction
12.	_____ seems to explain why the relationship between attitudes and behavior can some times be strong and at other times weak.	The Behavior-al Inten-tions Model
13.	An inward orientation with a focus on abstract ideas, personal feelings, etc., is known as _____.	introver-sion

14. Those who have a high _____ believe   internal
     events in their lives are of their own doing,   locus of
     whereas those with a high _____   control;
     believe they are not in control of events   external
     in their lives.   locus of
                                                            control

---

15. An _____ is useful for understanding   interact-
     behavior in complex social settings.   ionist
                                                            perspec-
                                                            tive

---

16. _____ refers to an individual's   cognitive
     level of moral judgment.   moral
                                                            develop-
                                                            ment

---

17. _____ are rules of behavior, or   norms
     or proper ways of acting, which have been
     accepted as appropriate by members of a
     group or by society.

---

18. The distinctive ways that different populations   culture
     or societies organize their lives comprise
     _____.

CHAPTER 4

PERCEPTION AND ATTRIBUTION

LEARNING OBJECTIVES

When you read and when you review Chapter 4, keep in mind the learning objectives which have been established by the authors. Look them over as a guide to picking out the most important parts of the chapter, and then think about them as you are going through the chapter. When you have finished the chapter, ask yourself whether you have met the objectives.

The authors intend that when you have finished studying this chapter you should be able to:

* Define perception and describe the major elements in the perceptual process.
* Explain the concepts of perceptual selection and organization.
* Describe the factors that determine how one person perceives another.
* Identify five kinds of perceptual errors.
* Explain the process of attribution and how attributions influence behavior.
* Describe important attributions that people make in the work setting.

CHAPTER OUTLINE

After you have read the chapter, complete the following outline.

I.   THE PERCEPTUAL PROCESS.

    A.   Perception is defined as *psychological process whereby people take info. from the envieonment + make sense of their world. It is the selection + organization of the envieonmental stimuli to provide meaningful experiences for the pierceiver.*

    B.   The basic elements in the perceptual process are

        1. *environmental stimuli — ~~all the 5 senses taste, smell, hear, sight, touch~~*

        2. *Observation — taste, smell, hear, sight, touch*

        3. *perceptual selection*

        4. *perceptual organization*

        5. *interpretation*

        6. *response*

II.   PERCEPTUAL SELECTION.

    A.   Perceptual selection is *the process by which people filter out most stimuli so they can deal w/ important ones.*

    B.   External factors of perception include *(Charact. that influence whether Stimuli will be noticed.*

        1. *Size — larger external factor — more likely to be piecewed(*

        2. *intensity — more intense, more likely pieceived*

        3. *contrast — external factors stand out against background or that are not what people expect → more likely*

        4. *motion — moving factor more so than stationary*

        5. *repetition — repeated factor more than single*

        6. *novelty & familiarity*

    C.   Internal factors of perception include

        1. *personality*

        2. *learning*

        3. *motivation*

4.

5.

D. A perceptual set is *an Expectation of a perception based on past Experiences w/same or similar stimuli.*

E. Field dependence/independence is *relationship btwn personality + perception is provided by an aspect of the personality*

    1. Examples of implications of field dependence for organizational behavior are

        a. *field dependent tends to pay more attention to external environmental cues*

        b. *field independent relies on bodily sensations (ie pull of gravity) interacts more independently w/ others in org. more aware of important diff. in roles, status, needs*

F. Learning affects perception by *past experiences & what was learned from those experiences. life experiences are determined by culture one's born into which influence perceptual process.*

G. Motivation affects perception by *people perceive things that promise to help satisfy their needs & that have been reward in past. Ignore mildly disturbing things but perceive ↓ dangerous ones. Pollyanna principle – states that pleasant stimuli are processed more efficiently + accurately than lesser or*

III. PERCEPTUAL ORGANIZATION. *Relationship btwn motivation a perception sum by pollyanna.*

A. Perceptual organization is *the process by which people group environmental stimuli into recognizable patterns.*

    1. The figure-ground principle states that *people tend to perceive the factor they are most attentive to as standing out against a background.*

    2. Perceptual grouping is *the tendency to form individual stimuli into a meaningful pattern by such means as: continuity, closure, proximity or similarity.*

        a. Continuity is *the tendency to perceive objects as continous pattern; useful as organizing principle*

        b. Closure is *the tendency to complete an object so that it is perceived as a constant, overall form. It is the ability to perceive a whole object, even though only part of the object is evident.*

        c. Proximity means *that a group of objects may be perceived as related because of their nearness to each other.*

        d. Similarity means *that the more alike objects are, the greater is the tendency to perceive them as a common group.*

IV.   PERSON PERCEPTION.

A.   Person perception is *the process by which individuals attribute characteristics or traits to other people*

1.   How is person perception related to the general process of perception? *the process follows same sequence of observation, selection org., interpretation, & response. However, the element that is being perceived is another human being.*

B.   Factors that influence how one person perceives another are

1. *Characteristics of the person being perceived*

2. *Characteristics of the perceiver*

3. *the situation or context w/in which the perception takes place.*

C.   Implicit personality theories are

V.   PERCEPTUAL ERRORS.

A.   How accurate are people in their perceptions of others?

1.   The more common interview errors include

a. *similarity error* – interviewers positive predispose *toward candidates who are similar to them, neg. biased against those unlike them.*

b. *contrast error* – *compare one candidate against another rather than against standard criteria.*

c. *overweighting of neg. info.* – *overreact on neg. info to/for excuse to disqualify candidate*

d. *first-impression error*

2.   Errors to avoid in forming perceptions of others include

a. *generalizing from a single trait to a whole constellation of traits*

b. *assuming that a single behavior will show itself in all situations*

c. *placing too much reliance on physical appearance*

B.   Perceptual defense is *the tendency for people to protect themselves against ideas, objects or situations that are threatening*

C.   Stereotyping is *the tendency to assign attributes to someone solely on the basis of a category in which a person has been placed.*

D.   The halo effect is *the process by which the perceiver evaluates all dimensions of another person based solely on one 1ˢᵗ impression, either favorably or unfavor.*

E.   Projection is *the tendency for people to see their own traits in other people that is, they project their own feelings tendencies or motives into their judgement of others.*

F.   Expectancy effects are *the extent to which prior expectations bias how events, objects, & people are actually perceived.*

1.   What is the name given to the situation where the behavior of the perceiver is shaped by expecting certain things to happen? *self-fulfilling prophecy.*

VI.   ATTRIBUTIONS: PERCEIVING THE CAUSES OF BEHAVIOR.

A.   The attribution process refers to *the ways in which people come to understand the causes of others & their own behavior.*

1.   Why do people make attributions? *in an attempt to understand the behavior of other people & to make better sense of their environment*

2.   Antecedents of attribution are *factors internal to perceiver*

a. *the amount of info. the perceiver has about a person & the situation & how that info is org. by perceiver.*

b. *the perceiver's beliefs - implicit personality traits, what other people do in similar situation*

c. *the motivation of the perceiver - importance to the perceiver of making accurate decision. ie:*

3.   Attributions made by the perceiver may identify the cause as either

a. *internal*

b. *External*

4.   Consequences of the attribution process include

a. *behavior of perceiver in response to behavior of others*

b. *implicit feelings - how perceiver feels about event, people, circumstances*

c. *Effects on the perceiver's expectation of future events.*

B.   Internal -vs- External Causes of Behavior.

1.   Kelley's Theory of Causal Attributions focuses on

a. *consensus* - the extent to which others, faced w/ same situations behave in a manner similar to person perceived

b. *consistency* - the extent to which the person perceived behaves in the same manner on other occasions when faced w/ sim. sits

c. *distinctiveness* - the extent to which the person perceived acts in the same manner in diff. situations

2.   The perceiver will tend to:

a.   Attribute the behavior of a person to external causes when *high consensus, high consistency, high distinctiveness*

b.   Attribute the behavior of a person to internal causes when *low consensus low ~~consistency~~ distinctiveness*

3.   The fundamental attribution error is *the tendency to underestimate the impact of external causes & to overestimate the impact of internal causes.*

C.   Attributions of Success and Failure.

1.   Success and failure are usually attributed to

a. *ability*

b. *effort*

c. *task difficulty*

d. *luck*

2.   Self-serving bias is the tendency to *attribute success to internal factors (ability, effort) & attribute failure to external factors (task diff, luck)*

DIRECTED QUESTIONS

I.   Major Elements in the Perceptual Process.

1.   Paying attention to some aspects of the environment and ignoring others is known as:
     a)   Perceptual organization;
     b)   Perceptual selection;   b

c)   Perceptual error;
d)   Attribution.
2.   Stimuli in the environment are observed through:
a)   The five senses;
b)   External and internal filters;   a
c)   Perceptual grouping;
d)   Attribution.
3.   The basic steps in the perceptual process:
a)   Are separate, distinct, and can be easily observed;
b)   Are observation and selection;   b
c)   Occur almost instantaneously;
d)   Vary from one individual to another.
4.   Which of the following affects our perceptions of an object:
a)   Our preconceptions about the object;
b)   The ways in which we organize objects;   d
c)   The meanings we attach to objects;
d)   All of the above.

II.   Internal and External Factors Affecting Perceptual Selection.

1.   Which of the following is **not** an internal factor affecting perceptual selection:
a)   Learning;
b)   Motivation;
c)   Contrast;   c
d)   Personality.
2.   Which of the following **is** an internal factor influencing one's perception:
a)   The novelty of the stimuli;
b)   Motion;   d
c)   Intensity;
d)   Cultural background of the perceiver.
3.   Characteristics of the stimuli influencing the probability that they will be noticed:
a)   Are known as internal factors of perception;
b)   Are known as external factors of perception;   b
c)   Include learning, motivation, and personality;
d)   Include the perceiver's background experience.
4.   Perceptual selection is:
a)   Filtering out unpleasant stimuli;
b)   Organizing stimuli into meaningful patterns;   c
c)   Filtering out less important stimuli;
d)   Making assumptions about people and things.

5.   An expectation of a perception based on past
     experience within the same or similar stimuli is
     known as:
     a)   Perceptual set;
     b)   Set of expectations;
     c)   Motivation;   a
     d)   Cultural distinction.
6.   An individual strongly concerned with family and
     peer relationships is influenced by which of the
     following orientations:
     a)   Power;
     b)   Learning;   d
     c)   Achievement;
     d)   Affiliation.
7.   According to the authors, which of the following
     is most likely to account for being able to
     follow a conversation in a noisy, crowded room,
     when another person might not be able to do so:
     a)   Learning;
     b)   Novelty;   d
     c)   Personality;
     d)   Motivation.
8.   Which of the following is likely to be the best
     explanation why miniature ponies capture most
     people's attention:
     a)   Size;
     b)   Novelty;   b
     c)   Intensity;
     d)   All of the above.

III.   Perceptual Organization.

1.   Perceptual organization is:
     a)   The filtering of environmental stimuli;
     b)   The grouping of environmental stimuli;   b
     c)   A predisposition to perceive an object in a
          given way;
     d)   The attribution of characteristics or traits
          to individuals.
2.   Perception of objects as standing out against
     other objects is known as:
     a)   Perceptual grouping;
     b)   Attribution;   d
     c)   The principle of similarity;
     d)   The figure-ground principle.
3.   The tendency to form individual stimuli into
     meaningful patterns is known as:
     a)   Perceptual grouping;
     b)   Attribution;   a

    c) The principle of similarity;
    d) The figure-ground principle.

4. A possible explanation for a manager's inflexibility and lack of creativity might be the tendency toward:
    a) Closure;
    b) Proximity;   c
    c) Continuity;
    d) None of the above.

5. Perception of a group of objects as related because of their nearness to each other can best be explained by the principle of:
    a) Similarity;
    b) Proximity;   b
    c) Closure;
    d) Continuity.

IV. Determinants of How People Perceive Each Other.

1. Person-perception is:
    a) Attributing characteristics or traits to individuals;
    b) Another name for the attribution process;   a
    c) The way in which persons perceive situations;
    d) All of the above.

2. Internal factors may affect person-perception in which of the following areas:
    a) Characteristics of the person being perceived;
    b) Characteristics of the perceiver;
    c) The situation or context within which the   d
       perception takes place;
    d) All of the above.

3. Implicit personality theories:
    a) Explain how personality operates as an internal factor influencing perception;
    b) Involve external factors influencing perception;   c
    c) Make assumptions about what a person is like based on limited interaction;
    d) Explain how the perceiver's personality influences his/her perceptions of others.

4. Which of the following increases the accuracy of person-perception:
    a) Generalizing from a single trait;
    b) Assuming that a single behavior will emerge in all situations;   d

    c)   Basing perceptions of individuals on their physical characteristics;

    d)   Using physical cues as possible partial sources of information.

5.   Characteristics of the perceiver affect perceptions of other people because:

    a)   External factors affect person-perception;

    b)   One can only arrive at accurate perceptions of other people if they are within the same culture;   c

    c)   Internal factors affect person-perception;

    d)   All of the above.

6.   "Primacy effects" on person-perception are:

    a)   The effects of the most important factor influencing the perception;

    b)   First impressions;   b

    c)   The situation in which perceptions first occur;

    d)   The most influential trait or characteristic of the person being perceived.

7.   Perceptual judgement is:

    a)   The process of organizing perceptions as "wholes";

    b)   Judgement as to what information the perceiver should supply beyond what has been gathered from the person/object being perceived;   c

    c)   The "final" judgement that is made about a person after all perceptions have been organized into a "whole";

    d)   None of the above.

V.   Perceptual Errors.

1.   The tendency to assign attributes to a person solely on the basis of a category to which that person belongs is known as:

    a)   Perceptual defense;

    b)   Stereotyping;   b

    c)   Projection;

    d)   Halo effect.

2.   The tendency to avoid unpleasant stimuli is known as:

    a)   Perceptual selection;

    b)   Stereotyping;   d

    c)   Expectancy;

    d)   Perceptual defense.

3.   A perceiver who evaluates all dimensions of a person solely according to one impression has engaged in which error:

a)   Perceptual defense;
b)   Stereotyping;   c
c)   Halo effect;
d)   None of the above.

4.   "Self-fulfilling prophecy" is a possible outcome
     of which perceptual error:
     a)   Stereotyping;
     b)   Expectancy;   b
     c)   Halo effect;
     d)   Projection.

5.   Seeing your own undesirable traits in others is
     known as:
     a)   Projection;
     b)   Halo effect;   a
     c)   Expectancy;
     d)   Stereotyping.

6.   A consumer interview error in which people
     compare job candidates to other candidates
     interviewed at the same time rather than to some
     absolute standard is:
     a)   Similarity;
     b)   Contrast;   b
     c)   Overweighting of negative information;
     d)   First impression.

7.   Reacting as though you are looking for an excuse
     to eliminate someone in an interview describes
     which error:
     a)   Similarity;
     b)   Contrast;   c
     c)   Overweighting of negative information;
     d)   First impression.

VI.   The Process of Attribution.

     1.   The process by which we come to understand the
          causes of behavior (including our own):
          a)   Projection;
          b)   Expectancy;   c
          c)   Attribution;
          d)   Stereotyping.

     2.   Attributions are based on:
          a)   Behavior, level of effect, expectancy;
          b)   Perceived causes of behavior;   c
          c)   Information, beliefs, and motivation;
          d)   All of the above.

     3.   Which of the following is a consequence of the
          attribution process:
          a)   Beliefs;
          b)   Expectancy;   b

    c)   Perceived causes;

    d)   All of the above.

4.   The assigned cause for a behavior:

    a)   Can be either internal or external;

    b)   Helps the perceiver attach meaning to the event;

    c)   Is important for understanding subsequent consequences for the perceiver;

    d)   All of the above.

            d

5.   The extent to which the person perceived behaves in the same manner on all occasions when faced with the same situation is called:

    a)   Consensus;

    b)   Consistency;

    c)   Distinctiveness;

    d)   Error.

            b

6.   The extent to which others would behave the same as the perceived in a given situation is called:

    a)   Consensus;

    b)   Consistency;

    c)   Distinctiveness;

    d)   Error.

            a

7.   Which of the following is likely to lead the perceiver to attribute behavior to internal causes:

    a)   Acting differently in other situations;

    b)   Acting differently than other people act in this situation;

    c)   Acting differently in this situation on other occasions;

    d)   None of the above are associated with internal causation.

            a

8.   Which of the following attributions will the perceiver be most likely to make when there is inconsistency in the behavior of the perceived:

    a)   Internal causes;

    b)   External causes;

    c)   Behavior is irrational;

    d)   Unable to make causal attribution.

            d

9.   Fundamental attribution error is:

    a)   The tendency to blame conflict on individuals rather than on the situation;

    b)   The tendency to underestimate the impact of external causes of behavior;

    c)   The tendency to overestimate the impact of internal causes of behavior;

    d)   All of the above.

            d

10.   There is a tendency to attribute one's failures to:

  a) External factors;
  b) Internal factors;   a
  c) Both;
  d) Neither.
  11. The tendency to attribute causation in one's own
      failure in a way which denies personal
      responsibility for failure is known as:
      a) Self-fulfilling prophecy;
      b) Fundamental attribution error;   d
      c) Projection;
      d) Self-serving bias.
  12. Which of the following is <u>not</u> an antecedent in
      the attribution process?
      a) Perceived causes of behavior;
      b) Information;   a
      c) Beliefs;
      d) Motivation.

APPLIED QUESTIONS

1. When managers from several functional areas of a
   business look at a situation and each notices first
   those issues which involve his/her own area, they
   are engaging in:
   a) Observation;
   b) Perceptual selection;   b
   c) Perceptual organization;
   d) Interpretation.
2. A firm has manufacturing facilities in South America.
   Numerous employee relations problems exist. The
   local workforce is responding poorly to the work
   rules that have been established at the home office
   in Houston, Texas. Plans to move the facilities are
   being considered because of the perception that the
   locals cannot adapt to the work rules necessary for
   industrial employment. This perception has most
   likely been influenced by:
   a) External factors;
   b) Internal factors;
   c) Sensory factors;   b
   d) Fundamental attribution error.
3. One of the first questions we tend to ask a new
   acquaintance is, "what do you do?" When we learn the
   person's occupation, we immediately develop certain
   perceptions beyond what we actually "know" about the
   person. That is because we have developed which of
   the following regarding people in that occupation:

   a) Perceptual set;
   b) Self-serving bias;   a
   c) Motivational set;
   d) Implicit personality theory.

4. You see yourself as a dedicated hard-worker, willing
   to devote yourself to doing your best to get the job
   done right and on time. You are surprised when you
   overhear two fellow employees describing you as
   someone who "likes to make others look bad" and who
   will "walk all over people." Which of the following
   is most likely to account for this <u>difference</u> in
   perceptions:
   a) Learning;
   b) Motivation;   b
   c) Intensity;
   d) Self-serving bias.

5. In your first days at work you spent a lot of time
   with a fellow employee who befriended you. He still
   works in the same general area where you are located,
   but you now realize that you seldom ever notice him,
   let alone spend time with him. Now, you spend most
   of your time with your boss, your assistant, and your
   project engineer. This is an example of:
   a) Perceptual grouping;
   b) Perceptual error;   d
   c) Perceptual set;
   d) Figure-ground principle.

6. A manager who rigidly insists that his employees go
   strictly "by the book" may be overly affected by what
   perceptual process:
   a) Closure;
   b) Repetition;   c
   c) Continuity;
   d) Similarity.

7. An employee who typically has trouble comprehending
   the meaning of any part of a project unless he/she is
   given great detail on the entirety of that project
   may be suffering from the inability to carry out what
   aspect of the perceptual process:
   a) Similarity;
   b) Continuity;   d
   c) Repetition;
   d) Closure.

8. Three new college graduates begin a management
   training program in a bank. It quickly becomes
   obvious that two do not take their training
   seriously. The third does. She drops out of their
   car pool, no longer sits with them at staff meetings,
   and begins eating her lunch with other people. She
   is recognizing the principle of:

a) Similarity;
b) Proximity;   b
c) Closure;
d) Continuity.
9.   In a 1985 motion picture, a stranger arrives at a
      work scene. He proceeds to a particular individual
      and says, "I noticed your height. You must be
      in charge here." This reflects:
      a) Projection;
      b) Motivation;   d
      c) Halo effect;
      d) Implicit personality theory.
10.   A co-worker (who is European) typically surprises you
      by her bluntness. You have just asked her opinion of
      your new car, and she has responded that she does not
      like its color. You decide she is the rudest person
      you have ever met. From the information here, which
      influence seems most likely to be responsible for
      your perceptions:
      a) Characteristics of your co-worker;
      b) Your characteristics;   b
      c) The situation within which the perception
         occurred.
      d) Perceptual grouping.
11.   Research on job interviewing warns us that applicants
      have a very short time at the beginning of the
      interview to favorably impress the interviewer, and
      that should they fail to do so it will be difficult
      to "recover." The explanation of this is known as:
      a) Stereotyping;
      b) Attribution error;   d
      c) Implicit personality theory;
      d) Primacy effect.
12.   Which of the following allows people to concentrate
      on their work while in crowded, noisy offices:
      a) Perceptual selection;
      b) Projection;   a
      c) Expectancy;
      d) Attribution.
13.   A supervisor who suffers from low self-esteem expects
      poor performance from his subordinates. He does not
      believe they can handle their jobs. This perceptual
      error is a result of: ·
      a) Expectancy;
      b) Stereotyping;   d
      c) Halo effect;
      d) Projection.
14.   It is not uncommon to hear a supervisor say about an
      employee, "There is no reason why he/she acted that
      way." Which of the following would **not** be a likely
      explanation of that perception:

a) Lack of perceiver motivation;
b) Inappropriate perceiver beliefs;
c) Lack of perceiver information;
d) Lack of perceiver understanding of consequences of subordinate behavior.

d

15. A baseball player has done poorly with one team. He is traded to a new team, where he does extremely well. Fans of his former team accuse him of having been lazy and unmotivated before the trade. While this is possible, the fans may also be guilty of:
a) Fundamental attribution error;
b) Self-serving bias;
c) Halo effect;
d) Self-fulfilling prophecy.

a

16. A worker says of his superior, "She's a time bomb. You never know when she's going to go off or what's going to set her off. I never know how she's going to react when I ask her a question. Sometime she's great; other times she blows sky high." This worker has just said that:
a) The supervisor's behavior stems mainly from external causes;
b) The supervisor's behavior stems mainly from internal causes;
c) The supervisor's behavior exhibits low consensus;
d) The supervisor's behavior exhibits low consistency.

d

17. An employee complains that he would have received a higher merit increase if he had been in another department "rather than in here with all these 'hot-shots'." This employee has just said that:
a) He had not failed;
b) He had failed because of internal causes;
c) He had failed because of external causes;
d) None of the above.

c

18. In explaining one's failures there is a tendency to attribute causality to:
a) Internal factors;
b) External factors;
c) Expectancy effects;
d) Halo effects.

b

19. Dennis, a graduate of the State University, has a tendency to spend more time interviewing applicants from State University that he does when interviewing others. This could be a result of which error:
a) Contrast;
b) First impression;
c) Similarity;
d) Overweighting negative information.

c

20. Research shows that you have only a short time to begin to get an interviewer to form a positive opinion of you in an interview. This may in part reflect which error:
    a) Contrast;
    b) First impression;   c
    c) Similarity;
    d) Overweighting negative information.

PROGRAMMED STUDY SUPPLEMENT

1.	The _____ states that pleasant stimuli are processed more efficiently and accurately than less pleasant ones.	pollyanna principle
2.	Self-fulfilling prophecy is one possible result of _____ effects in the perception process.	expectancy
3.	When we sort through environmental stimuli and discard those we believe unimportant while attending to the important ones, we are engaging in _____.	perceptual selection
4.	When you give insufficient consideration to the situation surrounding an employee's behavior and blame that behavior solely on, say, a lack of motivation on the employee's part, you may have committed a _____.	funda-mental attribu-tion error
5.	Continuity, closure, proximity, and similarity are types of _____.	perceptual grouping
6	The psychological process whereby people extract information from the environment and make sense of their world is known as _____.	perception
7.	_____ occurs as an attempt to understand the behavior of others and hence to better understand the environment.	attribu-tion

8. When the perceiver has experience with a   perceptual
    particular stimulus, a _____ may   set
    develop and influence subsequent encounters
    with like or similar stimuli.

---

9. A major part of an employee's job is getting   halo
    along with customers. Another important part   effect
    is keeping up with the required paper work.
    She does an excellent job of getting along
    with customers but she is extremely poor with
    the paper work side of her job. The employee
    gets an "outstanding" as an overall performance
    rating. This may reflect a _____.

---

10. The process of bringing together environmental   perceptual
    stimuli into recognizable patterns so that   organiza-
    we can interpret their meaning is known as   tion
    _____.

---

11. The tendency to avoid unpleasant stimuli is   perceptual
    called _____.   defense

---

12. The _____ is a partial explanation   figure-
    for having forgotten the name of (and rarely   ground
    thinking of) a former employee who had been   principle
    one of your very best but who has been gone
    from your work group for a year or two.

---

13. I may cope with one of my failures by   self-
    adopting a _____, such as blaming   serving
    the failure on the fact that the task was an   bias
    impossible one to perform.

---

14. _____ is the type of perceptual   stereo-
    error that would lead one to assume any   typing
    female job applicant who had school-age
    children at home would likely be absent
    frequently and thus to refuse to hire
    such applicants.

---

15. _____ error may explain why some   projection
    supervisors may fear that their employees
    would not work if left unwatched.

16. An aspect of the personality that affects whether a person pays more attention to external environmental clues or to bodily sensations is _____.

field dependence/independence

17. _____ is the process by which individuals attribute characteristics or traits to other people.

person perception

18. Views about which physical characteristics, personality traits, and specific behaviors are related to others are _____.

implicit personality theories

19. When expectations that certain things will happen shape the perceiver's behavior so that those events are more likely to happen, a _____ has occurred.

self-fulfulling prophecy

20. First impressions are also known as _____.

primacy effects

CHAPTER 5

INDIVIDUAL PROBLEM-SOLVING STYLES

LEARNING OBJECTIVES

When you read and review Chapter 5, keep in mind the learning objectives which have been established by the authors. Look them over as a first guide to picking out the most important parts of the chapter, and think about them as you are going through the chapter. When you have finished the chapter, ask yourself whether you have met the objectives.

The authors intend that when you have finished studying this chapter you should be able to:

* Describe the four stages of the problem-solving model.
* State two methods that individuals use to gather data.
* State two methods that individuals use to evaluate information.
* Identify your own problem-solving style.
* List the strengths and weaknesses of four individual problem-solving styles.

CHAPTER OUTLINE

After you have read the chapter, complete the following outline.

I.   INDIVIDUAL PROBLEM-SOLVING PROCESSES.

    A. Two major sources of stimuli affecting the decision maker are

        1.

        2.

    B. The decision maker's personal frame of reference is

    C. Perceptual filtering relates to

    D. Cognitive complexity measures

        1. Problem interpretation refers to

    E. How people define and rank problems is influenced by

        1.

        2.

II.   PSYCHOLOGICAL FUNCTIONS OF PROBLEM SOLVING.

    A. Four basic functions.

        1. Sensing

        2. Intuitive

        3. Thinking

        4. Feeling

B. Sensation -vs- Intuition in Gathering Information.

    1. Sensation-type person.

        a. A sensation-type person is

        b. The problem-solving style of a sensation-type person:

           (1)

           (2)

           (3)

           (4)

           (5)

           (6)

    2. Intuitive-type person.

        a. An intuitive-type person is

        b. The problem-solving style of an intuitive-type person:

           (1)

           (2)

           (3)

           (4)

           (5)

C. Feeling -vs- Thinking in Evaluating Information.

    1. Feeling-type person.

        a. A feeling-type person is

b.   The problem-solving style of a feeling-type person:

(1)

(2)

(3)

(4)

(5)

2.   Thinking-type person.

a.   An thinking-type person is

b.   The problem-solving style of an thinking-type person:

(1)

(2)

(3)

(4)

(5)

III.   INDIVIDUAL PROBLEM-SOLVING STYLES.

A.   A sensition-thinker is

1.   They deal with others by

2.   Their possible weaknesses include

3.   Appropriate occupations include

B. An intuitive-thinker is

1. They deal with others by

2. Their possible weaknesses include

3. Appropriate occupations include

C. A sensation-feeler is

1. They deal with others by

2. Their possible weaknesses include

3. Appropriate occupations include

D. An intuitive-feeler is

1. They deal with others by

2. Their possible weaknesses include

3. Appropriate occupations include

DIRECTED QUESTIONS

I. An Overview.

1. Two methods of data-gathering are:
    a) Sensation and intuition;
    b) Thinking and feeling;
    c) Sensation and thinking;
    d) Intuition and feeling.

a

2. According to Jung, for each individual:
   a) One data-gathering and one data-evaluation method become dominant;
   b) One of the four functions is dominant, backed up by any one of the other three functions;   c
   c) One of the four functions is dominant, backed up by one of the two functions in the opposite set of functions;
   d) One of the four functions is dominant, backed up by one of the two functions in the same set of functions.

3. The combination of functions which is most characteristic of Western Society is:
   a) Thinking-feeling;
   b) Sensation-thinking;   b
   c) Intuition-feeling;
   d) Sensation-intuition.

4. Which of the following is **not** true with respect to the general problem-solving process:
   a) Outcomes become inputs to next round;
   b) Defining and ranking problems are influenced by considerations of risk and consequence;
   c) Cognitive complexity refers to the perception filtering of information;   c
   d) Ability to make decisions is affected by the amount of information that can be processed.

II. Methods Used to Gather Data.

1. Which of the following best represents the pattern of preferences of the general population regarding the two data-gathering methods:
   a) 50% for sensation; and 50% for intuition;
   b) 35% for intuition, and 65% for sensation;   b
   c) 75% for intuition, and 25% for sensation;
   d) No convincing data have yet been gathered.

2. Which of the of the following is characteristic of intuitive type individuals:
   a) Decisions based on facts;
   b) Distrust of creativity;   d
   c) Orientation toward physical reality;
   d) Prefers solving new problems to engaging in routine activity.

3. Which of the following is characteristic of sensation type individuals:
   a) Willingness to re-define problems after work gets underway;

b) Reliance on hunches;
c) Simultaneous consideration of numerous alternatives;
d) Working a problem through to conclusion.

4. A sensation-oriented individual would be most likely to be:
   a) Impatient when details get complicated;
   b) Impatient with people who do not see the immediate value of his/her ideas;
   c) Future-oriented;
   d) All of the above.

d

a

III. Methods Used To Evaluate Data.

1. Thinking-type individuals base evaluations on:
   a) Human aspects of organizational problems;
   b) Subjective values;
   c) Application of impersonal criteria;
   d) Application of traditional values.

c

2. If carried to extreme, the "feeling" method may make one appear:
   a) Rigid;
   b) Boring;
   c) Manipulative;
   d) Dogmatic.

c

3. The "thinking" method:
   a) Is emphasized in the U.S. society as the "natural" problem-solving model;
   b) Has been over-emphasized as the superior method of evaluation;
   c) Is oriented toward past, present, and future;
   d) All of the above.

d

4. Evaluation based on "thinking":
   a) Tends to make the evaluator good at negotiation;
   b) Tends to give considerable weight to extenuating circumstances;
   c) Often results in the discovery of new facts;
   d) All of the above.

c

5. Which of the following is more likely to be associated with the "thinking" function:
   a) Conformity;
   b) Conservatism;
   c) Persuasiveness;
   d) All of the above.

b

IV.   Managerial Problem-Solving Profiles.

1.   Intuitive-thinkers are individuals who:
   a)   Focus on possibilities but analyze them impersonally;
   b)   Make decisions based on precise interpretations of facts and figures;
   c)   Are good negotiators and good at spotting system problems;
   d)   See abstract possibilities and prefer employee participation in decision-making.

a

2.   Which profile do the authors identify as the best for "troubleshooters":
   a)   Sensation-thinking;
   b)   Intuitive-thinking;
   c)   Sensation-feeling;
   d)   Intuitive-feeling;

c

3.   These managers are characterized as drawing from personal views when making decisions and as having a strong commitment to their subordinates:
   a)   Sensation-thinkers;
   b)   Intuitive-thinkers;
   c)   Sensation-feelers;
   d)   Intuitive-feelers.

d

4.   These managers like to clarify, settle, and conclude problems, and to do so based on fact:
   a)   Sensation-thinkers;
   b)   Intuitive-thinkers;
   c)   Sensation-feelers;
   d)   Intuitive-feelers.

a

5.   These managers want their subordinates' discussions to stick to the point and to be presentations of organized logical arguments of fact:
   a)   Sensation-thinkers;
   b)   Intuitive-thinkers;
   c)   Sensation-feelers;
   d)   Intuitive-feelers.

a

6.   These managers relate well with subordinates, but frequently allow personal likes and dislikes to enter into the decision-making process:
   a)   Sensation-thinkers;
   b)   Intuitive-thinkers;
   c)   Sensation-feelers;
   d)   Intuitive-feelers.

d

7.   One of the reasons that these managers get things done is that they are able to observe the factual details of a situation and then obtain the cooperation of their subordinates:

a)   Sensation-thinkers;
b)   Intuitive-thinkers;   c
c)   Sensation-feelers;
d)   Intuitive-feelers.

8. These managers have excellent analytical
    capabilities, but tend to be interested in an
    organization where stability is a goal:
    a)   Sensation-thinkers;
    b)   Intuitive-thinkers;   a
    c)   Sensation-feelers;
    d)   Intuitive-feelers.

9. Which of the following is <u>not</u> a basis upon which
    the model in the chapter was derived:
    a)   Each person's decisions are influenced by the
         different ways in which they perceive and
         organize their environment;
    b)   An individual's problem-solving styles have
         more influence on their decision-making than do
         the environments in which they operate;
    c)   The ways in which people gather information and   b
         evaluate it differ from person to person;
    d)   All of the above are consistent with the model.

V. Potential Weaknesses of Problem-Solving Styles.

1. Possible weaknesses of this style include:
    resistance to change; being too heavily rule-
    oriented; being unreceptive to new ideas; being
    overly committed to the immediate time frame:
    a)   Sensation-thinking;
    b)   Intuitive-thinking;   c
    c)   Sensation-feeling;
    d)   Intuitive-feeling.

2. Possible weaknesses of this style include: basis
    for decision-making is too personal and subjective;
    an uneven flow of energy and attention to
    problems; the need for approval gets in the way of
    decision-making:
    a)   Sensation-thinking;
    b)   Intuitive-thinking;   d
    c)   Sensation-feeling;
    d)   Intuitive-feeling.

3. Possible weaknesses of this style include:
    ignoring feelings of others; intolerance of others
    who may be thought not intellectually competent;
    unrealistically high expectations:
    a)   Sensation-thinking;

    b)   Intuitive-thinking;   b
    c)   Sensation-feeling;
    d)   Intuitive-feeling.
4. Possible weaknesses of this style include:
    impatience with delays due to complications; acting
    too quickly; over-emphasis on stability; tendency
    to blame others for problems encountered:
    a)   Sensation-thinking;
    b)   Intuitive-thinking;   a
    c)   Sensation-feeling;
    d)   Intuitive-feeling.

VI. Occupations Linked to Problem-Solving Styles.

    1. Occupations that require close personal contact with
        others are best held by individuals with which
        problem-solving style:
        a)   Sensation-thinking;
        b)   Intuitive-thinking;   c
        c)   Sensation-feeling;
        d)   Intuitive-feeling.
    2. Occupations that deal with the human side of the
        organization, and that deal with groups of people,
        either directly or indirectly, are best held by
        individuals with which problem-solving style:
        a)   Sensation-thinking;
        b)   Intuitive-thinking;   d
        c)   Sensation-feeling;
        d)   Intuitive-feeling.
    3. Occupations that require an overall view of
        organizations and that deal with the impersonal
        side of organizations are best held by individuals
        with which problem-solving style:
        a)   Sensation-thinking;
        b)   Intuitive-thinking;   b
        c)   Sensation-feeling;
        d)   Intuitive-feeling.
    4. Occupations that require decisions based on facts
        and figures relating to the impersonal side of
        the organization are best held by individuals with
        which problem-solving style:
        a)   Sensation-thinking;
        b)   Intuitive-thinking;   a
        c)   Sensation-feeling;
        d)   Intuitive-feeling.

VII. "Measures of Excellence" and Problem-Solving Types.

   1.   Match items a-h with items 1-8:
        a. Feeling   b. Sensation   c. Intuitive   d. Thinking
        e. Sensation-thinking   f. Intuitive-thinking
        g. Sensation-feeling   h. Intuitive-feeling

   ++

   1. ____Bias for action.   b

   2. ____Staying close to the customer.   g

   3. ____Autonomy through encouraging creativity.   c

   4. ____Productivity through people.   a

   5. ____Hands-on, value-driven management.   a

   6. ____Sticking with what you do best.   f

   7. ____Simple structure.   b

   8. ____Simultaneous tight and loose controls.   f

APPLIED QUESTIONS

1.   If the person interviewing you for a job places great
     emphasis on learning about your prior work experience,
     which of the following terms best describes him/her:
     a)   Intuition;
     b)   Sensations;   b
     c)   Thinking;
     d)   Feeling.
2.   An intuitive-type individual would be most likely to do
     which of the following when solving a business problem:
     a)   Have a difficult time deciding which path to
          follow;
     b)   Stick with an old tried and true method of dealing
          with the problem;   a
     c)   Believe the problem is caused by interpersonal
          difficulties;
     d)   Search for and obtain additional facts and figures.
3.   People who emphasize "feelings" in evaluating
     situations tend to:

a) Distrust creativity;
b) Dislike new problems unless there are structured
    ways of dealing with them;
c) Spend a great deal of time formulating problem-
    solving methods;
d) Dislike confrontations.

d

4. A manager who spends so much time analyzing a problem
    that actions sometimes come too late could best be
    described as a(n):
    a) Sensation-type;
    b) Intuitive-type;
    c) Feelings-type;
    d) Thinking-type.

d

5. Some labor arbitrators base their decisions almost
    entirely on "the facts," while others place more weight
    on extenuating circumstances. The latter could be said
    to interpret situations on the basis of:
    a) Feelings;
    b) Intuition;
    c) Thinking;
    d) Sensation.

a

6. Which type of manager would be most likely to reward
    employees even though there might be no clear data to
    show that reward was warranted:
    a) Intuitive-thinking;
    b) Intuitive-feeling;
    c) Sensation-thinking;
    d) Sensation-feeling.

b

7. Which type of manager would be most likely to have a
    reward system that consisted of rewards based on
    measurable performance standards:
    a) Intuitive-thinking;
    b) Intuitive-feeling;
    c) Sensation-thinking;
    d) Sensation-feeling.

c

8. These managers base their decisions largely on "the
    numbers," and thus sometimes act without considering
    the human aspects of a problem:
    a) Sensation-feeling;
    b) Sensation-thinking;
    c) Intuitive-feeling;
    d) Intuitive-thinking.

b

9. A manager who would be most likely to analyze a
    subordinate's proposal for a new product would be:
    a) Intuitive-thinking;
    b) Intuitive-feeling;
    c) Sensation-thinking;
    d) Sensation-feeling.

a

10. A manager who had kept good records and had all the hard data necessary to terminate an employee, but who just could not bring himself to do it could best be classified as:
    a) Intuitive-thinking;
    b) Intuitive-feeling;
    c) Sensation-thinking;
    d) Sensation-feeling.

    d

11. These managers run formal, well-planned, efficient, impersonal meetings:
    a) Sensation-thinking;
    b) Sensation-feeling;
    c) Intuitive-thinking;
    d) Intuitive-feeling.

    a

12. If the primary need is for a manager who will come into the organization, help shape a direction for it, shake things up, and make the necessary changes, what sort of manager would likely be best:
    a) Sensation-thinking;
    b) Sensation-feeling;
    c) Intuitive-thinking;
    d) Intuitive-feeling.

    c

13. If you want a boss who will take most interest in and be supportive of your development as you move up the ladder, you will be in the best possible position if you boss is:
    a) Sensation-thinking;
    b) Sensation-feeling;
    c) Intuitive-thinking;
    d) Intuitive-feeling.

    d

14. Which of the following types of managers would be most likely to get into trouble by making inconsistent decisions where "people issues" are concerned:
    a) Sensation-thinking;
    b) Sensation-feeling;
    c) Intuitive-thinking;
    d) Intuitive-feeling.

    d

15. Which of the following sets of occupations is best suited to the intuitive-thinking type individual:
    a) Accountant, computer programmer, statistician;
    b) Design architect, economics teacher, research engineer;
    c) Negotiator, sales, trouble-shooter;
    d) Public relations, politics, advertising.

    b

16. Intuitive-thinking type individuals tend to assess organizational effectiveness by looking at variables containing such measures as:
    a) Various sales and cost ratios;
    b) Rate of new product development;

    b

    c)   Absenteeism, turnover, and grievances;
    d)   Consumer satisfaction, social responsibility, and quality of life.

17. A weakness that sensation-feeling type individuals may have is that they may:
    a)   Preserve some procedures and rules that should be changed;
    b)   Let the "need to be loved" get in the way of managing;
    c)   Lose interest in a project once the design stage and the challenge of initial implementation is over;
    d)   Do not see the value of abstract ideas.

d

18. A weakness that intuitive-feeling type individuals may have is that they may:
    a)   Preserve some procedures and rules that should be changed;
    b)   Let the "need to be loved" get in the way of managing;
    c)   Lose interest in a project once the design stage and the challenge of initial implementation is over;
    d)   Do not see the value of abstract ideas.

b

19. A strategy in dealing with some bosses is to be the "last person in to them." Earlier agreements frequently are forgotten. They "flow with the wind." They always go along with the last person who has made an appeal to them. Bosses like this are:
    a) Sensation-thinking;
    b) Sensation-feeling;
    c) Intuitive-thinking;
    d) Intuitive-feeling.

d

20. This type of manager has particular need for someone to "do the paperwork" and "dig out the facts," so that he/she can complete the analysis and make rational decisions:
    a) Sensation-thinking;
    b) Sensation-feeling;
    c) Intuitive-thinking;
    d) Intuitive-feeling.

c

21. In hopes of returning to the favorable profit position it once had, the management of a large retail store chain decides to divest itself of a recently acquired financial services division. This represents which of the following types of problem-solving:
    a) Intuitive-thinking;
    b) Intuitive-feeling;
    c) Sensation-thinking;
    d) Sensation-feeling.

a

PROGRAMMED STUDY SUPPLEMENT

1.	Of the types of managers described in the chapter, the _____ would be the most comfortable with an unstructured, group-centered management system that allows employee participation in decision-making.	intuitive-feeler
2.	A(n) _____ places greatest emphasis on human interaction, feelings, and emotion.	feeling-type person
3.	A(n) _____ places greatest emphasis on ideas, concepts, theories, innovations, and long-range thinking.	intuitive-type person
4.	An ability to see creative possibilities but yet analyze the potential of these possibilities on an impersonal basis is characteristic of the _____.	intuitive-thinker
5.	Logical and analytical bases for decisions characterize the _____.	thinking-type person
6.	An employee says, "My boss expects a lot, but he takes care of you if you do your job." That employee is probably describing a(n) _____.	sensation-feeler
7.	A(n) _____ is decisive and makes decisions based on precise interpretations of facts and figures.	sensation-thinker
8.	A(n) _____ uses facts and relies on past experience in approaching current problems.	sensation-type person
9.	_____ refers to a person's ability to process information.	cognitive complexity

10. _____ means that you would rather work with known facts than look for possibilities.   sensing

---

11. _____ means that you would rather look for possibilities than work with known facts.   intuition

---

12. _____ means that your judgments are based on impersonal analysis and logic more than on personal values.   thinking

---

13. _____ means that you base your judgments more on personal values than impersonal analysis.   feeling

---

14. _____ refers to the process of giving meaning and definition to those problems that have been recognized by the individual.   problem interpretation

---

15. A person's _____ reflects the way they visualize and think about situations.   problem-solving style

---

16. A _____ is a Korean business group consisting of large diversified companies owned and managed by a family.   chaebol

CHAPTER 6

LEARNING AND REINFORCEMENT

LEARNING OBJECTIVES

When you read and when you review Chapter 6, keep in mind the learning objectives which have been established by the authors. Look them over first as a guide to picking out the most important parts of the chapter, and then think about them as you are going through the chapter. When you have finished the chapter, ask yourself whether you have met the objectives.

The authors intend that when you have finished studying this chapter you should be able to:

* Discuss the differences among classical, operant, and social learning.
* Describe the contingencies of reinforcement.
* List the methods used to increase desired behaviors and reduce undesired behaviors.
* Describe the procedures and principles of behavioral modification.
* State two limitations of behavioral modification.

CHAPTER OUTLINE

After you have read the chapter, complete the following outline.

I.   TYPES OF LEARNING.

   A.   Learning is a permanent Δ in frequency of occurrence of a specific individual behavior. Learning depends on environmental factors.

   B.   Three types of learning:

      1. Classical conditioning - process ind. learn reflex beh. (involun.)

      2. Operant conditioning - process learn voluntary beh

      3. Social learning - behav. learn from observing others & imitating their beh.

   C.   Social learning theory.

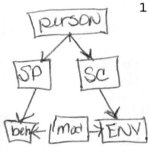

      1.   Components of the social learning theory model are

         a. modeling - behaviors acquired by observ. & imitate others

         b. environment

         c. behavior

         d. symbolic process - mental images that help guide a person's behavior

         e. self control - a person's self-efficacy controls his/her behavior

         f. person

      2.   Self-efficacy is the belief that one can perform adequately in a situation

         a.   Managers with high self-efficacy believe

            (1) they have the ability needed

            (2) they are capable of the effort required to achieve the goal

            (3) no outside events will prevent them from obtaining a desired level of performance

      3.   Learned helplessness is

4. Applications of social learning theory for improving behavior in organizations include:

    a.

    b.

    c.

    d.

    e.

    f.

II. CONTINGENCIES OF REINFORCEMENT.

A. A contingency of reinforcement is *the relationship btwn a behavior & the preceding & following environmental events that influence that behavior.*

1. A contingency of reinforcement consists of

    a. *antecedent - precedes & is a stimulus to a behavior*

    b. *consequence - result of a behavior. ; applied or w/d.*

    c. *behavior*

2. Positive events are *desired, or pleasing to employees*

3. Aversive events are *undesired, or displeasing, to employee.*

B. Positive reinforcement is *a pleasant consequence for occurence of a desired behavior.*

1. Reinforcement is *a behavioral contingency that ↑ the frequency of a particular behavior that it follows*

2. Reward is *an event that a person finds desireable or pleasing*

3. A primary reinforcer is *an event for which the individual doesn't have to learn the value of the reinforcer*

4. A secondary reinforcer is *an event that once had neutral value but has taken on some value (+ or −) for an individual because of past experience*

5. The principles of positive reinforcement are

    a. _principle of contingent reinforcement states reinforcer must be administered only if desired beh. is performed._

    b. _Immediate reinf._

    c.

    d.

C. Organizational rewards include

    1.

    2.

    3.

    4.

    5.

    6.

D. Negative reinforcement is

    1. Escape learning is

    2. Avoidance learning is

E. Omission is

    1. Steps in the omission procedure:

        a.

        b.

        c.

F. Punishment is

1. Potential effects of punishment are

    a.

    b.

    c.

    d.

    e.

    f.

2. Effective use of punishment includes

G. Guidelines for using contingencies of reinforcement in the workplace:

    1.

    2.

    3.

    4.

    5.

    6.

III. SCHEDULES OF REINFORCEMENT.

A. Continuous reinforcement is

B. Intermittent reinforcement is

    1. A fixed interval schedule is one in which

    2. A variable interval schedule is one in which

    3. A fixed ratio schedule is one in which

   4.   A variable ratio schedule is one in which

IV.   BEHAVIORAL MODIFICATION.

   A.   Behavioral modification is based on

   B.   Principles and procedures of behavioral modification.

       1.   Pinpointing relevant behavior consists of three
            activities:

            a.

            b.

            c.

       2.   Charting behavior:

            a.   Involves two periods

                 (1)

                 (2)

            b.   Has two overall objectives:
                 (1)

                 (2)

       3.   Choosing a contingency of reinforcement requires a
            judgement about

       4.   Depending upon whether the problem has been solved,
            the manager will either

            a.

            b.

C.   Limitations of behavior modification are:

1.

  a.   Can be managed by

    (1)

    (2)

2.

  a.   Can be dealt with by

D.   Ethical questions regarding behavior modification center around

DIRECTED QUESTIONS

I.   Theories of Learning.

1.   Classical conditioning involves:
     a)   Observational learning;
     b)   Learning through direct experience;   d
     c)   Changes in voluntary work behavior;
     d)   Reflexive responses.
2.   Social learning occurs through:
     a)   Involuntary or automatic responses;
     b)   Observing others performing the desired   b
          behavior;
     c)   Provoking changes in an individual's voluntary
          behavior;
     d)   Unconditional stimuli eliciting reflexive
          responses.
3.   Operant conditioning:
     a)   Relies on the consequences of the responses;
     b)   Is also known as modelling or imitation;   a
     c)   Involves involuntary or automatic responses;
     d)   Utilizes observational learning.
4.   Pavlov's dog is an example of:
     a)   Classical conditioning;
     b)   Operant conditioning;   a
     c)   Social learning;
     d)   Imitation.

5. Operant work behaviors are of interest to managers because:
    a) They are involuntary behaviors and need to be controlled;
    b) They can be learned without actually having been performed;
    c) They can be controlled by their environmental consequences;
    d) All of the above.

    c

6. Social learning:
    a) Consists of experiencing the consequences that follow behavior;
    b) Does not directly result in performance;
    c) Can be described as "learning by doing";
    d) All of the above.

    b

7. Employees with high self-efficacy believe:
    a) They have the ability needed;
    b) They are capable of achieving their goals;
    c) Only outside events will prevent them from achieving their goals;
    d) All of the above;
    e) a and b.

    e

8. When people's motivation drops off because they believe they are not capable of doing the job, the condition is called:
    a) Learned helplessness;
    b) High self-efficacy;
    c) Reinforcement antecedent;
    d) None of the above.

    a

II. Contingencies of Reinforcement.

1. A contingency of reinforcement:
    a) Consists of antecedents, behaviors, and consequences;
    b) May include application or withdrawal of environmental events;
    c) Is the relationship between a behavior and preceding and subsequent environmental events;
    d) All of the above.

    d

2. A stimulus that precedes a behavior and sets the stage for the behavior to occur is called a(n):
    a) Consequence;
    b) Behavior;
    c) Antecedent;
    d) Primary reinforcer.

    c

3. To say that a consequence is contingent upon a behavior is to say that it:
    a) Follows the antecedent of the behavior;
    b) Requires positive reinforcement;

    c

      c)   Occurs only if that behavior occurs;
      d)   Can be classified as a positive environmental
          event.
4. Which of the following illustrates types of
    contingency:
    a)   An environmental event is presented;
    b)   An environmental event is withdrawn;   d
    c)   An environmental event is aversive;
    d)   All of the above.

III. Methods to Increase Desired and Reduce Undesired Behavior.

1. Rewards:
    a)   Are aversive;
    b)   And reinforcers are the same thing;   c
    c)   Can be reinforcers if they increase occurrence
         of desirable behavior;
    d)   Increase the frequency of the behaviors they
         follow.
2. A primary reinforcer:
    a)   Always reinforces the desired behavior;
    b)   Is a neutral event that has taken on positive
         value;   d
    c)   Is the type of reinforcer that typically
         enforces behavior in organizations;
    d)   Does not require that an individual has learned
         its reinforcement value.
3. A secondary reinforcer:
    a)   Does not directly satisfy a base need but can
         be used to attain satisfaction;
    b)   Operates without reference to whether the
         individual has experienced it;   a
    c)   Automatically activates after a primary
         reinforcer's effects have occurred;
    d)   Is a negative reinforcer.
4. Reinforcement:
    a)   May not always occur when primary reinforcers
         are used;
    b)   Occurs whenever rewards are administered;   a
    c)   Requires the linking of primary and secondary
         reinforcers;
    d)   None of the above.
5. The principle of contingent reinforcement states
    that a reinforcer's effectiveness:
    a)   Depends on being used only when the desired
         behavior is performed;
    b)   Will be greatest if the individual has been
         deprived of the particular event;   a

c)   Depends on the amount of the reinforcer that is
     used;
d)   Depends on the willingness of the party
     involved to administer it.

6.   Which of the following relates to the principle of
     reinforcement deprivation:
     a)   What might seem like a "noticeable" reinforcer
          to one person might be so minimal as to go
          unnoticed by another;
     b)   If a person has recently been satiated with
          reinforcer, the reinforcer's effect will be
          reduced;   b
     c)   A reinforcer loses effect if administered in
          the absence of the desired behavior;
     d)   Reinforcement should closely follow behavior.

7.   A concern that rewards be distributed at regular
     intervals reflects which of the following
     principles:
     a)   Contingent reinforcement;
     b)   Immediate reinforcement;   b
     c)   Reinforcement size;
     d)   Reinforcement deprivation.

8.   The less satiated an individual is with a
     reinforcer, the greater effect it will have.
     This reflects which of the following principles:
     a)   Contingent reinforcement;
     b)   Immediate reinforcement;   d
     c)   Reinforcement size;
     d)   Reinforcement deprivation.

9.   The principle of reinforcement size says that:
     a)   What is or is not an effective size depends on
          the individual involved;
     b)   What is or is not an effective size depends
          partly on the behavior involved;   d
     c)   A large reinforcer will have more effect than a
          small reinforcer;
     d)   All of the above.

10. Self-administered rewards:
     a)   Are less important than other organizational
          rewards;
     b)   Can be a form of organizational reward;   d
     c)   Are rewards but not reinforcers;
     d)   Can be important reinforcers.

11. Organizational rewards:
     a)   Focus primarily on material rewards;
     b)   Are primary reinforcers;   c
     c)   May be given by fellow workers as well as
          supervisors;
     d)   Are totally controlled by supervisors.

12. Negative reinforcement:
    a) Occurs as a consequence of undesirable
       behavior;
    b) Is used to increase the frequency of desired
       behavior;   b
    c) Is a type of avoidance response;
    d) Is used to decrease the frequency of an
       undesired behavior.
13. Escape is a procedure whereby:
    a) A person prevents an undesirable event by
       performing the target behavior before the
       undesirable event occurs;
    b) The frequency of an undesirable behavior is
       decreased;   c
    c) A person performs a target behavior to cause
       an undesirable event to be discontinued;
    d) An unpleasant event follows a behavior and
       decreases its frequency.
14. Avoidance is a procedure whereby:
    a) A person prevents an undesirable event by
       performing the target behavior before the
       undesirable event occurs;
    b) The frequency of an undesirable behavior is
       decreased;   a
    c) A person performs a target behavior to cause an
       undesirable event to be discontinued;
    d) An unpleasant event follows a behavior and
       decreases its frequency.
15. Extinction is a procedure that:
    a) Can be useful for reducing undesirable
       behavior;
    b) Can be going on without the knowledge of the
       parties bringing it about;   d
    c) Should be used in combination with other
       reinforcers which develop desirable behavior;
    d) All of the above.
16. Which of the following are steps in the extinction
    procedure:
    a) Identifying the behavior to be reduced;
    b) Identifying the reinforcer that maintains the
       undesired behavior;   d
    c) Getting rid of the reinforcer that maintains
       the undesired behavior;
    d) All of the above.
17. A punishment contingency:
    a) Suppresses the frequency of a target behavior;
    b) Encourages the frequency of a target behavior;   a
    c) Exists when any unpleasant event is applied;
    d) Most often involves material consequences.

18. An individual should be able to recognize that a
     punishment contingency exists because:
     a) An unpleasant event is involved;
     b) An antecedent cues the individual that an
         unpleasant consequence will follow a certain   b
         behavior;
     c) Unpleasant interpersonal consequences will
         follow a certain behavior.

19. Advantages of using punishment include:
     a) Once it is instituted, it operates
         automatically with or without the presence of
         the punishing agent;
     b) It ensures that individuals will replace the
         undesired behavior with desired behavior;   c
     c) It often produces fast results in the short
         run;
     d) All of the above.

20. Which of the following is a potential side effect
     of punishment:
     a) Creativity and flexibility may be suppressed;
     b) Escape and avoidance behavior;   d
     c) Undesirable emotional reactions;
     d) All of the above.

21. Punishment:
     a) In some cases needs to be done publicly for it
         to have the strength needed;
     b) Is most effective in long-term management of
         employees;   c
     c) Focuses on specific undesired behavior rather
         than on the person;
     d) All of the above.

22. Punishment, to be effective, must:
     a) Be used in conjunction with appropriate
         positive reinforcement;
     b) Be the dominant form of reinforcement used;   a
     c) Be in written form;
     d) Train a person in what to do, as well as in
         what not to do.

IV. Schedules of Reinforcement.

1.   Reinforcers which are delivered after a constant
     number of behaviors have been performed are:
     a) Known as continuous reinforcers;
     b) On a schedule known as a continuous ratio
         schedule;   d
     c) On a schedule known as a variable ratio
         schedule;
     d) On a schedule known as a fixed ratio schedule.

2. Reinforcers which are delivered after passage of time are on a schedule known as a(n):
   a) Interval schedule;
   b) Ratio schedule;
   c) Variable schedule;
   d) Fixed schedule.

   a

3. A fixed interval schedule means that:
   a) The target behavior must occur a certain number of times before it is reinforced;
   b) The interval varies around some average length of time;
   c) The number of target behaviors that must occur varies around some average;
   d) A constant amount of time must pass before a reinforcer can be provided.

   d

4. Which of the following schedules provide reinforcers based on the passage of time:
   a) Fixed ratio schedule;
   b) Fixed interval schedule;
   c) Continuous reinforcement;
   d) None of the above.

   b

5. The "variable" in a variable interval schedule is:
   a) The number of times which a target behavior must occur before it is reinforced;
   b) The constant amount of time that must occur before a reinforcer is provided;
   c) Whether or not the reinforcement is continuous;
   d) None of the above.

   d

6. If reinforcement is provided when the first desired behavior occurs following a constant amount of time, the schedule is:
   a) Fixed ratio;
   b) Variable ratio;
   c) Fixed interval;
   d) Variable interval.

   c

7. The primary difference between a fixed interval schedule and a fixed ratio schedule is that:
   a) In a fixed ratio schedule the target behavior may not be reinforced the first time it occurs;
   b) The variable in a fixed ratio schedule is time, while it is the number of behavior occurrences in fixed interval schedules;
   c) Intervals are based on time whereas ratios are based on target behavior occurrences;
   d) None of the above.

   c

8. Which of the following schedules tends to produce the most uneven pattern of responses:
   a) Fixed interval;
   b) Fixed ratio;
   c) Continuous;
   d) Variable ratio.

   a

9. Which of the following <u>pairs</u> of schedules are most
    directly based on output:
    a) Fixed ratio and variable ratio;
    b) Fixed interval and variable interval;   a
    c) Fixed ratio and fixed interval;
    d) Variable ratio and variable interval.
10. Which of the following <u>pairs</u> of schedules
    do the authors see as leading to the highest
    performance levels:
    a) Fixed ratio and variable ratio;
    b) Fixed interval and variable interval;   a
    c) Fixed ratio and fixed interval;
    d) Variable ratio and variable interval.

V. Procedures for Behavior Modification.

1. The first step in applying operant conditioning is:
    a) Choosing a strategy;
    b) Pinpointing the target behavior;   b
    c) Charting a target behavior;
    d) Maintaining the contingency of reinforcement
        for the target behavior.
2. "Target behaviors" are those which are:
    a) Either desirable, undesirable, or neutral;
    b) Desirable;   c
    c) Desirable or undesirable;
    d) Desirable or neutral.
3. The objectives in charting target behavior include:
    a) Identify the actual frequency of a target
        behavior;
    b) Evaluating the effectiveness of an intervention
        strategy;   d
    c) Keeping track of a target behavior;
    d) All of the above.
4. During the intervention period:
    a) Feedback from charting sometimes is sufficient
        to cause behavioral change;
    b) Rewards or penalties sometimes accompany
        feedback;
    c) The individual's behavior is measured after   d
        some positive reinforcement or punishment;
    d) All of the above.
5. In behavioral modification:
    a) Choosing a strategy is done first so other
        procedures which will fit within that
        strategy can be identified;
    b) Positive reinforcement is the first alternative
        to consider;   b

    c) Extinction is inappropriate if the target behavior is undesirable;

    d) A decision has to be made concerning whether to deal with the desirable or the undesirable behaviors that have been identified.

6. When an intervention has been found to be effective in affecting target behavior:

    a) It should be discontinued so that it does not lose its effect;

    b) It should be changed because a set of new experiences will have greater effect on the individual affected;

    c) The target behavior should be re-identified;

    d) The contingency of reinforcement should be maintained.

                  d

7. Which of the following is a reasonable response if it is determined that an intervention strategy has failed:

    a) Re-identification of the target behavior;

    b) Change the reward;

    c) Try a different form of reinforcement contingency;

    d) All of the above.

                  d

VI. Limitations of Behavioral Modification.

1. Individual differences:

    a) Are often ignored by the behavioral modification approach;

    b) Are the basis on which behavioral modification works;

    c) Will make it impossible to effectively apply behavioral modification;

    d) Cannot be determined prior to application of contingent reinforcement.

                  a

2. When an atmosphere of trust between employees and managers exists:

    a) Individual differences less likely to exist;

    b) Group norms will be less likely to exist;

    c) Group norms to restrict cooperation will be less likely to emerge;

    d) Individual differences will not affect attempts at behavioral modification.

                  c

3. Group norms:

    a) Exist primarily in situations wherein the group is experiencing attempts to control it;

    b) Will not emerge if employees feel they are going to receive adequate pay;

                  d

     c)   Cause individuals to feel they are being exploited;

     d)   Are likely to reduce the effectiveness of reward systems if individuals feel exploited.

APPLIED QUESTIONS

1.   Which of the following areas is <u>not</u> stressed by the learning theory approach advanced in Chapter 6:
    a)   Objective behavior;
    b)   Measurable behavior;   c
    c)   Cognitive behavior;
    d)   Work behavior.

2.   Which of the following factors is <u>not</u> a true determinant of whether a particular behavior from an individual would be "undesirable":
    a)   An objective measure of "desirable" behavior;
    b)   The viewpoint of the individual's supervisor;   a
    c)   The individual's viewpoint;
    d)   Organizational norms.

3.   Which of the following is <u>not</u> a true statement:
    a)   A worker's personality and values influence his/her behavior;
    b)   A manager should try to modify or control a worker's personality and values;   b
    c)   Environmental conditions in the workplace influence a worker's behavior;
    d)   A manager should try to modify or control environmental conditions in the workplace.

4.   Which of the following types of learning is usually <u>not</u> considered applicable to the workplace:
    a)   Classical conditioning;
    b)   Social learning;   a
    c)   Observational learning;
    d)   Operant conditioning.

5.   When an ambitious young comedienne tries to improve her act by watching every TV comic possible and by going to see live comedy wherever she can find it, she is engaging in:
    a)   Operant conditioning;
    b)   Social learning;   b
    c)   Classical conditioning;
    d)   Behavior modification.

6.   Which of the following is an example of a circumstance in which the failure to elicit the desired response is most likely attributable to a breakdown in operant conditioning:

a) An employee is put on a job before completing a training program and subsequently fails due to a lack of job knowledge;

b) An employee has observed people performing a certain set of tasks but has not really developed an understanding of the principles behind the job as a whole;

c) An employee who values 2 hours free time far more than she values the loss of a half day's pay disrupts the work flow by leaving 2 hours early even though threatened with the loss of 4 hours of pay;

d) None of the above.

7. The brief staff meeting a manager has at the beginning of a week to make sure his people understand his priorities for that week is what part of a contingency of reinforcement:
a) Behavior;
b) Consequence;
c) Antecedent;
d) None of the above.

8. When, after being briefed on the manager's priorities, the employee completes a task high on that list of priorities, such completion comprises what part of a contingency of reinforcement:
a) Behavior;
b) Consequence;
c) Antecedent;
d) None of the above.

9. The presentation of a cash bonus to someone who places a positive value on extra cash as a reward for accomplishing a goal which management has set is an example of:
a) Positive reinforcement;
b) Extinction;
c) Punishment;
d) Negative reinforcement.

10. The angry shouting of a supervisor at an employee who has just disobeyed a work rule is an example of:
a) Positive reinforcement;
b) Extinction;
c) Punishment;
d) Negative reinforcement.

11. When a manager tells a group of workers that they will not be able to leave for lunch until they complete a set of tasks, that manager is engaging in:
a) Positive reinforcement;
b) Extinction;
c) Punishment;
d) Negative reinforcement.

c

c

a

a

c

d

12. An employee has been able to get his supervisor to do
     certain difficult parts of his job for him by
     constantly asking the supervisor questions to the point
     where the supervisor found it quicker to do the job.
     When that supervisor stops this practice and tells the
     employee to figure it out on his own, which of the
     following procedures will be involved:
     a)   Positive reinforcement;
     b)   Extinction;   b
     c)   Punishment;
     d)   Negative reinforcement.
13. Employees are pleased at the prospects of earning
     additional money when it is first announced that a
     period of incentive pay possibilities will be coming
     up.   After an extended time they begin to grumble and
     refuse to try to exceed quotas.   This may be partially
     explained by:
     a)   The principle of reinforcement deprivation;
     b)   The principle of operant conditioning;   a
     c)   The principle of extinction;
     d)   The principle of immediate reinforcement.
14. Which of the following is an example of avoidance:
     a)   Involuntary turnover;
     b)   Quickly performing the task upon being yelled at by
          the supervisor;   c
     c)   Absenteeism;
     d)   All of the above.
15. Which of the following statements regarding the
     effective use of punishment is true:
     a)   A manager who uses positive reinforcement correctly
          will not need to resort to punishment;
     b)   A manager may ensure a smoothly-running operation
          by reprimanding employees who have bad attitudes;   d
     c)   The long-run side effects of punishment will
          counter-act short-run benefits so that punishment
          should not be used;
     d)   None of the above statements is true.
16. A piece-rate incentive system is an example of which
     type of reinforcement schedule:
     a)   Fixed interval;
     b)   Fixed ratio;   b
     c)   Variable interval;
     d)   Variable ratio.
17. A bonus paid each time your sales for the quarter
     exceed the average of last quarter's sales in your
     division of the company is an example of which type of
     reinforcement schedule:
     a)   Fixed interval;
     b)   Fixed ratio;   d
     c)   Variable interval;
     d)   Variable ratio.

18. Some employees may tend to work hardest toward the end of each 6-month period when they know they are about to be reviewed for a pay increase. This is an example of which type of reinforcement schedule:
    a) Fixed interval;
    b) Fixed ratio;
    c) Variable interval;
    d) Variable ratio.

    a

19. A firm believes that it is not getting a good return on its expenditures for employee benefits because it is unable to fill the wide range of employee needs. Which of the following strategies would appear best:
    a) Hire people with more closely related needs;
    b) Allow employee participation in determining benefits to be offered;
    c) Change the set of preferences held by the existing employees;
    d) Build a better atmosphere of trust between employees and management.

    b

20. An unemployed worker searches diligently for work about six weeks and finds nothing. Discouraged, she quits looking. She's an example of:
    a) High self-efficacy;
    b) Reinforcement defense;
    c) Learned helplessness;
    d) Social learning.

    c

PROGRAMMED STUDY SUPPLEMENT

1. A(n) _____ is a stimulus that precedes a behavior and sets the stage for the behavior to occur.

   antecedent

2. Disciplinary suspensions are examples of _____.

   aversive events

3. To determine whether an attempt to change an employee's behavior has been successful, one may need to utilize a _____ procedure.

   charting

4. _____ involves involuntary or automatic responses or behaviors that are not under an individual's conscious control.

   classical conditioning

5. Receiving praise would be one possible _____ an employee might encounter from a behavior that a manager believed desirable.

conse-
quence

---

6. A _____ is the relationship between a behavior, its antecedents, and its consequence.

contingen-
cy of
reinforce-
ment

---

7. Payment in the form of weekly paychecks would represent reinforcement on a(n) _____.

fixed
interval
schedule

---

8. A payment system that included a feature whereby an employee would receive 115% of base rate after output reached 100% of standard would represent reinforcement on a(n) _____.

fixed
ratio
schedule

---

9. Interval schedules and ratio schedules are types of _____.

intermit-
tent rein-
forcement

---

10. _____ typically does not occur in the workplace.

continuous
reinforce-
ment

---

11. _____ is a relatively permanent change in the frequency of occurrence of a behavior.

learning

---

12. _____ is an area of psychology that approaches behavior management by objective, measurable assessments of behavior.

learning
theory

---

13. The instructor tells the students that if they are unable to answer his questions in class next week there will be an extra exam given in the week following that. The instructor is using _____.

negative
reinforce-
ment

14. Once a new behavior is learned it is the consequences of that behavior that are important in maintaining its frequency. That concept is known as _____.

operant conditioning

---

15. It would make sense for an employer to attempt to withdraw a _____ from an employee if its existence had reinforced that employee's undesirable behavior.

positive event

---

16. A cash bonus can be a(n)_____ even though it is not a(n) _____ if it serves as a(n) _____.

positive reinforcement; primary reinforcement; secondary reinforcement

---

17. A "merit increase" which is not really based on merit but instead is given out almost automatically to any employee who stays out of serious trouble is not effective in stimulating performance because it is not based on the _____.

principle of contingent reinforcement

---

18. To tell a student that he/she should get the most they can out of this course because it will help them later on when they become managers may not be terribly effective. A partial explanation can be found in the _____.

principle of immediate reinforcement

---

19. After some point, the praise that initially caused the employee to keep his productivity high no longer works. One reason may be found in the _____.

principle of reinforcement deprivation

---

20. A certain incentive pay formula might reinforce desirable behavior in one employee but not in another, because the _____ is a relative concept.

principle of reinforcement size

21. One characteristic of _____ is that   punishment
     while it may eliminate an undesirable behavior
     it does not replace that behavior with one that
     is desirable.

---

22. Classical conditioning is generally thought to   reflexive
     be of little use for affecting employee
     behaviors because it involves _____
     responses that by and large are not the
     behaviors managers seek to control.

---

23. A behavioral contingency that increases the   reinforce-
     frequency of some behavior that it follows is   ment
     known as a(n)_____.

---

24. Employees who "keep one eye out for the boss"   variable
     who comes around every so often so they will be   interval
     seen doing something meriting praise are   schedule
     responding to a _____ of
     reinforcement.

---

25. A baseball club offers a bonus each month to   variable
     every player whose number of hits at the end of   ratio
     the month is within 15 hits of the league   schedule
     leader. That is a _____ of
     reinforcement.

---

26. An event that a person defines as desirable   reward
     or pleasant is called a _____.

---

27. In _____ a person prevents an   avoidance
     unpleasant event from occurring by   learning
     performing the proper behavior before
     the unpleasant event is presented.

---

28. In _____ a person performs a behavior   escape
     to terminate an unpleasant event that is   learning
     present.

---

29. An _____ means that reinforcers are   interval
     delivered after the passage of a certain   schedule
     amount of time.

30. In a _____, reinforcers are delivered
     after a certain number of behaviors have
     been performed.

     ratio
     schedule

---

31. _____ refers to procedures and prin-
     ciples that are based on operant condi-
     tioning.

     behavior
     modifica-
     tion

---

32. _____ refers to those behaviors we learn
     from observing others and imitating their
     behavior.

     social
     learning

---

33. The belief that one can perform adequately in
     a situation is _____.

     self-
     efficacy

---

34. _____ occurs when the motivation to
     perform the task is so low that the worker
     gives up.

     learned
     helpless-
     ness

---

35. _____ means all reinforcing events are
     stopped.

     omission

CHAPTER 7

WORK MOTIVATION

<u>**LEARNING OBJECTIVES**</u>

When you read and when you review Chapter 7, keep in mind the learning objectives which have been established by the authors. Look them over first as a guide to picking out the most important parts of the chapter and then think about them as you are going through the chapter. When you have finished the chapter, ask yourself whether you have met the objectives.

The authors intend that when you have finished studying this chapter you should be able to:

* Define motivation and describe the process of motivation.
* Explain and apply four content theories of motivation: needs hierarchy theory, ERG theory, achievement motivation theory, and motivator-hygiene theory.
* Describe and apply two process theories of motivation: expectancy theory and equity theory.
* State the organizational implications for each of the motivation theories.

CHAPTER OUTLINE

After you have read the chapter, complete the following outline.

I.   THE CONCEPT OF MOTIVATION.

    A.   Motivation is *the forces acting on or w/in a person that cause the person to behave in a specific, goal-directed manner.*

        1.   In the workplace, motivation must, at the minimum, accomplish

           a. *people must be attracted not only to join org. but also to remain in it.*

           b. *people must perform the task for which they are hired.*

           c. *people must go beyond routine performance & become creative & innovative in their work*

II.   BASIC MOTIVATIONAL PROCESSES.

    A.   The key motivational principle is that *people's performance is based on their level of ability & motivation.*

        1.   The study of motivation is concerned with

           a. *what drives behavior*

           b. *what direction behavior takes*

           c. *how to maintain this behavior*

    B.   Core phases of the motivational process.

        1. *identifying a person's needs - needs can be psychological, physiological, social*

        2. *Employee searches for ways to satisfy needs*

        3. *Employee selects goal-directed behaviors*

        4. *Employee performs*

        5. *Employee receives either reward/punishment*

        6. *employee reassesses need deficiencies*

C.   Complications in the process include

1. motives can only be inferred; they cannot be seen.

2. dynamic nature of needs - needs, desires, expect-ations change + conflict w/each other.

3. Considerable differences in the way people select certain motives over others & in the energy w/ which people pursue these motives.

III. CONTENT THEORIES OF MOTIVATION.

A.   Content theories focus on the factors w/in a person that energize, direct, + stop behavior. → these factors focus on specific factors that motivate people

B.   Needs Hierarchy Theory.
     Maslow Hierarcy

1.   Basic assumptions:

a. A satisfied need does not motivate. However, when one need is met, another arises → people always striving to satisfy a need.

b. The needs network for most people is v. complex. w/ several needs affecting the behavior of each person @ any time.

c. Lower-level needs must be satisfied before higher-level needs are activated sufficiently to drive behavior.

d. There are more ways to satisfy higher-level needs than lower-level.

2.   The five need categories:

a. phsiological needs - food, H₂O, air shelter lowest level.

b. security needs - safety, stability, absence of threat, illness, pain.

c. affiliation needs - friendship, love, feeling of belonging

d. esteem needs - personal feeling of achievement + self worth + recognition or respect from others

e. self-actualization - self-fullment.

3.   Organizational implications are that
     - states goals that people value
     - types of behaviors that will help filfull various needs

C.   ERG Theory.

1.   Focuses on three sets of basic needs:

a. Existence needs - mat'l needs, food, air, H₂O pay, fringe benefits + working conditions

b. relatedness needs - est + maintaining interpersonal relationships w/co-workers, superiors, subordinates, friends

c. + family

(c) growth needs - expressed by individual's attempt to find opp. for unique personal dev. by making creative or productive contrib. at work

2. ERG Theory is based on the frustration-regression process, which means if a person is continually frustrated in attempts to satisfy growth needs, relatedness needs will reemerge as a major motivating force. the indiv. return to satisfy lower-level needs instead attempt satisfy growth needs. frustration lead to regressing

a. Needs Hierarchy Theory is based on the fulfillment-progression process, which means that a person progresses up the needs hierarch as each set of lower-level needs are satisfied

3. Organizational implications are that

D. Achievement Motivation Theory. ~~epleqleare~~

1. Focuses on three needs:

a. for achievement

b. affliation

c. power

2. Achievement Motivation Theory states that people are motivated according to the strength of their desire either to perform in terms of a standard of excellence or to succeed in competitive situations

a. The amount of achievement motivation that one has depends on their childhood, their personal + occupational experiences & the type of org. for which they work

b. How are "daydreams" a critical part of the theory? people can be taught to change their motivation by changing these daydreams

3. Achievement motivation is measured by Thematic Apperception test

4. Characteristics of high achievers:

a. set own goals - prefer to work at problem then leave to chance or other people

b. avoid selecting extremely difficult goals

c. prefer task provide immediate feedback

5.   The effect of money on high achievers is

6.   Organizational implications are

a.   arrange tasks so that employees receive periodic feedback on their performance. Feedback enables employees to modify performance

b.   provide good role models of achievement. Employees should be encouraged to copy heros.

c.   Modify employee self-images. High-achievement individuals accept themselves & seek job challenges & responsibilities

d.   Control employee imaginations. Employees should think about setting realistic goals & ways to attain them.

E.   Motivator-Hygiene Theory.

1.   Unique features of the Motivator-Hygiene Theory are

a.

b.

2.   Motivator factors are

a.   Examples include

b.   Another name for motivator factors is

3.   Hygiene factors are

a.   Examples include

b.   Another name for hygiene factors is

4.   Organizational implications are that

IV.   PROCESS THEORIES OF MOTIVATION.

    A.   Process theories focus on

    B.   Expectancy Theory.

        1.   Expectancy Theory states that

        2.   Assumptions underlying Expectancy Theory.

           a.

           b.

           c.

           d.

        3.   Components of Expectancy Theory.

           a.   First-level outcomes:

           b.   Second-level outcomes:

           c.   Expectancy:

           d.   Instrumentality:

           e.   Valence:

        4.   Research on Expectancy Theory has focused on

           a.

           b.

           c.

        5.   Organizational implications are that

           a.

      b.

      c.

      d.

      e.

      f.

C. Equity Theory.

    1. Equity theory focuses on

    2. Assumptions underlying Equity Theory.

       a.

       b.

    3. The General Equity Model.

       a. Inputs are

          (1) Examples include

       b. Outputs are

          (2) Examples include

       c. Equity exists when

       d. Inequity exists when

          (1) Consequences of inequity

             (a)

(b)

(c)

(d)

(e)

(f)

4. Research on Equity Theory has focused on

   a.

   b.

      (1)   Procedural justice is

DIRECTED QUESTIONS

I.   The Role of Motivation.

   1. Which of the following behavioral requirements cause
      organizations to be interested in motivation:
      a)   Attracting and keeping employees;
      b)   Getting employees to perform tasks for which
           they are hired;   d
      c)   Getting employees to go beyond the tasks for
           which they are hired;
      d)   All of the above.

II. The Motivational Process.

   1. Performance:
      a)   Is a function of ability and motivation;
      b)   Can occur where ability is great enough,
           even if motivation is absent;   a
      c)   Can occur where motivation is high enough,
           even if ability is absent;
      d)   All of the above.
   2. Which of the following is <u>not</u> one of the
      reasons why motivation in the real world is a
      more complex issue than in the general model
      of the motivational process:

a) Motives cannot be seen;   c
b) Motives are dynamic;
c) People have different types and levels of
    abilities;
d) People differ in their selection of motives
    and in their drives to pursue their motives.

III. Content Theories of Motivation.

1. Which of the needs in Maslow's hierarchy involves
    people wanting others to accept them for what they
    are and to perceive them as competent and able:
    a) Physiological;   c
    b) Affiliation;
    c) Esteem;
    d) Self-actualization.
2. Which of the following is one of the basic
    assumptions underlying Maslow's need hierarchy:
    a) A satisfied need does not motivate;
    b) The needs network for most people is very   a
        simple;
    c) Higher level needs must be satisfied first;
    d) There are more ways to satisfy lower level needs
        than there are to satisfy higher level needs.
3. To make work more meaningful, managers who
    specialize in self-actualization might:
    a) Involve employees in designing jobs;
    b) Make special assignments capitalizing on
        employees' unique skills;
    c) Provide leeway to employee groups in designing   d
        work procedures;
    d) All of the above.
4. Managerial implications of Maslow's need hierarchy
    include:
    a) Top managers are generally more able to satisfy
        their higher level needs than are lower level
        managers;   a
    b) Line managers are less likely to feel
        fulfillment of self-actualization needs than are
        staff managers;
    c) Young workers are more likely to meet self-
        actualization needs than are older workers;
    d) All of the above.
5. In ERG theory, growth needs:
    a) Are similar to Maslow's affiliation needs;
    b) Are similar to Maslow's self-actualization   b
        needs;
    c) Are needs involving personal development;
    d) All of the above.

6. ERG theory differs from Needs Hierarchy theory:
    a) In the way in which people satisfy the different sets of needs;
    b) In that ERG considers the fulfillment-progression process but not the frustration-regression process;   a
    c) In that ERG says that lower-level needs must be met before higher-level needs are activated.
7. According to ERG theory, when a manager finds that a subordinate's higher-level needs are blocked that manager should:
    a) Change the subordinate's needs;   b
    b) Re-direct the subordinate's behavior toward satisfying lower-level needs;
    c) Counsel the subordinate to accept the fact that his/her higher level needs cannot be met in the organization;
    d) All of the above.
8. Which of the following is <u>not</u> one of the three needs upon which Achievement Motivation theory focuses:
    a) Achievement;   b
    b) Growth;
    c) Affiliation;
    d) Power.
9. Achievement Motivation theory states that:
    a) People are motivated according to the strength of their desire to perform in terms of a standard of excellence;
    b) People are motivated according to the strength of their desire to succeed in competitive situations;   d
    c) The amount of achievement motivation people have depends partly on their background;
    d) All of the above.
10. Which of the following is <u>not</u> a characteristic of a high achiever:
    a) High achievers like to set their own goals;
    b) High achievers tend to pick out goals at the highest level of difficulty;   b
    c) High achievers prefer tasks that provide immediate feedback;
    d) High achievers prefer to be as fully responsible for their own goal attainment as possible.
11. Which of the following statements is true regarding the role of money where achievers are concerned:
    a) Incentive plans tend to be very effective;
    b) It is often the one measure that they accept as   c
        adequately reflecting their contribution;

c) High achievers tend to put a high price tag on
    themselves;
d) All of the above.
12. McClelland's research suggests that the managerial
    implications of Achievement Motivation theory
    include which of the following:
    a) Free workers' imaginations so they can pursue
        goals at the highest levels they can imagine;   c
    b) Rather than trying to be a role model of
        achievement, understand that workers set their
        own targets;
    c) Arrange tasks so that workers will receive
        periodic performance feedback;
    d) All of the above.
13. Hygiene factors include:
    a) Contextual factors;   a
    b) Intrinsic factors;
    c) Content factors;
    d) Internal factors.
14. Which of the following is not classified as a
    motivator in the Motivator-Hygiene theory
    construct: d
    a) Achievement;
    b) Recognition;
    c) Responsibility;
    d) Interpersonal relations.
15. The Motivator-Hygiene theory states that:
    a) A person can be satisfied and dissatisfied at
        at the same time;
    b) Hygiene factors cannot increase or decrease   d
        job satisfaction;
    c) Extrinsic outcomes are largely determined by
        the organizations, which intrinsic outcomes
        are largely administered internally by the
        individual;
    d) All of the above.
16. Which of the following statements is true regarding
    Motivator-Hygiene theory:
    a) The terms "hygiene" and "contextual" refer to
        the same set of factors;
    b) Researchers have found that motivators
        contribute to satisfaction and hygiene factors   d
        contribute to dissatisfaction;
    c) Little has been done to explain why certain
        factors affect performance positively or
        negatively;
    d) All of the above.

IV.   Process Theories of Motivation.

    1.   Process theories:
       a)   Attempt to explain factors within a person that energize, direct, and stop behavior;
       b)   Focus on specific factors that motivate people;
       c)   Attempt to describe and analyze how the personal factors interact and influence each other to produce certain kinds of behavior;   c
       d)   All of the above.
    2.   Expectancy theory:
       a)   Focuses on an individual's feelings of how fairly he or she is treated in comparison with others;   b
       b)   Assumes that individuals assign probabilities to efforts leading to desired outcomes;
       c)   Deals with the ratio inputs and outcomes to another person's inputs and outcomes;
       d)   None of the above.
    3.   First-level outcomes:
       a)   Are the results of behaviors associated with doing the jobs itself;
       b)   Includes such outcomes as pay increases, promotion, and job security;   a
       c)   Exist when ratios of outcomes to inputs are not equal;
       d)   All of the above.
    4.   The events that first-level outcomes are likely to produce are called:
       a)   Expectancies;   d
       b)   Valences;
       c)   Instrumentalities;
       d)   Second-level outcomes.
    5.   The belief that a particular level of effort will be followed by a particular level of performance is called:
       a)   Expectancy;   a
       b)   Valence;
       c)   Instrumentality;
       d)   Equity.
    6.   An individual's preference for a second-level outcome is called:
       a)   Expectancy;   b
       b)   Valence;
       c)   Instrumentality;
       d)   Equity.
    7.   The relationship between first- and second-level outcomes is called:
       a)   Expectancy;   c
       b)   Valence;

c) Instrumentality;
d) Equity.

8. Which of the following is <u>not</u> a basic assumption
    underlying expectancy theory:
    a) A combination of individual and environmental
        forces determine behavior;
    b) People make decisions about their own behavior   c
        in organizations;
    c) In any given organization, people have the same
        types of needs and goals;
    d) People choose among alternative behaviors based
        on which they believe will produce desired
        outcomes.

9. The general model of expectancy theory says that:
    a) Motivation is the force that causes individuals
        to expend effort;
    b) Individuals must believe that effort will lead   d
        to desired performance;
    c) Effort-performance expectancy is based on a
        perception of how difficult it will be to
        achieve a particular behavior;
    d) All of the above.

10. Managerial implications of expectancy theory include:
    a) Managers should try to determine the outcomes
        which each employee values;
    b) Managers should set the desired levels of
        performance slightly higher than the employees
        will be able to attain;
    c) Criteria for attainment of performance levels   a
        may either be measurable and observable or non-
        measurable and non-observable;
    d) All of the above.

11. From expectancy theory, managers learn that:
    a) It is reality, and not people's perceptions,
        that determines motivation;
    b) Any amount of reward provided will be   c
        significant and will therefore motivate
        significant behavior;
    c) Management must follow through on its promises
        that performance will be linked to reward;
    d) Even if negative outcomes are likely, motivation
        will be high if there are rewards.

12. Equity theory:
    a) Focuses on an individual's feelings of how
        fairly they are treated in comparison with
        others;
    b) Is based on the relationship between inputs   d
        and outcomes;
    c) Says that individuals assign weights to inputs
        and outcomes according to their perceived
        performance;

d) All of the above;
e) None of the above.

13. Which of the following is a key element in equity theory:
    a) Social relationships are viewed as an exchange process in which individuals make contributions and expect certain results;
    b) Each person compares his/her own situation with that of others;
    c) Individuals evaluate their social relationships in much the same way they evaluate economic exchanges;
    d) All of the above.

    d

14. Which of the following is a typical second-level outcome in an organizational setting:
    a) Performance;
    b) Experience;
    c) Past experience;
    d) Challenging assignments.

    d

15. Which of the following is a typical input in an organizational setting:
    a) Being held responsible;
    b) Status symbols;
    c) Job effort;
    d) Job security.

    c

16. Equity is said to exist when:
    a) The ratio of one's outcomes to inputs equals the perceived ratio for others;
    b) The ratios of outcomes to inputs among group members are not equal;
    c) People think they are overpaid, but not when they think they are underpaid;
    d) Someone believes their inputs and outcomes exceed those of others.

    a

17. Inequity:
    a) Leads to tension-reducing behavior;
    b) Occurs when the ratio of outcomes to inputs for one person equals that ratio for others;
    c) Creates tension between but not within individuals;
    d) May lead people to distort inputs or outcomes of others but not their own inputs or outcomes.

    a

18. Which of the following is consistent with most of the existing research on equity theory:
    a) The theory is too narrow in its specifying the actions that people choose in order to reduce inequity;
    b) The research focuses mainly on short-term comparisons;

    a

    c)   The research focuses mainly on long-term
         comparisons;
    d)   Too little of it deals with compensation issues.
19. Which of the following is an accurate statement
     regarding the managerial implications of equity
     theory:
    a)   Individuals who think they have not been treated
         fairly will engage in tension-reduction
         behavior;   a
    b)   People engage in only one tension-reduction
         behavior at a time;
    c)   Employees typically make decisions about equity
         without reference to the inputs and outcomes
         of other people;
    d)   All of the above.
20. Procedural justice means:
    a)   Procedures are just;
    b)   Rules are just;   d
    c)   Administration of procedures and rules is just;
    d)   All of the above;
    e)   None of the above.

APPLIED QUESTIONS

I.   Basic Model of Motivation.

    1.   When GM agreed to a labor contract with a $1 billion
         job security program, it was responding to the
         pressures of:
        a)   The labor union;
        b)   The hourly employee's fear of automation;
        c)   Foreign competition;   d
        d)   All of the above.
    2.   An organization has cut back on its training
         expenditures, relying instead upon its heavy
         emphasis on motivational programs. Which of the
         following is most likely to cause problems:
        a)   Motives are dynamic in nature;   b
        b)   Performance requires ability as well as
             motivation;
        c)   Motivation is goal directed;
        d)   People have different motives.
    3.   Managers need to be able to implement a variety of
         motivational schemes because:
        a)   Different motives drive different people;
        b)   Performance requires ability as well as   a
             motivation;

   c) Motives are second-level outcomes;
   d) Employees are concerned with equitable treatment.
4. Which of the following is the accurate statement of the basic management principle involving motivation:
   a) Motivation = f(ability x performance);   c
   b) Ability = f(motivation x performance);
   c) Performance = f(ability x motivation);
   d) None of the above.
5. Managers should not expect all employees to respond in the same way to the same motivational approaches because:
   a) People have different needs;
   b) There are differences in the ways people select   d
      certain motives over others;
   c) There are differences in the level of drive with which people pursue their motives;
   d) All of the above;
   e) None of the above.

II. Content and Process Theories of Motivation.

   1. Which of the following fall within the concepts of the content theories of motivation:
      a) Employees pressure their union to prevent management from installing new limits on promotion;
      b) An employee believes that working hard will not   a
         result in a merit increase, and so does not work hard;
      c) An employee reduces her output because she received the same merit increase as another employee who did practically no work at all;
      d) All of the above.
   2. Which of the following fall within process theories of motivation:
      a) An employee is disappointed with her pay increase, but then decides it's not so bad because she doesn't plan to work all that hard next year anyway;
      b) A manager assumes that all he needs to do for   a
         his employees is to provide them with wage increases that exceed the cost-of-living increases;
      c) A manager assumes that his employees will respond favorably to "employee-of-the-month" awards;
      d) All of the above;
      e) None of the above.

3. Which of the following is a process theory of
    motivation:
    a) Equity theory;   a
    b) ERG theory;
    c) Two-factor theory;
    d) Needs hierarchy theory.
4. Which of the following is <u>not</u> a content theory
    of motivation:
    a) ERG theory;   c
    b) Achievement motivation theory;
    c) Expectancy theory;
    d) Needs hierarchy theory.

III. Basic Dimensions of Content Theories of Motivation.

1. Employers who attempt to motivate employees by
    promoting their pride in their work are focusing on:
    a) Physiological needs;   d
    b) Security needs;
    c) Affiliation needs;
    d) Esteem needs.
2. Employers who attempt to motivate employees by
    emphasizing job security, pension plans, guaranteed
    work plans, etc., are focusing on:
    a) Self-actualization needs;   b
    b) Security needs;
    c) Affiliation needs;
    d) Esteem needs.
3. Employers who attempt to motivate employees by
    utilizing such programs as job enrichment, employee
    participation plans, and the like are focusing on:
    a) Affiliation needs;   c
    b) Physiological needs;
    c) Self-actualization needs;
    d) Security needs.
4. ERG theory adds an extra dimension beyond needs
    hierarchy theory to understanding employee behavior
    in that:
    a) It offers clues as to what employees may do if
        attainment of higher level needs is blocked;
    b) It has a great deal more research behind it to   a
        back it up;
    c) It points out that employees will continue to
        engage in activity toward the attainment of
        higher level needs even if blocked by the
        organization;
    d) It looks at a larger, more complete number of
        needs.

5. An employee is highly motivated to increase her work capacity, become more productive, and attain levels of responsibility in the organization. When the "old boy" network holds her down, she focuses all her energies on becoming a social favorite in the organization. Which of the following best explains her behavior:
    a) Needs hierarchy theory;
    b) Two-factor theory;
    c) ERG theory;
    d) Achievement motivation theory.

    c

6. Which of the following content theories offers the best explanation for why a manager should be certain to provide appropriate feedback to employees:
    a) Needs hierarchy theory;
    b) Two-factor theory;
    c) ERG theory;
    d) Achievement motivation theory.

    d

7. A manager looks at the goals employees have set for themselves. Which of the following should the manager expect of the high achievers:
    a) Goals that can be met with relative ease;
    b) Goals that are within the capability of relatively few people;
    c) Goals that are not at either the high extreme or the low extreme;
    d) Could be any of the above.

    c

8. According to Herzberg, an employer who wishes to keep employees from being dissatisfied should:
    a) Make certain they have interesting work;
    b) Provide ample amounts of recognition for work well done;
    c) Make certain the relationships between employees and supervisors are good;
    d) Provide workers the opportunity to accept responsibility.

    c

9. According to Herzberg, an employer who wishes to make the workplace one that offers motivation for the employees should:
    a) Provide employees with adequate salaries;
    b) Provide full explanations of company policies;
    c) Provide adequate technical supervision;
    d) Provide significant opportunities for advancement.

    d

10. An employer needs to understand that employee behaviors that look inconsistent may not be, since:
    a) A person can be satisfied and dissatisfied at the same time;
    b) Employee motives may change;

    d

c)   Any individual employee may have conflicting
     motives at any one time;
d)   All of the above.

IV.   Basic Dimensions of Process Theories of Motivation.

1.   An employee who has experienced an absence of
     relationship between good performance and reward
     has experienced an absence of:
     a)   First-level outcome;   b
     b)   Instrumentality;
     c)   Valence;
     d)   Expectancy.

2.   I play racquetball three times a week, and I work
     hard at improving but in fact I have not improved
     any over the last 5 or 6 years. (I may have gotten
     worse!) Which of the following is low for me:
     a)   Effort;
     b)   Instrumentality;   d
     c)   Valence;
     d)   Expectancy.

3.   You are told that if you get a grade of 90 or better
     on the two quizzes you will not have to take the
     third quiz, so you work hard to do so. The
     attractiveness to avoiding the third quiz is very
     high to you. For you, avoiding the quiz can be
     said to have a positive:
     a)   First-level outcome;
     b)   Expectancy;   c
     c)   Valence;
     d)   None of the above.

4.   Which of the following is most directly tied in
     with equity theory:
     a)   Employee health plans;   d
     b)   Pension benefits;
     c)   Employee assistance plans;
     d)   Comparable worth.

5.   Which of the following theories is most directly
     related to the potential effects of an employer's
     policy to require employees to refrain from
     revealing their salaries to each other:
     a)   Equity;   a
     b)   Maslow;
     c)   Expectancy;
     d)   Herzberg.

6.   You learn that a co-worker who works less time and
     turns out poorer quality of work than you do
     receives a higher salary than you do. Equity
     theory suggests that you may:

    a)   Work harder in the hopes that you can get a pay
increase;   d
    b)   Work less since you are not being paid enough
for what you do;
    c)   Threaten to quit unless you are given a pay
increase;
    d)   Any of the above.

7. Which theory is <u>most</u> directly related to the
statement, "Getting to the national convention was a
real eye-opening. I had no idea we were so under-
paid here":
    a)   Equity;
    b)   Maslow;   a
    c)   Expectancy;
    d)   Herzberg.

8. If you typically discard mail offerings of
opportunities to win a fortune, you probably do it
because of which of the following:
    a)   Valence;   b
    b)   Expectancy;
    c)   Equity;
    d)   Needs.

9. Which of the following relates to procedural
justice:
    a)   People think the rules are fair, but the
administration of the rules is unfair;
    b)   People think the pay they get is unfair in
light of how hard they work;   a
    c)   People think the pay they get is unfair
compared to what other people in other firms
get;
    d)   All of the above.

PROGRAMMED STUDY SUPPLEMENT

1.   _____ is the term used to describe the   motivation
forces that cause a person to behave in a
specific way.

---

2.   The term _____ refers to a person's talent   ability
for doing goal-related tasks.

---

3.   _____ are deficiencies that an individual   needs
experiences at a particular time.

4. A _____ is a specific result that the
    individual wants to achieve.   goal

5. The _____ covers physiological, security,   needs
    affiliation, esteem, and self-actualization   hierarchy
    needs.   theory

6. _____ are the lowest level in Maslow's   physiolog-
    hierarchy.   ical needs

7. _____ include safety, stability, and the   security
    absence of pain, threat, or illness.   needs

8. The needs for friendship, love, and a feeling   affiliation
    of belonging are all _____.   needs

9. _____ holds that when one set of an   ERG theory
    employee's needs are blocked the manager may
    redirect the subordinate's behavior toward
    satisfying lower level needs.

10. Needs involving an individual's quest for   growth
    personal development are _____.   needs

11. The perceived fairness of rules and procedures   procedural
    is referred to as _____.   justice

12. Reward systems that permit employees to select   cafeteria
    from a set of alternative benefits are called   benefit
    _____.   plans

13. _____ are also known as intrinsic or   motivators;
    content factors, while _____ are also known   hygiene
    as extrinsic or context factors.   factors

14. _____ states that people are motivated   achievement
    according to the strength of their desire to   motivation
    perform in terms of a standard or their desire   theory
    to succeed against competition.

15. _____ attempts to explain the factors within a person that energize, direct, and stop behavior.

content theories

16. _____ attempt to describe and analyze how personal factors interact to produce certain kinds of behavior.

process theories

17. One method of assessing achievement motivation is through use of the _____.

TAT

18. _____ factors are associated with an individual's negative feelings about a job, while _____ factors are associated with positive feelings.

extrinsic; intrinsic

19. _____ is an internally oriented theory in which individuals assign probabilities to efforts leading to desired first- and second-level outcomes.

expectancy theory

20. _____ exists when the ratio of a person's outcomes to inputs equals the perceived ratio of outcomes to inputs for others.

equity

21. Feelings of self-worth meet an individual's _____.

esteem needs

22. At the top of Maslow's need hierarchy is _____.

self act-ualization

23. An individual's preference for a second-level outcome is called _____.

valence

24. Results of efforts associated with doing the job are called _____.

first-level outcomes

25. The relationship between first-level outcomes and second-level outcomes is called _____.

instru-mentality

26. _____ states that job satisfaction and dissatisfaction do not exist on a single continuum.

motivator-hygiene theory

27. In equity theory, _____ are what an individual receives from an exchange.

outcomes

28. _____ are such things as pay increases, promotions, job security, etc., that are produced by first-level outcomes.

second level outcomes

29. In ERG theory, needs for establishing and maintaining relationships are known as _____.

relatedness needs

30. _____ represent what an individual contributes to an exchange.

inputs

31. _____ exists when the ratios of outcomes to inputs are not equal.

inequity

32. _____ focuses on an individual's feelings of how fairly he or she is treated in comparison with others.

equity theory

33. _____ consists of the material needs in ERG theory.

existence

34. The belief that a particular level of effort will be followed by a particular level of performance is called _____.

expectancy

CHAPTER 8

GOAL SETTING AND PERFORMANCE ENHANCEMENT

LEARNING OBJECTIVES

When you read and when you review Chapter 8, keep in mind the learning objectives which have been established by the authors. Look them over first as a guide to picking out the most important parts of the chapter, and then think about them as you are going through the chapter. When you have finished the chapter, ask yourself whether you have met the objectives.

The authors intend that when you have finished studying this chapter you should be able to:

* Explain the role of customers, suppliers, and others in the goal-setting process.
* List the key factors in individual goal setting and performance and describe their relationships.
* Discuss how management by objectives (MBO) can be applied as a management philosophy and system.
* Describe how performance can be enhanced through an appropriately designed and implemented performance appraisal process.
* Explain three contemporary reward systems for enhancing performance.

CHAPTER OUTLINE

After you have read the chapter, complete the following outline.

I.   INTRODUCTION TO GOAL SETTING.

A.   Goal setting is

B.   Goals are

C.   Purposes of goal setting are

1.

2.

3.

4.

5.

D.   Role of Stakeholders.

1.   Stakeholders are

2.   Stakeholders increase the complexity of goal setting most in situations wherein

a.

b.

c.

d.

3.   Examples of typical stakeholders are

a.

b.

c.

d.

e.

f.

g.

h.

II. GOAL SETTING AND PERFORMANCE.

A. Locke and Latham Goals Model.

1. Challenges provided for

a. Goal difficulty requirement:

b. Goal clarity requirement:

c. Self-efficacy requirement:

2. What do moderators do?

a. Ability:

b. Goal commitment:

c. Feedback:

d. Task complexity:

3. What do mediators do?

a. Direction of attention:

b. Effort:

c. Persistence:

4. Task performance is likely to be high when

    a.

    b.

    c.

5. Rewards are important so that

6. The primary focus of satisfaction in the Locke-Latham Model is

7. Consequences of

    a. Satisfaction include

    b. Dissatisfaction include

8. Organizational implications are

    a.

    b.

B. Individual-Focused Management by Objectives.

    1. Management by objectives is

    2. Components of the Individual-Focused MBO Model:

        a. Goal setting with subordinates, by

            (1)

            (2)

            (3)

            (4)

(5)

(6)

b.   Participation.

  (1)   The most effective level of participation is

  (2)   A prerequisite for participation is

c.   Implementation requires

d.   Performance appraisal and feedback requires

  (1)

  (2)

  (3)

  (4)

3.   Criticisms of Individual MBO usage include

  a.

  b.

  c.

  d.

  e.

  f.

C.   Team-Focused Management by Objectives.

  1.   Attempts to overcome two major deficiencies of individual MBO:

  a.

  b.

2.   Greatest potential for success occurs when

a.

b.

c.

III. ENHANCING PERFORMANCE THROUGH APPRAISAL.

A.   The performance appraisal process is

1.   The goal of a good performance appraisal system is

a.   The system can accomplish that goal by

(1)

(2)

(3)

2.   Performance appraisal information is used for

a.

b.

c.

B.   Problems in appraisal include

1.

2.

3.

4.

C.   Methods of Appraisal.

1.   Ranking methods involve

    a.   Advantages of ranking methods include

        (1)

        (2)

        (3)

    b.   Disadvantages of ranking methods include

        (1)

        (2)

        (3)

2.   Graphic rating involves

3.   Behavioral Anchored Rating Scales indicate

    a.   Advantages of BARS include

        (1)

        (2)

        (3)

        (4)

    b.   Disadvantages of BARS include

        (1)

        (2)

        (3)

4.   Goals-Based Ratings involve

    a.   Characteristics of effective goals-based systems are

        (1)

                    (2)

                    (3)

                    (4)

                    (5)

          b.   Goals-based systems require managers to

IV. ENHANCING PERFORMANCE THROUGH REWARD SYSTEMS.

    A. Flexible benefit plans are

       1. Advantages of flexible benefit plans include

          a.

          b.

          c.

       2. Problems of flexible benefit plans include

          a.

          b.

          c.

    B. "Banking time off" means

       1. Potential problems with banking time off include

          a.

          b.

    C. Skill-based pay is

       1. The principal advantage of skill-based pay is

2. Disadvantages of skill-based pay include

    a.

    b.

DIRECTED QUESTIONS

I.   Goal Setting.

1. Which of the following is <u>not</u> one of the purposes
    of goal setting:
    a) Guide and direct behavior;
    b) Provide standards for assessment;   c
    c) Bring about evaluation of part performance;
    d) Justify organizational activities.
2. Which of the following situations make goal
    setting most difficult:
    a) Individual stakeholders have minimal power
        in relation to the organization;
    b) Stakeholders tend to perceive their interest   c
        to be compatible;
    c) Stakeholder expectations vary from time
        to time;
    d) All of the above.
3. Goals can be:
    a) Implicit;
    b) Vague;   d
    c) Externally imposed;
    d) All of the above;
    e) None of the above.
4. Goal clarity and goal difficulty are examples of:
    a) Goal incentives;
    b) Feedback;   d
    c) Role outcomes;
    d) Goal attributes.
5. Self-efficacy is a goal:
    a) Attribute;
    b) Moderator;   a
    c) Mediator;
    d) Consequence.
6. Role clarity and role challenge:
    a) Result in goal clarity and goal difficulty;
    b) Are a result of goal clarity and goal   b
        difficulty;
    c) Are a result of high levels of performance;
    d) Result in good goal setting.

7. Factors that mediate goal attainment are:
   a) Direction;
   b) Effort;
   c) Persistence;
   d) All of the above.

d

8. Factors that moderate the strength of the relationship between goals and performance include:
   a) Effort;
   b) Clarity;
   c) Ability;
   d) Satisfaction;
   e) All of the above.

c

9. Which of the following makes goal setting and individual responses to goal achievement a dynamic process:
   a) Goal commitment;
   b) Task complexity;
   c) Feedback;
   d) Challenge.

c

10. Task performance is likely to be high when:
    a) Challenging goals are present;
    b) Moderators are absent;
    c) Mediators are not in operation;
    d) All of the above;
    e) b and c.

a

11. Consequences of goal pursuit may turn out badly and lead to dissatisfaction, which in turn may lead to:
    a) Job avoidance;
    b) Work avoidance;
    c) Psychological defenses;
    d) Defiance;
    e) All of the above.

e

II. Management by Objectives.

1. MBO is intended to serve which of the following purposes:
   a) Joint superior-subordinate goal setting;
   b) Evaluating progress toward goals;
   c) Integrating goals set at various levels within the organization;
   d) All of the above;
   e) None of the above.

d

2. Which of the following is <u>not</u> a step in MBO goal setting:
   a) Design the job;
   b) State what must be done;
   c) Set standards;

a

d) Set deadlines or timetables;
e) None of the above (i.e., all are steps in MBO goal setting).

3. Regarding participation in MBO goal setting:
a) If a job does not contain sufficient discretionary content, MBO cannot be used;
b) It is not essential that a job has discretionary content for MBO to be successful;
c) Planning and control tasks must be increased or stimulated if MBO is to be successful;
d) MBO can generally be used successfully even on routine or programmed jobs;
e) Both a and c.

      e

4. MBO:
a) Requires that, once set, goals remain unchanged so that employees will know what is expected of them;
b) Relies on performance evaluation by superiors rather than on self-evaluation;
c) Recognizes that factors other than the employee's own behavior may affect outcomes;
d) All of the above.

      c

5. Which of the following statements is <u>not</u> true about MBO:
a) Significant parts of jobs may be difficult or impossible to measure;
b) MBO prescribes a passive role for supervisors;
c) It is as much a developmental as a review process;
d) Feedback is a key element.

      b

6. Which of the following is cited by the authors as a criticism of how MBO has been used:
a) Too little emphasis on reward-punishment psychology;
b) Too little control from the top;
c) Qualitative aspects of jobs receive too little attention;
d) Too much emphasis on group goals.

      c

7. One principal way in which team-focused MBO differs from individual-focused MBO is that:
a) The team model recognizes interdependencies between jobs;
b) The team model requires both superior and subordinate participation;
c) The team model gives the common superior the responsibility for integrating the goals of different jobs;
d) All of the above.

      a

8.   The team-focus MBO model works best when:
  a)   A need for integration among individuals exists;
  b)   Top management is supportive;   d
  c)   Participants have at least minimal skills in group processes;
  d)   All of the above.

III. Enhancing Performance Through Appraisal.

1.   A good performance appraisal system will help employees reach their potential and increase their effectiveness by:
  a)   Providing feedback;
  b)   Providing a means for short-run development;   d
  c)   Helping managers make decisions;
  d)   All of the above;
  e)   a and b.
2.   Uses of performance appraisals include:
  a)   Bases for performance-based pay decisions;
  b)   Personnel movement decisions;   e
  c)   Justification for decisions already made;
  d)   All of the above;
  e)   a and b.
3.   When a rater bases performance appraisal on one aspect of an employee's work without considering other aspects, which error is occurring:
  a)   Halo;
  b)   Central tendency;   a
  c)   Stereotyping;
  d)   Leniency.
4.   Which appraisal method is most appropriate for comparing employees doing the same or similar work:
  a)   Ranking;
  b)   Graphic rating;   a
  c)   BARS;
  d)   Goal based ratings.
5.   Which appraisal method is based on whether the employee has performed certain job behaviors and how frequently:
  a)   Ranking;
  b)   Graphic rating;   c
  c)   BARS;
  d)   Goal based ratings.

IV. Enhancing Performance Through Reward Systems.

1.   Use of plans tailored to fit employee needs is a strength of:

a)   Flexible benefit systems;
b)   Banking time off;   a
c)   Skill-based pay;
d)   None of the above.

2.   High training costs are a problem in which of the
     following:
     a)   Flexible benefit systems;
     b)   Banking time off;   c
     c)   Skill-based pay;
     d)   None of the above.

3.   Being based on employee performance is an advantage
     of:
     a)   Flexible benefit systems;
     b)   Banking time off;   b
     c)   Skill-based pay;
     d)   None of the above.

APPLIED QUESTIONS

I.   Goal Setting.

   1.   Which of the following increases the difficulty of
        goal setting:
        a)   Stakeholders have little power;
        b)   Stakeholders know what they want and they stick
             to it;   c
        c)   Great competition between divergent stakeholder
             groups;
        d)   All of the above.

   2.   Which of the following represents an appropriate
        goal challenge:
        a)   Employees are delighted at the new set of goals
             because it is clear that all employees can
             meet those goals;
        b)   Employees are anxious because their is   c
             substantial evidence that no one will be able
             to meet the goals;
        c)   In discussion with employees, it seems apparent
             that they all know and understand the specifics
             of the new goals;
        d)   All of the above.

   3.   The workers are told to, "Do your best and you'll
        probably be O.K. at wage time." That is a bad
        statement in terms of:
        a)   Challenge;
        b)   Moderators;   a
        c)   Mediators;
        d)   All of the above.

4. Performance will tend to be higher when goals are:
   a) Vague;
   b) Rejected by employees;
   c) Easily attained;   e
   d) Extremely difficult to attain;
   e) Set participatively.

5. Skill-based pay might be one way to approach
   proper management of goal:
   a) Clarity;
   b) Mediators;   c
   c) Moderators;
   d) Consequences.

6. In which of the following is effort most likely
   to lead to goal attainment:
   a) Scoring high on achievement tests;
   b) Scoring high on aptitude tests;   c
   c) Unloading boxes from a truck;
   d) All of the above;
   e) b and c.

7. Task performance is likely to be high in which of
   the following:
   a) Tasks are complex;
   b) Extremely challenging goals are set;
   c) Many different tasks are presented   e
      simultaneously;
   d) All of the above;
   e) None of the above.

8. "High goals may lead to less experienced
   satisfaction than low goals." Is that statement
   consistent or inconsistent with the Locke and
   Latham model:
   a) Consistent;   a
   b) Inconsistent.

III. Management by Objectives.

1. Which of the following jobs is <u>least</u> appropriate
   for an MBO approach:
   a) Salesperson;
   b) College instructor;   c
   c) Assembly line worker;
   d) Design engineer.

2. What effect is MBO most likely to have on the
   level of responsibility associated with a job:
   a) Increase;
   b) Decrease;   a
   c) No relationship.

3. The argument that the MBO process is "managerially
   weak" is:

a) Irrelevant because under MBO managers do not
   need to be strong;
b) Unfortunately accurate;   c
c) Incorrect, and in fact MBO results help
   managers be stronger;
d) True where subordinate participation becomes
   too strong.

4. Team-focused MBO would be <u>least</u> appropriate for
   which of the following situations:
   a) Commission retail clothing salespersons;
   b) Where employees involved have participated in   a
      many team projects;
   c) Top management's style is basically
      "facilitating";
   d) A matrix management organization.

III. Enhancing Performance Through Appraisal.

1. Which of the following does <u>not</u> support the
   effectiveness of the performance appraisal process:
   a) Managers fully discuss performance evaluations
      with employees;
   b) Managers work out career development plans with c
      employees;
   c) Pay increases and promotion based on seniority;
   d) Merit pay systems.

2. The new performance appraisal instrument requires
   that ratings be normally distributed within each
   department. This method will present:
   a) Leniency errors;
   b) Control tendency errors;   e
   c) Halo effect;
   d) All of the above;
   e) a and b.

3. Managers who have an excessive drive to be "loved"
   by all their employees may be especially subject to:
   a) Leniency errors;
   b) Control tendency errors;   a
   c) Halo effect;
   d) All of the above;
   e) a and b.

4. I have 14 employees: 2 secretaries, a bookkeeper,
   5 salespeople, an office manager, and 5 sales
   assistants. Which would be the least appropriate
   appraisal method for me to use:
   a) Ranking;
   b) Graphic rating;   a
   c) BARS;
   d) Goal-based.

5. One of my concerns is that we use employee
    participation wherever possible. Which would be
    the most appropriate appraisal method for me to
    use:
    a) Ranking;
    b) Graphic rating;   d
    c) BARS;
    d) Goal-based.

IV. Enhancing Performance Through Reward Systems.

1. Which reward plan most directly meets the needs of
    a demographically diverse work force:
    a) Flexible benefits;
    b) Banking time off;   a
    c) Skill-based.
2. We have had to keep our employment levels down in
    order to keep our labor costs down. We don't have
    any "extra" people. So, we need the ones we have
    to be as flexible as possible. Which reward plan
    would best address this need:
    a) Flexible benefits;
    b) Banking time off;   c
    c) Skill-based.
3. Our primary concern is labor costs. Which reward
    plan would likely cause us the <u>most</u> trouble (as
    far as labor costs are concerned):
    a) Flexible benefits;
    b) Banking time off;   c
    c) Skill-based.

PROGRAMMED STUDY SUPPLEMENT

1. _____ indicate whether the employee   BARS
    has performed certain job behaviors and how
    frequently.

---

2. _____ provides employees knowledge   perform-
    about how well their outcomes correspond to   ance ap-
    the goals which they were pursuing.   praisal

---

3. Managers use _____ to increase   goal set-
    efficiency and effectiveness by specifying   ting
    desired outcomes.

4. In _____ the individual is evaluated on a series of performance dimensions, usually through the use of a 5- or 7-point scale.   graphic ratings

5. Future outcomes that individuals and groups desire and strive to achieve are called _____.   goals

6. _____ are used to compare employees doing the same or similar work.   ranking methods

7. _____ is a goal setting process which recognizes job interdependencies and integrates individual goals.   team-focused MBO

8. _____ occurs when the rater judges all employees to be average.   central tendency

9. _____ should be challenging but not unreasonable.   goal difficulty

10. Rating all employees higher that they should be is called _____.   leniency

11. In _____ subordinates meet one-on-one with supervisors to set goals and plan actions.   individual focused MBO

12. _____ are the groups having potential or real power to influence decisions.   stakehold-ers

13. _____ must be high so that employees know what is expected of them.   goal clarity

14. _____ refers to the individual's determination to reach a goal, regardless of where the goal came from.   goal commitment

15. A system that allows employees to choose
    benefits rather than having benefits chosen
    for them is called _____.

    flexible
    benefit
    plan

---

16. _____ is a system that rewards
    employees for learning.

    skill-
    based pay

---

17. A term coined by Peter Drucker to designate
    a philosophy and system of participative
    management is _____.

    MBO

CHAPTER 9

WORK STRESS

LEARNING OBJECTIVES

When you read and when you review Chapter 9, keep in mind the learning objectives which have been established by the authors. Look them over first as a guide to picking out the most important parts of the chapter, and then think about them as you are going through the chapter. When you have finished the chapter, ask yourself whether you have met the objectives.

The authors intend that when you have finished studying this chapter you should be able to:

* Explain the concepts of stress and stressors.
* Describe the general nature of the body's response to stressors.
* Diagnose the sources of stress in organizations.
* Describe the effects of stress on health.
* Explain the relationship between stress and job performance.
* Understand the nature and causes of job burnout.
* Identify some methods that individuals and organizations can use to cope with stress.

CHAPTER OUTLINE

After you have read the chapter, complete the following outline.

I.   NATURE OF STRESS.

    A.   Some definitions:

        1.   Stress is

        2.   Stressors are

        3.   The "fight-or-flight" response is

    B.   Whether or not an individual experiences stress in a particular situation depends on

        1.

        2.

        3.

        4.

II. SOURCES OF STRESS.

        1.   Work stressors are

            a.

            b.

            c.

            d.

            e.

            f.

        2.   Life stressors are

a.   How are work stressors and life stressors
     related?

III. EFFECTS OF STRESS.

A.   Work stress effects are in three major areas:

1.

2.

3.

B.   Implications of work stress on

1.   Health:

2.   Performance:

a.   What is the typical relationship between
     performance and stress?

C.   Job burnout refers to

1.   Components of job burnout are

a.

b.

c.

2.   Characteristics associated with a high probability
     of burnout are

a.

b.

c.

IV.   PERSONALITY AND STRESS.

    A.   Personality influences

        1.

        2.

    B.   Type A personality.

        1.   Characteristics of Type A personality are

            a.

            b.

            c.

        2.   Behaviors and tendencies associated with Type A
           personality are

            a.

            b.

            c.

            d.

        3.   Aspects of Type A personality associated with stress
           reactions and heart disease are

            a.

            b.

            c.

    C.   The hardy personality is

        1.   Behaviors and tendencies associated with hardiness
           are

            a.

     b.

     c.

  2.   What is the relationship between hardiness and stress?

V.   STRESS MANAGEMENT.

  A. Individual stress coping methods.

    1. Purposes are

      a.

      b.

    2. An example of ways to work on "hardiness" includes

      a.

      b.

      c.

      d.

      e.

  B. Organizational stress coping mechanisms.

    1. Three directions of organizational stress coping are

      a.

      b.

      c.

    2. Programs of stress management focusing on workload include

      a.

      b.

        c.

        d.

        e.

        f.

3. Programs of stress management focusing on job conditions, role conflict, and role ambiguity include

        a.

        b.

        c.

        d.

        e.

        f.

4. Wellness programs are

        a. Major types of wellness programs:

           (1)

           (2)

           (3)

DIRECTED QUESTIONS

I. Nature of Stress.

  1. Stress:
    a) Involves the interaction of a person and that person's environment;
    b) Is the set of physical or psychological demands from the environment;
    c) Is the set of demands that stem from such sources as the job, the family, friends, or co-workers;
    d) All of the above.

a

2. Biochemical and bodily changes representing natural
    responses to environment stressors:
    a) Constitute what is called a "fight-or-flight"
        response;
    b) Must be overcome in the work environment;   d
    c) Are difficult to overcome when the strength
        of the negative threat is great;
    d) All of the above.
3. Which of the following factors affect the
    likelihood that an individual will experience work
    stress:
    a) Perception of the current situation;
    b) Past experiences;   d
    c) Social support;
    d) All of the above.
4. The process whereby an individual selects and
    organizes information regarding stressors is:
    a) Role ambiguity;
    b) Perception;   b
    c) Tolerance for ambiguity;
    d) None of the above.
5. Positive reinforcement may reduce the level of
    stress an individual feels in a given situation,
    depending on which of the following factors:
    a) Perception;
    b) Past experience;   b
    c) Social support;
    d) Performance levels.
6. The presence or absence of others influences how
    an individual will respond to stress in a work
    setting by:
    a) Allowing the individual to cope more
        effectively;
    b) Reducing the individual's ability to cope;   d
    c) Giving the individual greater confidence;
    d) All of the above;
    e) None of the above.

II. Stressors.

1. The lack of participation in decision making is a
    stressor related most directly to:
    a) Career development;
    b) Interpersonal relations in the organization;   c
    c) Role conflict and role ambiguity;
    d) Conflict between work and other roles.
2. Difficulty in delegating responsibility is a
    stressor related most directly to:
    a) Career development;
    b) Interpersonal relations in the organization;   b

    c)   Role conflict and role ambiguity;
    d)   Conflict between work and other roles.

3. Experiencing differing expectations or demands on the role which one plays in an organization is known as:
    a)   Role conflict;
    b)   Role ambiguity;   a
    c)   Role overload;
    d)   Role reversal.

4. As a stressor, shift work falls within which of the following categories of sources of stress:
    a)   Stressors at work;
    b)   Being part of the organization;   d
    c)   Conflict between work and other roles;
    d)   All of the above.

5. Life stressors:
    a)   Result from an individual's role in the organization;
    b)   Include having responsibility for the behavior   c
        of others at work;
    c)   May cause stress that reduces the ability to cope with stress created by stressors at work;
    d)   Are a result of factors intrinsic to the job.

6. Environmental stressors:
    a)   Accumulate across time;
    b)   Interact with other stressors;   d
    c)   Include temperature and lighting;
    d)   All of the above;
    e)   a and b.

III. Effects of Stress.

1. The effects of stress:
    a)   Are negative;
    b)   Result in five to ten times as much industrial   d
        lost time as do strikes;
    c)   Include such emotional effects as impulsive behavior, alcohol abuse, and drug abuse;
    d)   All of the above.

2. Which of the following health problems have been found to have proven or likely links to stress:
    a)   Cancer;
    b)   Heart disease;   d
    c)   Industrial accidents;
    d)   All of the above.

3. Stress is related to performance in that:
    a)   Stress needs to be eliminated in order that performance may peak;

b) For any given task or set of tasks an optimum level of stress can be identified as applicable to all individuals performing that task or set of tasks;

c) Too little stress has a positive effect on performance, whereas too much stress has a negative effect;

d) Optimum points of stress are difficult to identify because they are different for each individual.

d

4. Job burnout:
   a) Occurs with least frequency in occupations that provide the opportunity to help people;
   b) Includes feelings of high personal accomplishments;
   c) Is frequently found among individuals who tend to be idealistic and/or self-motivating achievers;
   d) All of the above.

c

5. Which of the following statements about job burnout is correct:
   a) Comes on suddenly in most victims;
   b) Burnout occurs more frequently among people who do not have the opportunity to interact with others in their work;
   c) Burnout candidates tend to seek unattainable goals;
   d) All of the above.

c

IV. Personality and Stress.

1. Which of the following personality dimensions is related to stress:
   a) Self-esteem;
   b) Tolerance for ambiguity;
   c) Introversion/extroversion;
   d) Dogmatism;
   e) All of the above.

e

2. Which of the following is not an accurate link between personality dimensions and stress:
   a) Low self-esteem--higher stress;
   b) Low tolerance for ambiguity--higher stress;
   c) Low dogmatism--high stress;
   d) High internal locus of control--low stress.

c

3. Which of the following is not characteristic of people with Type-A personality:
   a) Unconcerned about barriers to accomplishment;
   b) Time urgency;
   c) Competitive;
   d) Aversion to idleness.

a

4. Which of the following is <u>not</u> a Type-A behavior:
   a) Self-preoccupation;
   b) General satisfaction with life;   b
   c) Accelerated speech;
   d) Fast paced living.

5. Which of the following is a Type-A pattern:
   a) Free-floating hostility;
   b) Strong focus and commitment to completing an   a
      activity before moving on to another;
   c) Heavy emphasis on planning;
   d) Evaluation of one's own activities focus on
      the quality of accomplishment rather than on
      the number of accomplishments.

6. Which of the following is <u>not</u> true regarding people
   with Type-B personality:
   a) Lack of desire for career success or goal
      accomplishment;
   b) Emphasis on setting goals and examining   a
      alternatives;
   c) Less status conscious and less insistent on
      recognition than Type-A's;
   d) Less likely to behave competitively or act
      aggressively than Type-A's.

7. Which of the following is an aspect of the hardy
   personality:
   a) Isolation from others;
   b) High internal locus of control score;   b
   c) Indifference to major life changes;
   d) All of the above;
   e) None of the above.

V. Stress Management.

1. In analyzing an employee's behavior for signs of
   stress, one should look at:
   a) Behavior in isolated events that reveal
      something different than that which typically
      occurs;
   b) Whether the employee develops a pattern of   b
      preoccupation with mistakes and personal
      failure;
   c) Whether the employee is ever absent or tardy;
   d) Whether the employee misses any deadlines.

2. Which of the following have the authors cited as
   programs that have been reported to reduce stress
   related problems in corporations:
   a) Corporate wellness programs;
   b) Programs to reduce uncertainty and increase   d
      control of the workplace;

    c)   Workshops dealing with role clarity and role analysis;
    d)   All of the above.

3. Effective managers:
    a)   Will make employees more stress-resistant;
    b)   Will learn to recognize the symptoms that   d
        occur when an employee faces too much stress;
    c)   Will learn to eliminate or control the sources of stress;
    d)   All of the above.

4. Individual coping mechanisms include:
    a)   Take time to have fun;
    b)   Establish an MBO program;   a
    c)   Redesign your job;
    d)   All of the above;
    e)   a and c.

5. Organizational coping mechanisms include:
    a)   Increase employee participation;
    b)   Learn relaxation techniques;   a
    c)   Stick with decisions;
    d)   All of the above;
    e)   b and c.

6. Which of the following is not a type of employer provided wellness program:
    a)   Treating employee illness at work;
    b)   Providing information;   a
    c)   Efforts to modify life-styles;
    d)   Creating more healthy environments.

APPLIED QUESTIONS

I. The Concept of Stress.

1. Which of the following are stressors:
    a)   An individual's spouse pressures the individual to earn greater amounts of money;
    b)   An individual explodes at a co-worker;
    c)   An individual feels her body tighten as she   a
        approaches her office each morning;
    d)   All of the above.

2. Stress:
    a)   Is a consequence of special physical or psychological demands;
    b)   Is a general response to special physical or   e
        psychological demands;
    c)   Involves the interaction of a person with his/her environment;

    d)   Occurs when a person believes they cannot
        meet the demands which face them;
    e)   All of the above;
    f)   None of the above.

II.   Responses to Stressors.

    1.   You are swamped with work on the job, and have been
        for as long as you can remember. Today at work
        your boss told you that you would be taking over
        part of a co-worker's job while she goes on
        vacation. You screamed at your boss, punched out
        early, and went home. This might be called:
        a)   An absence of positive reinforcement;
        b)   A fight-or-flight response;   b
        c)   Selective perception;
        d)   A result of life stressors.
    2.   Two managers are transferred from corporate
        headquarters to a production facility. One
        interprets this as an opportunity to gain the
        field experience necessary for further advancement;
        the other sees it as "banishment." Which of the
        following statements best describe(s) the
        situation:
        a)   The event is stressful for one of the managers
            but not for the other;
        b)   The one viewing the move as an opportunity is   c
            likely to perform well, while the other is
            likely to perform poorly;
        c)   In both cases, the stress could produce either
            negative or positive results;
        d)   The two managers clearly have very different
            personality characteristics.
    3.   A football team has an 8-0-1 record for the year.
        They travel to play an opponent with a 2-7-0
        record. They are badly beaten. Which of the
        following probably best explains that event:
        a)   The losing team did not have a realistic
            perception of the relative abilities of the
            two teams;
        b)   The losing team felt too little stress going   b
            into the game;
        c)   The losing team felt too much stress going
            into the game;
        d)   Players on the two teams approached the game
            differently because of the differences in their
            personalities.
    4.   You have decided that you cannot wait any longer.
        You must confront your boss and ask for a pay
        increase. As you near your boss' office door,

you can feel your face getting flush and your
throat begin to tighten. You wonder if you can
speak. This sort of response is:

a) A natural bodily change that occurs in the
    face of stress;
b) Unacceptable in the work place;   a
c) Likely to lead to poor performance;
d) Probably the result of your inability to
    accurately perceive how your boss will react.

5. You have been well trained to perform the tasks
    included in your job. Your friend has not. As a
    consequence you do not feel excessive stress from
    the demands of the job whereas your friend does.
    Which of the following factors is <u>unlikely</u> to be
    applicable as an explanation of your different
    responses:
    a) Past experiences;
    b) Social support;   d
    c) Individual differences;
    d) All may be applicable as partial explanations.

III. Stressors.

1. A foreman's workers expect him to represent them
    to management, while management expects the foreman
    to act in its behalf and keep the workers in line.
    This potential source of stress is an example of:
    a) Role overload;
    b) Role conflict;   b
    c) Role ambiguity;
    d) Role feedback.

2. "We're supposed to watch the gauges, but that is
    just two or three times a shift . . . and nothing
    ever changes anyway. This job drives me nuts."
    This statement indicates a potential source of
    stress resulting from:
    a) Stressors intrinsic to the job;
    b) Interpersonal relations in the organization;   a
    c) Conflict between work and other roles;
    d) Simply being in the organization.

3. "I think I'm in over my head in this job," and
    "I'm topped out . . . there's no place to go," are
    statements suggesting the potential for stress
    involving one's:
    a) Role conflict and role ambiguity;
    b) Career development;   b
    c) Being part of the organization;
    d) Interpersonal relations in the organization.

4. Which of the following statements is <u>not</u> related to
    role ambiguity:

    a)   My job duties are unclear to me;
    b)   I'm not sure who I report to and who reports   c
        to me;
    c)   I work on a lot of unnecessary tasks or
        projects;
    d)   I don't really understand what's expected of
        me.

5.   Which of the following statements is related to
     role conflict:
    a)   I have more projects than I can handle at one
        time;
    b)   I simply have more to do than can be done in   c
        an ordinary day;
    c)   I get caught in the middle between my boss
        and my subordinates;
    d)   I don't really have the training to do this
        job.

6.   Major sources of potential stress include which
     of the following life stressors:
    a)   Having trouble with a boss;
    b)   Keeping up with new technology at work;   d
    c)   Lack of power and influence in the workplace;
    d)   Personal injury or illness;

IV. Positive and Negative Effects of Stress.

1.   Which of the following is true regarding the
     effects of stress:
    a)   Too much "comfort" can kill an organization;
    b)   Absenteeism may result from either too little   d
        or too much stress;
    c)   Life stressors can have either negative or
        positive results;
    d)   All of the above.

2.   If an employee experienced increasing blood
     pressure levels, greatly heightened anxiety, and
     became unable to communicate as well as in the
     past, that employee might be exhibiting:
    a)   Physiological effects of stress;
    b)   Emotional effects of stress;   d
    c)   Behavioral effects of stress;
    d)   All of the above;
    e)   None of the above.

3.   Positive effects of stress include:
    a)   Producing enough motivation or challenge to
        cause an individual to be interested in
        performing well;
    b)   Pressure that causes people to leave the job   a
        if they don't like it;

    c) Behaviors aimed at trying to avoid stress;
    d) All of the above.

V. Nature and Causes of Burnout.

1. Which of the following occupations would seem most
   likely to contain conditions leading to burnout:
   a) Probation officers;
   b) Postal clerk;   a
   c) Bailiff;
   d) Computer repair service person.
2. An individual says that she feels "trapped" by the
   job. She hates the job because it has just become
   too time consuming, but she is unable to leave.
   She does not think she can find another job that
   pays enough. She is likely to:
   a) Feel as though no sources of relief are
      available;
   b) Experience physical, mental, or emotional   e
      exhaustion;
   c) Depersonalize everyone in the work setting;
   d) Have feelings of low personal accomplishment;
   e) All of the above;
   f) None of the above.
3. Which of the following is <u>not</u> a description of
   a condition likely to result in job burnout:
   a) A salesperson seeks to double his predecessor's
      annual sales results, even though other
      experienced salespeople (including personal
      friends) have pointed out the impossibility of
      doing so;
   b) A social worker believes that if he works hard   d
      enough he can get people throughout the
      community to change their views on society;
   c) Being an Air Traffic Controller;
   d) Constantly meeting with your supervisor to revise
      MBO goals to reflect changes in interests and
      changes in constraints.

VI. The Relationship Between Stress and Job Performance.

1. One task for a manager is to:
   a) Remove all stress so that employee performances
      will improve;
   b) Try to get to know his/her subordinates well   b
      enough to understand something about where
      their optimum stress points lie for each task;

    c)   Make sure that people feeling high stress are adequately challenged;

    d)   All of the above.

2.   A person who goes through the motions of the job unenthusiastically and without involvement may be experiencing:

    a)   Too little stress;

    b)   A Type-A personality;   a

    c)   Optimum stress;

    d)   All of the above.

3.   An aversion to idleness is associated with:

    a)   Hardy personalities;

    b)   Type A personality;   b

    c)   Type B personality;

    d)   Social support.

4.   The current trend to empower workers is partially a stress management technique that involves:

    a)   Job redesign;

    b)   Structured reorganization;

    c)   Goal-setting;   e

    d)   Greater employee participation;

    e)   All of the above.

PROGRAMMED STUDY SUPPLEMENT

1.   _____ create stress or the potential for stress.   stressors

---

2.   _____ occurs when the demands on an individual exceed that individual's capacity to meet them all, thereby constituting a source of stress in the organization.   role overload

---

3.   People with _____ may have strong desires for career success but are not driven by urgency of time and do not feel compelled to accomplish increasingly larger numbers of tasks.   Type-B personality

---

4.   _____ results from special physical or psychological demands that exceed an individual's ability or capacity to respond.   stress

5. Some part of the stress felt by employees at work stems from _____ originating from their personal circumstances.

    life stressors

---

6. A natural response to stress is the _____, something which must be overcome in a work setting.

    fight-or-flight response

---

7. Performance decreases, absenteeism, turnover, and communication difficulties are examples of _____.

    behavioral effects of stress

---

8. Tendencies toward time urgency, competitiveness, hostility, an aversion to idleness, and failure to plan are signs of _____.

    Type-A personality

---

9. A source of stress that exists in the organization when differing expectations or demands are placed on a person's role is _____.

    role conflict

---

10. A condition under which an individual can no longer cope with the demands of a job and the willingness to try to do so therefore drops off dramatically is called _____.

    job burnout

---

11. Increased blood pressure, heart rate, and gastrointestinal disorders are examples of _____.

    physiological effects of stress

---

12. A source of stress in the organization that exists when there is uncertainty about job duties and responsibilities is known as _____.

    role ambiguity

---

13. Anger, anxiety, nervousness, irritability, and inability to concentrate are examples of _____.

    emotional effects of stress

14. _____ is defined as a cluster of
    characteristics that includes a sense of
    commitment and perceiving that one has
    control over one's own life.

    hardiness

15. _____ refers to treating people like
    objects.

    deperson-
    alization

16. _____ are activities organizations
    engage in to promote good health habits or
    to identify and correct health problems.

    wellness
    programs

17. Eliminating or controlling the source of
    stress and/or making the individual more
    resistant to stress is called _____.

    stress
    management

CHAPTER 10

DYNAMICS WITHIN GROUPS

LEARNING OBJECTIVES

When you read and when you review Chapter 10, keep in mind
the learning objectives which have been established by the
authors. Look them over first as a guide to picking out the most
important parts of the chapter and then think about them as you
are going through the chapter. When you have finished the
chapter, ask yourself whether you have met the objectives.

The authors intend that when you have finished studying this
chapter you should be able to:

* Explain the tensions between group interests and
  individual interest.
* State the different types of groups and teams found
  in organizations.
* Describe the five-stages model and the punctuated
  equilibrium model of group development.
* Discuss seven of the major factors that can
  influence group behaviors and effectiveness.
* Identify and explain the six phases of effective
  group decision making.
* Diagnose why groups and teams may be ineffective and
  inefficient.
* Explain how group or team creativity can be
  stimulated through the nominal group technique and
  electronic brainstorming.

CHAPTER OUTLINE

After you have read the chapter, complete the following outline.

I.   GROUPS.

A.   A group is *those persons w/shared goals who communicate w/one another often over a span of time & are few enough so that each person may communicate w/all the others face to face*

B.   Conditions that must be met for a group to exist are

1. *members are able to see + hear each other*

2. *each member engages in personal communication w/ every other member*

3. *the individuals see themselves as members of the group w/shared goals.*

II. INDIVIDUAL-GROUP RELATIONS.

A.   Individualism vs. Collectivism.

1.   The effect that a cultural belief in individualism has on behavior is *it creates uneasiness & ambivalence over the influence that groups should have in org. decision making*

2.   The effect that a cultural belief in collectivism has on behaviors is ~~creates~~ *relative influence + assertiveness of the individual in groups.*

B.   Group vs. individual interests.

1.   These may conflict because

a. *groups mobilize powerful forces that produce important effects for individuals*

b. *groups may produce both good + bad results*

c. *groups can be managed to ↑ the benefits for them*

2.   A free rider is *a group member who obtains benefits from membership but does not bear a proportional share of the responsibility for generating benefit*

3.   The sucker effect is *one or more individuals in the group decide to w/hold effort in the belief that the free riders are planning to w/hold effort.*

III. GROUP TYPES AND DEVELOPMENT.

    A.   Categorization of groups according to primary purposes.

        1.   A friendship group is *informally evolves to serve the primary purpose of meeting its members personal needs of security, esteem & belonging.*

        2.   A task group is *formally created by mhgt. to accomplish org. defined goals.*

    B.   Categorization of groups according to interdependencies of members

        1.   A counteracting group is *when members interact to resolve some type of conflict, usually thru negotiation & compromise.*

        2.   A coacting group is *when members perform their jobs relatively independently in the short-run.*

        3.   An interacting group is *when a group can't accomplish its goal(s) until all members have completed their share of the task or jobs.*

    C.   Types of interacting teams.

        1.   A problem-solving team is *5-21 employees discussing ways to improve quality, productivity (efficiency) & work environment.*

        2.   A special purpose team is *5-30 employees, designing & introducing work reforms & new technology to improve input/output, strategic decision/plans.*

        3.   A self-managing team is *5-15 employees to produce an entire good or service*

    D.   Coalitions are *org. or individuals who band together to pursue a specific goal.*

        1.   Key features of a coalition include

            a. *deliberately created by members*

            b. *operates independently of the formal org. structure*

            c. *formed to achieve a specific & mutual goals*

            d. *requires united action*

E.   Some groups go through a 5-stage developmental sequence.

   1.

   2.

   3.

   4.

   5.

F.   Some groups develop through a punctuated equilibrium
     process, which means

IV.   GROUP BEHAVIORS AND EFFECTIVENESS.

   A.   Factors that influence group behaviors and effectiveness
        are

      1.

      2.

      3.

      4.

      5.

      6.

      7.

   B.   Context includes

      1.   Information technology is

         a.   Groupware is

C. Group goals are

D. Effective group size is

   1. Size affects the following group variables:

      a.

      b.

      c.

E. Similarities or differences among member composition and roles.

   1. How do problem-solving styles influence groups?

   2. Task-oriented roles include the following sub-roles:

      a.

      b.

      c.

      d.

      e.

   3. Relations-oriented roles include the following subroles:

      a.

      b.

      c.

      d.

      e.

      f.

    4. Self-oriented roles include the following sub-roles:

        a.

        b.

        c.

        d.

    5. How does work force diversity influence groups?

F. Norms are

    1. Norms differ from organizational rules in that

    2. The relationship between norms and group goals is that

    3. Group norms are most likely to be enforced if they

        a.

        b.

        c.

        d.

    4. Two basic types of conformity to norms are

        a.

        b.

G. Cohesiveness is

    1. The relationship between cohesiveness and conformity is

2.   Groupthink is

  a.   The initial conditions for groupthink are

      (1)

      (2)

      (3)

      (4)

      (5)

      (6)

  b.   The characteristics of groupthink are

      (1)

      (2)

      (3)

      (4)

      (5)

      (6)

      (7)

      (8)

  c.   Groupthink leads to defective decision making in terms of

      (1)

      (2)

      (3)

      (4)

      (5)

(6)

(7)

H. Leadership.

1. An informal leader is

2. Groups have multiple leaders because

3. Examples of what effective group leaders do:

a.

b.

c.

V. EFFECTIVE GROUP DECISION MAKING.

A. What happens when a group deals with decisions of increasing importance?

B. The six phases of group decision making are

1.

2.

3.

4.

5.

6.

VI.   STIMULATING GROUP CREATIVITY.

    A.   The nominal group technique is

        1.   It is especially useful for

           a.

           b.

           c.

        2.   It consists of four steps:

           a.

           b.

           c.

           d.

    B.   Electronic brainstorming is

DIRECTED QUESTIONS

I.   Individual-Group Relations.

    1.   A "group" is:
      a)   A number of people who communicate directly
          with each other over time;
      b)   A number of people who communicate directly
          or through intermediate persons over time;   a
      c)   A number of people at the same level in the
          organizational hierarchy;
      d)   A number of people of the same status or
          relative influence in the organization.
    2.   The Western cultural influence has:
      a)   Led to the easy acceptance of group
          functioning in organizations;
      b)   Led to "fitting into the group" at work;   d
      c)   Had less impact on U.S. organizations
          than the cultures of Japan and China have
          had in those countries;

       d)   Made it more difficult for individuals
           to adapt to collectivism within
           organizations.

3. Where the dominant value is individualism:
    a)   The impact of groups on individuals is generally
       insignificant;
    b)   Those adhering to that value argue that   d
       group processes should have no influence
       on organizational outcomes;
    c)   Groups will not exist in the long run;
    d)   None of the above.

4. Groups will:
    a)   Always exist, regardless of people's
       views on individualism -vs- collectivism;
    b)   Generate outputs that strongly   d
       influence the lives of individualists
       as well as collectivists;
    c)   Generally be capable of being managed;
    d)   All of the above.

5. Which of the following is a true statement:
    a)   Individual interests and group interests
       inherently conflict;
    b)   Group members sometimes obtain the benefits   b
       without sharing the costs;
    c)   Organizations can be managed in such a
       way that groups do not form;
    d)   All of the above.

II. Group Types and Development.

1. A group with the principle purpose of
accomplishing organizationally defined   c
goals is a(n):
    a)   Open group;
    b)   Closed group;
    c)   Task group;
    d)   Primary group.

2. Which of the following is <u>not</u> a type of
task group:
    a)   Open group;
    b)   Interacting group;   a
    c)   Counteracting group;
    d)   Coacting group.

3. Which of the following is a true statement:
    a)   A single group can either serve
       friendship purposes or task purposes;
    b)   An interacting group works primarily   c
       through compromise and negotiation;

   c) Temporary independence is characteristic
      of coacting groups;
   d) All of the above are true.

4. Interdependence means that:
   a) A group cannot perform its task until
      all members have completed their shares;
   b) The members interact to resolve some   d
      type of conflict;
   c) Even if slight and/or only in the short
      run, it is the linkage that is necessary
      to constitute a group;
   d) All of the above.

5. At which of the following stages of group
   development is it possible for a group to fail:
   a) Forming;
   b) Storming;   d
   c) Performing;
   d) All of the above.

6. At which of the following stages of group
   development do task behaviors emerge with
   respect to relative goal priorities,
   individual responsibilities, and
   leadership:
   a) Forming;
   b) Storming;   b
   c) Norming;
   d) Performing.

7. Which stage is dominated by a conflict which
   must be managed with particular care so that
   the group can effectively evolve into the
   next without bitterness:
   a) Forming;
   b) Storming;   b
   c) Norming;
   d) Performing.

8. The stage at which task-oriented behaviors
   evolve into sharing of information, acceptance
   of others' opinions, and attempts to agree
   or compromise on a set of rules by which the
   group will operate:
   a) Forming;
   b) Storming;   •   c
   c) Norming;
   d) Performing.

9. At what stage do members come to understand
   when it is best for them to work independently
   of each other and when it is best to work
   cooperatively:
   a) Storming;
   b) Norming;   c

      c)   Performing;

      d)   Adjourning.

10. Which of the following types of groups is a set of individuals or organizations that band together to pursue a specific goal:
    a)   Coalition;
    b)   Counteracting group;   a
    c)   Coacting group;
    d)   Interacting group.

11. Quality circles is an example of which kind of group:
    a)   Problem solving team;
    b)   Special purpose team;   a
    c)   Co-acting group;
    d)   Self-managing work team.

12. A group wherein each member learns all the jobs and tasks that have to be performed by the groups is a:
    a)   Problem solving team;
    b)   Special purpose team;   d
    c)   Co-acting group;
    d)   Self-managing work team.

13. Which of the following developmental sequences is illustrative of a punctuated equilibrium developmental process:
    a)   Forming, storming, norming, performing, adjourning;
    b)   Forming, adjourning;   c
    c)   Forming, performing, adjourning;
    d)   All of the above.

III. Influences of Group Behavior and Effectiveness.

1.   Which of the following presents the <u>least</u> problems as the size of the group increases:
    a)   Domination of group interaction by a few members;
    b)   Tendency for subgroups to form;   c
    c)   Formalization of rules and procedures;
    d)   Demands on the leader.

2.   Which combination of problem-solving styles would likely lead to the most conflict if each were powerful in a group:
    a)   Sensation-thinker/intuitive-feeler;
    b)   Sensation-thinker/sensation-feeler;   a
    c)   Sensation-thinker/intuitive-thinker;
    d)   Sensation feeler/intuitive-feeler.

3.   Which of the following is <u>not</u> a task-oriented role:
    a)   Information-seeker;
    b)   Gatekeeper;   b

    c)   Evaluator;
    d)   Coordinator.

4. Group member roles which build group-centered activities, sentiment, and viewpoints are known as:
    a)   Relations-oriented roles;
    b)   Self-oriented roles;   a
    c)   Task-oriented roles;
    d)   None of the above.

5. Which of the following is likely to lead to highest status within the group for the group members involved:
    a)   Playing task-oriented roles;
    b)   Playing relations-oriented roles;   d
    c)   Playing self-oriented roles;
    d)   Playing whichever set of roles is valued most by the group.

6. Rules which have been adopted by the group as appropriate ways for its members to act are known as:
    a)   Goals;
    b)   Objectives;   c
    c)   Norms;
    d)   Strategies.

7. Norms differ from organizational rules in that they:
    a)   Are written down and distributed by management;
    b)   Have penalties which management has   c
          specified for violators;
    c)   Must be accepted and substantially implemented before they can be said to exist;
    d)   All of the above.

8. Subconscious group norms:
    a)   Have no impact since they are not at the level of consciousness;
    b)   Have been developed by someone other than   c
          group members;
    c)   Should be brought to the level of consciousness;
    d)   All of the above.

9. Norms are most likely to be enforced if:
    a)   Management issues written warnings specifying penalties for non-compliance;
    b)   They simplify or make predictable the   b
          behavior that is expected of group members; .
    c)   They relate to matters other than interpersonal concerns;
    d)   All of the above.

10. Personal acceptance conformity:
    a) Occurs when a person's behavior is similar
       to that of the rest of the group due to
       group pressure;
    b) May be absent even if compliance occurs;   b
    c) Accounts for the majority of conformity in
       organizations today;
    d) Is a lesser level of commitment than is
       compliance.

11. Group goals:
    a) Emerge out of group norms;
    b) May be compatible with or may conflict with   b
       some member goals;
    c) Will not be attained if there are group
       norms in contradiction with those goals;
    d) All of the above.

12. When there are group norms in contradiction of
    certain group goals:
    a) Group members may well not be aware of the
       contradiction;
    b) Group members may rationalize those norms as   d
       being necessary to achieve some wider or
       longer-run goal;
    c) Some individual member behaviors may then be
       counter-productive to group or organization
       goals;
    d) All of the above.

13. Cohesiveness is:
    a) When individuals conform because of real or
       imagined group pressures;
    b) When individual behaviors, attitudes, and   c
       beliefs are consistent with the group's
       norms and wishes;
    c) The strength of the members' desires to remain
       in the group and their commitment to the group;
    d) All of the above.

14. Which of the following is a true statement:
    a) There is no relationship between cohesiveness
       and conformity;
    b) Low cohesiveness is usually associated with   b
       low conformity;
    c) High cohesiveness is dependent upon high
       conformity;
    d) Low conformity and low cohesiveness is
       referred to as groupthink.

15. Groupthink occurs when:
    a) Decision-making groups are both conforming
       and cohesive;
    b) There is a complex and dynamic environment;   d
    c) The group is insulated from outsiders;
    d) All of the above.

16. Which of the following statements is <u>not</u> true:
    a) Groupthink leads to a more complete search for alternatives in decision-making;
    b) One of the characteristics of a groupthink is an illusion of unanimity;   a
    c) An initial condition conducive to groupthink is high group cohesiveness;
    d) Groupthink tends to lead to a failure to work at contingency plans.

17. Regarding leadership:
    a) Informal task leaders are less likely to emerge than are informal relations leaders;
    b) Relations-oriented goals and task-oriented goals conflict with each other;   a
    c) Effective groups have one individual who is both the task-oriented leader and the relations-oriented leader;
    d) All of the above.

18. The external environment:
    a) Exerts influences on the task group;
    b) Is influenced by the task group;   d
    c) Includes new information technologies;
    d) All of the above.

IV. Effective Group Decision-Making.

1. Which of the following has the relative ascending order correct, as indicated by the continuum of group decisions:
    a) Groups decide on internal leadership, recruitment of new members, internal distribution of tasks, and methods to use;
    b) Groups decide on recruitment of new members, internal leadership, additional tasks to undertake, and quantitative goals;   a
    c) Groups decide on additional tasks to undertake; methods to use, and internal distribution of tasks;
    d) Groups decide on methods to use, additional tasks to undertake, qualitative goals, and quantitative goals.

2. In group decision-making, "evaluating alternatives" occurs in which of the following phases:
    a) Problem definition;
    b) Translating ideas to actions;   b
    c) Solution evaluation planning;
    d) Evaluation of the product and the process.

3. Which of the following sets of activities occur in Phase V of the Group Decision-Making Mode (the Solution Evaluation Planning phase):

   a) Explaining the situation, generating
       information, and clarifying the problem;
   b) Evaluating probable effects and comparing them   c
       with desired outcomes, revising ideas, and
       developing final action alternatives;
   c) Creating a monitoring plan, developing
       contingency plans, and assigning
       responsibilities;
   d) None of the above.

4. Of the following phases of group decision-making,
   which is the first to occur:
   a) Solution action planning;
   b) Solution evaluation planning;   d
   c) Evaluation of the product and the process;
   d) Ideas to actions.

V.   Stimulating Group Creativity.

   1. The nominal group technique is designed for use
      when:
      a) Collective judgement is more important than
          individual judgement;
      b) There is incomplete knowledge concerning the   b
          nature of the problem;
      c) Members are likely to be in agreement;
      d) All of the above.

   2. Specifically, the nominal group technique is
      most useful for:
      a) Establishing priorities;
      b) Exchanging information;   a
      c) Coordinating activities;
      d) Negotiating or bargaining.

   3. The advantage of the nominal group technique
      over the usual interacting group methods is
      most likely to be felt when:
      a) Idea generation is important;
      b) Directed leadership is important;   a
      c) Group members are aware of problem
          identification;
      d) All of the above.

   4. Key guidelines to brainstorming include:
      a) Prepare ideas by discarding the most unlikely;
      b) Be prepared to challenge the ideas of others;   c
      c) Be prepared to combine your ideas with others;
      d) All of the above.

APPLIED QUESTIONS

I.   Individual-Group Relations.

    1.   Which of the following issues involves the
        question of individualism -vs- collectivism:
        a)   A professional employee resists joining a union
            because he believes he can obtain a better
            salary by dealing directly with management;
        b)   Cultural differences have caused a U.S.   a
            executive and a Canadian executive a difficult
            time completing a business transaction;
        c)   Managers must make certain decisions on their
            own, while others can be delegated;
        d)   All of the above.

II. Group Types and Development.

    1.   The local unit of a labor union might fit into
        which of the following classifications:
        a)   Friendship group;
        b)   Task group;   d
        c)   Counteracting group;
        d)   All of the above.
    2.   A student group working on a project wherein
        each member is assigned a topic to research and
        prepare an individual report to present in the
        class is a(n):
        a)   Counteracting group;
        b)   Coacting group;   b
        c)   Interacting group;
        d)   Open group.
    3.   A student group working on a project wherein
        each member is assigned part of a topic to research
        and then bring back and fit in with parts that
        other members have researched is a(n):
        a)   Counteracting group;
        b)   Coacting group;   c
        c)   Interacting group;
        d)   Open group.
    4.   A task force of managers representing several
        of a corporation's plants from different
        locations across the country has come together to
        resolve some highly conflictive issues. The
        first night was a social get-together, designed
        to bring people together under friendly terms,
        followed by a brief meeting to outline the
        problems and assign responsibilities. During the
        discussions that followed, several managers

refused to have anything to do with the project,
or gave it only surface attention. The group
could not agree on goals or on ways to proceed.
At what stage of group development does the
breakdown appear to have begun:
   a)   Adjourning;
   b)   Forming;   d
   c)   Performing;
   d)   Storming.

5.   In the situation just described, at what stage
     do they appear to be when the impact of the
     breakdown is felt:
   a)   Norming;
   b)   Performing;   a
   c)   Adjourning;
   d)   Forming.

6.   In which of the following group situations is
     the adjourning stage likely to be most obvious:
   a)   A firm's board of directors;
   b)   A firm's affirmative action committee;   c
   c)   A city's centennial committee;
   d)   A firm's task force on creativity and innovation.

7.   Which type of group should be attempted if the goal
     is to get the maximum contribution and development
     in employees:
   a)   Problem-solving;
   b)   Special purpose;   d
   c)   Co-acting;
   d)   Self-managing.

8.   Which of the following would most appropriately
     lead to a punctuated equilibrium developmental
     process:
   a)   Need for high quality group output;   c
   b)   Need to resolve interpersonal differences in
        order for the group to work effectively;
   c)   Need for the group to "hit the ground running."

III. Influences on Group Behaviors and Effectiveness.

1.   In which of the following would the negative
     effects of large group size be of least concern:
   a)   There is conflict within the group and
        individuals have little commitment to the
        group;
   b)   The group has been formed to handle a project   c
        on a "rush" basis;
   c)   The group's task is highly technical and
        expertise in all aspects of the task is
        essential;

   d)   The decisions before the group primarily
        involve value judgments.
2. One problem facing a particular group is that
    the members tend to decide on paths of action
    too early, and thus frequently are faced with
    having adopted the wrong path of action. This
    may be a result of not having anyone in which
    of the following roles:
    a)   Initiator;
    b)   Information seeker;   d
    c)   Coordinator;
    d)   Evaluator.
3. A group is dominated by a few members, thus
    losing the value of having people with varied
    backgrounds. This may be a result of not having
    anyone in which of the following roles:
    a)   Group observers;
    b)   Standard setters;   d
    c)   Coordinators;
    d)   Gatekeepers.
4. In resolving a dispute between two factions
    within a group, individuals playing which of the
    following roles would be _least_ productive:
    a)   Information seekers;
    b)   Harmonizers;   c
    c)   Blockers;
    d)   Coordinators.
5. Which of the following is a task-oriented behavior:
    a)   Checking for consensus;
    b)   Trying to keep peace;   a
    c)   Avoiding involvement;
    d)   Reducing tension.
6. Which of the following is an example of a sanction
    for a violation of a norm:
    a)   An employee is suspended in accordance with the
         union contract for having fallen asleep
         on the job;
    b)   The work group is angry with a co-worker who   c
         has violated one of the firm's safety rules;
    c)   The work group refuses to speak to a woman who
         is the only group member who eats lunch with
         the supervisor;
    d)   The union fines a member who crosses the
         picket line.
7. After a heated debate and a 52%-to-48% vote to
    support the state political party's platform on
    an issue, the county organization publicly
    announces that it is in support of the platform.
    This is an example of:
    a)   Compliance;
    b)   Groupthink;   a

     c)   Personal acceptance conformity;
     d)   None of the above.

8.   A newly-installed computer-based information network was developed so that the University's Records Office and the teaching departments across campus can communicate more effectively. For each, this is an example of which category of factors:
     a)   Multiple leaders;
     b)   External environment;   b
     c)   Cohesiveness;
     d)   Norms.

9.   Individual group members may be asked to draw up their ideas on a list of goals, but the group goals that finally emerge are not simply an accumulation of those individual goals. The reason for this is:
     a)   The simple accumulation of individual goals would result in too large a number of goals;
     b)   Some of those goals might conflict;   c
     c)   Group goals focus on what is desired for the group, rather than on simply what each individual member desires;
     d)   Such an accumulation process would require more cohesiveness than could be found in most groups.

10.   A work group's goal may be to exceed the "standard" so that its members may receive incentive pay. A group norm may be that the standard will not be exceeded by very much, however. This norm:
     a)   Is counter productive to the expressed goal;
     b)   May be rationalization on the part of the   d
           group members;
     c)   May be consistent with the expressed goal in the longer run;
     d)   All of the above.

11.   A bipartisan political group formed to wrestle with a common problem of complex international relations:
     a)   Is unlikely to have high cohesiveness but may have high conformity;
     b)   Is likely to have high cohesiveness but may   b
           tolerate low conformity;
     c)   Is likely to have both low cohesiveness and low conformity;
     d)   Is likely to have high cohesiveness and high conformity.

12.   In which of the following groups would groupthink be most likely to occur:
     a)   An extremist religious cult;
     b)   An executive management team within a large   a
           corporate organization;

    c) A fraternal organization, such as the Elks
       Lodge or the Masonic Lodge;

    d) A community organization, such as the local
       Rotary Club or Chamber of Commerce.

13. Which of the following is likely to be a defective
    effect of groupthink:
    a) The group is insulated from outside;
    b) The illusion of invulnerability;   c
    c) Selective bias in processing information
       at hand;
    d) Collective rationalization.

14. The relationship between cohesion and productivity
    is as follows:
    a) Cohesion contributes to productivity;
    b) Productivity contributes to cohesion;   c
    c) Productivity and cohesion are interdependent;
    d) Productivity and cohesion are independent.

15. A supervisor is moved to a post for which he has
    insufficient training or experience. Someone from
    within the work group begins to perform some of the
    managerial and supervisory duties which that manager
    should be doing. This is an example of one of the
    few instances in which:
    a) There is both a task leader and a relations
       leader;
    b) There is no task leader;   c
    c) An informal task leader emerges;
    d) There is no relations leader.

16. The concept of "multiple leaders" refers to which
    of the following:
    a) A work group is large enough to require more
       than one leader;
    b) The tasks of the work group are complex enough   c
       to require more than one leader;
    c) A work group may have one person as a task
       leader and another as a relations leader;
    d) The fact that task leadership and relations
       leadership are necessarily provided by
       different people.

17. A company has decided to move its assembly
    operation to a new location in a state other than
    the one in which it is currently located. The
    assembly workers are told that they will have to
    relocate or look for another job. They join
    together and persuade management to stagger the
    relocation over the next year so that those who
    are not going to make the move will have time to
    find a job. In this example:
    a) The external environment has had an influence
       on the internal environment;

b)   The internal environment has had an influence   c
     on the external environment;
c)   Two-way influences between the internal and
     external environments have occurred;
d)   There has been no influence either way between
     the two environments.

IV.   Effective Group Decision-Making.

1.   "Alright--we know something about this problem,
     but before we get into a discussion of what we're
     going to do about it, let's make sure we know what
     we're trying to accomplish ...what outcome do we
     want?" This statement indicated that the group
     is in what phase of the decision-making model:
     a)   Problem definition;
     b)   Problem solution generation;   a
     c)   Ideas to action;
     d)   Solution action planning.
2.   "Let's don't just jump into this thing. Let's
     brainstorm it for a while...Get as many
     possibilities out on the table as possible...Then
     we'll decide which way to go..." This statement
     indicates that the group is in what phase of the
     decision-making model:
     a)   Problem definition;
     b)   Problem solution generation;   b
     c)   Solution evaluation planning;
     d)   Evaluation of the product and the process.
3.   "OK. Our plan seems to have worked pretty well.
     But there are still a few loose ends that look
     like they need to be tied up. Let's see what
     they are and then we'll decide what to do about
     them." What phase of the decision-making model
     is the group in here:
     a)   Problem solution generation;
     b)   Solution action planning;   d
     c)   Solution evaluation planning;
     d)   Evaluation of the product and the process.

V.   Stimulating Group Creativity: Nominal Group Technique.

1.   Which of the following statements is accurate:
     a)   NGT is useful when necessary to generate
          new ideas;
     b)   NGT is useful when it is necessary to elicit   d
          equal opportunity for participation from all
          group members;

    c) NGT is useful when it is necessary to make sure group members understand the reasoning behind the ideas that are being considered;

    d) All of the above.

2. For which of the following situations would NGT be most appropriate:

    a) A work group is going to meet with management representatives to discuss the group's demand that the company pay for the safety clothing which they are required to wear;

    b) Plans have been finalized for the annual company picnic, and there is going to be a meeting to hand out the assignments and make sure all the logistics are settled;

    c) A merger of two companies has occurred and a new management team is being established with the first task being to develop sets of corporate purposes, objectives, and strategies;

    d) None of the above.

c

3. Which of the following is most appropriate for brainstorming:

    a) Whether to comply with the new law;

    b) What zoning regulation must be changed for us to start our new business here;

    c) What can be done to get Harry to participate more;

    d) None of the above.

c

PROGRAMMED STUDY SUPPLEMENT

1. When, in the short run, group members perform their jobs relatively independently of one another, a _____ exists.

coacting group

---

2. _____ is the strength of the members' commitment to the group.

cohesive-ness

---

3. _____ occurs when a member's behavior becomes or remains similar to the group's desired behavior because of real or imagined group pressure.

compliance conformity

---

4. A _____ exists when members interact to resolve some type of conflict.

counter-acting group

5. The _____ occurs when a group member withholds effort in the belief that free riders are planning to withhold efforts.

    sucker effect

---

6. A _____ serves the primary purpose of meeting members' needs for security, esteem, and belonging.

    friendship group

---

7. A number of individuals all of whom communicate frequently over time in face-to-face fashion is known as a _____ .

    group

---

8. _____ are the objectives or states desired for the group as a whole.

    group goals

---

9. _____, which can occur when decision-making groups are both conforming and collusive leads to weak decision-making.

    groupthink

---

10. In any group, _____ may emerge over time and exert a relatively high influence in the group.

    informal leaders

---

11. To stimulate creative group decision-making where members lack agreement or there is incomplete knowledge about the nature of the problem, the _____ may be used.

    nominal group technique

---

12. _____ are rules of behavior which have been accepted and implemented by members of a group.

    norms

---

13. In _____, the individual's own behavior and attitudes or beliefs are consistent with the group's norms.

    personal acceptance

---

14. _____ work on ways of improving quality, productivity, and the work environment.

    problem-solving teams

15. The _____ of group members builds group-centered activities, sentiments, and viewpoints.

relations oriented role

---

16. The _____ focuses only on members' individual needs.

self-oriented role

---

17. A _____ operates primarily to accomplish organizationally defined goals.

task group

---

18. The _____ of group members facilitates and coordinates decision-making activities.

task-oriented role

---

19. The term _____ refers to a member of a group who obtains benefits from group membership but does not bear a proportionate share of the cost.

free rider

---

20. An _____ exists when a group cannot perform a task until all members have completed their shares of the task.

inter-acting group

---

21. A _____ is a set of individuals or organizations that band together to pursue a specific goal.

coalition

---

22. _____ refers to the many means of assembling and electronically storing, transmitting, processing, and retrieving words, numbers, images, and sounds, as well as to the electronic means for controlling machines of all kinds.

informa-tion technology

---

23. _____ usually operate with more empowerment that problem-solving teams.

special-purpose teams

---

24. One or more managerial levels are usually eliminated by the introduction of _____.

self-managing teams

25. A group's _____ encompasses the outside conditions and factors that it cannot directly control.

context

---

26. An approach to using specialized computer aids, communication tools, and designated physical facilities that enable teams to be more effective is known as _____.

groupware

---

27. The relationship between inputs consumed and outputs produced is called _____.

efficiency

---

28. _____ is a group process in which individuals offer as many ideas as possible within a limited time.

brain-storming

---

29. _____ is the use of computer technology to facilitate the generation and communication of ideas to group members.

electronic brain-storming

CHAPTER 11

DYNAMICS BETWEEN GROUPS

LEARNING OBJECTIVES

When you have read and when you review Chapter 11, keep in mind the learning objectives which have been established by the authors. Look them over first as a guide to picking out the most important parts of the chapter and then think about them as you are going through the chapter. When you have finished the chapter, ask yourself whether you have met the objectives.

The authors intend that when you have finished studying this chapter you should be able to:

* Describe the impact of intergroup relations on organizational effectiveness.
* Explain how each of six major factors can affect intergroup behaviors and effectiveness.
* Diagnose the causes of cooperative versus competitive relations between two or more groups.
* Explain how winning or losing in intergroup competition can affect the dynamics within a group.
* Describe seven approaches that can be used to create effective intergroup dynamics.

CHAPTER OUTLINE

After you have read the chapter, complete the following outline.

I.   KEY INFLUENCES ON INTERGROUP DYNAMICS AND EFFECTIVENESS.

    A.   Uncertainty.

        1.   Types of uncertainty.

            a.   State uncertainty is

            b.   Effect uncertainty is

            c.   Response uncertainty is

        2.   Uncertainty absorption occurs when

            a.   Dimensions of a group's power are

                (1)

                (2)

                (3)

            b.   Uncertainty absorption is important because

                (1)

                (2)

                (3)

    B.   Group goals.

        1.   Goal conflict occurs when

            a.   Mixed goal conflict means

2.   Outcomes of competition between interdependent groups are predictable in terms of:

   a.   What happens within each competing group?

   b.   What happens between competing groups?

   c.   What happens to the winner?

   d.   What happens to the loser?

C.   Substitutability is

   1.   Limits on substitutability might include

   2.   The relationship between substitutability and power is that

D.   Basic types of intergroup task relations.

   1.   Independent task relations are

      a.   Loose coupling occurs when

   2.   Interdependent task relations are

   3.   Dependent task relations are

      a.   Dependence occurs when

         (1)

         (2)

         (3)

4. Diagnosis of intergroup task relations is important because

   a.

   b.

   c.

E. Resource sharing is

F. Attitudinal sets are

   1. Are attitudinal sets the cause or the results of intergroup behavior and effectiveness?

   2. What is the relationship between attitudinal sets and intergroup task relations?

II. CREATING EFFECTIVE INTERGROUP DYNAMICS.

   A. Superordinate group goals are

   B. Superordinate group rewards are

      1. Examples of superordinate group rewards are

         a.

         b.

   C. Information technologies that aid interpersonal relations within and between groups include

      1.

      2.

3.

4.

D. Organizational hierarchy is

E. Plans set forth the organization's

    1.

    2.

    3.

    4.

    5.

F. Linking roles are

    1. Boundary spanning roles are

        a. The basic types of boundary spanning roles are

            (1)

            (2)

            (3)

            (4)

G. Task forces are

H.   Integrating roles and groups are

1.   Integrating groups are used when

a.

b.

c.

DIRECTED QUESTIONS

I.   Key Influences on Intergroup Dynamics and Effectiveness.

1.   The most common goal conflict is:
   a)   Mixed goal conflict;
   b)   Win-lose conflict;   a
   c)   Lose-lose conflict;
   d)   Win-win conflict.
2.   Win-lose goal conflict:
   a)   Is typically widespread in organizations;
   b)   Occurs when one group wins at the expense of   b
        another;
   c)   Occurs when a group attains some of its
        objectives and fails at others;
   d)   Cannot occur within an organization if that
        organization is to survive.
3.   Mixed goal conflict:
   a)   May serve as a basis for creating coalitions;
   b)   May arise at a certain level of goal attainment   d
        even though no conflict had existed earlier;
   c)   Is more common than win-lose situations;
   d)   All of the above.
4.   When competing groups are interdependent and
     interact:
   a)   Group cohesiveness breaks down;
   b)   Task orientations diminish relative to social   c
        orientations;
   c)   Intragroup differences diminish;
   d)   All of the above.
5.   "Losers" in intergroup competition:
   a)   Develop greater internal harmony;
   b)   Increase intragroup cooperation;   e
   c)   Become more realistic in self-assessment;
   d)   All of the above;
   e)   None of the above.

6. When groups compete, they:
   a) Take each other's statements more seriously and at face value;
   b) Develop more respect for and lose some of the hostile feelings toward each other;   c
   c) Decrease interaction and communication with each other;
   d) All of the above;
   e) None of the above.

7. Uncertainty absorption occurs when:
   a) Uncertainty within an organization is absorbed relatively evenly among all groups in the organization;
   b) There is no uncertainty within an organization;   b
   c) One group (or a small number of groups) has all the decision-making power within an organization;
   d) None of the above.

8. The degree to which one group can affect the behavior of another group is known as the:
   a) Domain of its power;
   b) Scope of its power;   c
   c) Weight of its power;
   d) Absorption of its power.

9. The number of groups that any group can affect is known as the:
   a) Domain of its power;
   b) Scope of its power;   a
   c) Weight of its power;
   d) Absorption of its power.

10. The impact of a group's technical expertise:
    a) Influences uncertainty absorption;
    b) Once established, extends over all areas of knowledge and skills;   a
    c) Is independent of how important others think this technical expertise may be;
    d) All of the above.

11. Substitutability:
    a) Reduces the power of the "buyer" group relative to the power of the "seller" group;
    b) Increases the power of the "buyer" group relative to the power of the "seller" group;   b
    c) Is neutral with regard to the relative power of the "buyer" and "seller" groups;
    d) None of the above.

12. Organizational rules regarding limits on substitutability:
    a) Are usually to protect existing power relationships between groups;

b)   Occur only if such rules increase the speed
     and/or hold down the costs of transactions;   c
c)   Are usually to promote full utilization of
     organizational resources;
d)   None of the above.

13. When groups engage in interaction and mutual
    decision-making only at their discretion, task
    relations are said to be:
    a)   Independent;
    b)   Dependent;   a
    c)   Interdependent.

14. When collaboration, integration, and mutual
    decision-making are necessary and desirable for
    both, task relations are said to be:
    a)   Independent;
    b)   Dependent;   c
    c)   Interdependent.

15. When one group has the power and ability to
    determine the behaviors and outcomes from
    interactions with other groups, the task relations
    are said to be:
    a)   Independent;
    b)   Dependent;   b
    c)   Interdependent.

16. Which of the following conditions is associated
    with interdependent task relations:
    a)   One group absorbs uncertainty for others;
    b)   The services that one group provides for others d
         are not readily substitutable;
    c)   One or more groups depend on another for needed
         resources;
    d)   No one group can dictate the outcome of all
         interactions.

17. Resource sharing:
    a)   Refers to the degree to which groups must obtain
         a needed resource from a common group;
    b)   Refers to the degree to which resources are   d
         sufficient to meet the needs of all groups;
    c)   Can result in either competition or cooperation;
    d)   All of the above.

18. Attitudinal sets between groups:
    a)   Can cause the behaviors and outcomes of the
         interactions;
    b)   Can result from the behaviors and outcomes of   d
         the interactions;
    c)   Are the thoughts and feelings groups have
         toward each other;
    d)   All of the above.

II. Creating Effective Intergroup Dynamics.

   1. Which of the following is <u>not</u> a condition for
       lateral relations:
       a) Groups are interdependent;
       b) Groups are able to influence each other;   c
       c) Groups are independent;
       d) Groups are at similar organizational levels.
   2. Which of the following is <u>not</u> a major mechanism for
       managing lateral relationships:
       a) Hierarchy;
       b) Substitutability;   b
       c) Plans;
       d) Task forces.
   3. Superordinate group goals:
       a) Replace individual group goals;
       b) Are benefits received by members of two or   c
           more groups;
       c) Are common ends that cannot be achieved by
           independent efforts of each group separately;
       d) All of the above.
   4. Superordinate group rewards:
       a) Stimulate willingness of groups to cooperate in
           pursuit of superordinate group goals;
       b) Are tangible benefits received by the members   d
           of two or more groups;
       c) Are intangible benefits received by the members
           of two or more groups;
       d) All of the above.
   5. Which of the following mechanisms for achieving
       integration do the authors assert as the simplest:
       a) Hierarchy;
       b) Plans;   a
       c) Linking roles;
       d) Integrating roles.
   6. Which of the following mechanisms for achieving
       integration do the authors assert to involve the
       least additional cost:
       a) Hierarchy;
       b) Plans;   a
       c) Linking roles;
       d) Integrating roles.
   7. Planning involves which of the following:
       a) Deciding on whether or not to actually
           engage in planning;
       b) Setting organizational goals;   b
       c) Making sure there is constant interaction
           between groups which have to act and make
           decisions that affect each other;
       d) All of the above.

8. Boundary-spanning roles:
   a) Are a specialized category of integrating roles;
   b) Link an organization to other external groups   b
      of organizations;
   c) Constitute a method for obtaining integration
      through use of a common superior;
   d) All of the above.
9. Task forces:
   a) Are positions filled by one person who is
      assigned to assist groups in their relationships
      with each other;
   b) Consist of several persons given the task of   c
      ensuring integration between groups;
   c) Are specialized groups consisting of represen-
      tatives from each in a series of interdependent
      groups working on specific problems of mutual
      concern;
   d) None of the above.
10. Managers are more likely to use integrating groups
    of increasing complexity when:
    a) The differences between groups needing
       integration decreases;
    b) The need to deal with non-routine problems   c
       between the groups decreases;
    c) The need for integration increases because of
       interdependent task relations;
    d) All of the above.
11. Information technologies assist in creating
    effective intergroup dynamics by:
    a) Fitting in at the top of the hierarchy of
       complexity;
    b) Supplementing the hierarchy of complexity;   b
    c) Reducing the need for superordinate goals and
       rewards;
    d) All of the above.
12. Which boundary-spanning role involves obtaining
    resources from other groups:
    a) Ambassador;
    b) Task coordinator;
    c) Scout;   a
    d) Guard.

APPLIED QUESTIONS

I. Key Influences on Intergroup Dynamics and Effectiveness.

1. Which of the following is an example of a win-lose
   goal conflict:

a) A year-long coal miners' strike;
b) The 1981 strike by the Professional Air   d
Traffic Controllers Organization;
c) A manager announces that the company's Board of
Directors will pursue the path he suggests or he
will resign;
d) All of the above;
e) None of the above.

2. In the case of the air traffic controllers:
a) Compatible goals could have been adopted;
b) Goal conflict might have occurred without   b
win-lose conflict if things had been better
managed;
c) Union-management goal conflict is always win-lose
conflict;
d) All of the above.

3. Uncertainty absorption by groups is important for
which of the following reasons:
a) It forces top management to decide which groups
will have the discretion to make decisions that
affect others;
b) It influences the relative power of groups in   d
organizations;
c) It requires that organizations ensure that
uncertainty absorption by groups is consistent
with the groups' expertise;
d) All of the above;
e) None of the above.

4. Diagnosis of task relations between two or more
groups is important because:
a) Achievement of organizational goals is often
influenced by nature and degree of task
relations;
b) Some degree of interdependent task relations   d
between lateral groups is inevitable and must
be managed;
c) There is no single set of "right" task
relations that should exist;
d) All of the above;
e) None of the above.

5. Regarding resource sharing:
a) Management encourages collaborative problem-
solving;
b) Management must help set priorities to   d
minimize unnecessary competition and
destructive conflict;
c) Management can influence attitudinal sets as
one way of managing conflict;
d) All of the above;
e) None of the above.

6. Where groups are interdependent:
   a) Competitive attitudinal sets will probably reduce goal achievement;
   b) Competitive attitudinal sets will probably increase goal attainment;
   c) Competitive attitudinal sets are unrelated to the probability of goal attainment;
   d) Competitive attitudinal sets are unlikely to emerge.

   a

7. If management keeps track of people in group "A" by means of data furnished by group "B", then:
   a) Group "A" and group "B" are likely to be mutually cooperative;
   b) Group "B" and management are likely to be very competitive;
   c) Group "B" is to be competitive with group "A";
   d) None of the above.

   c

II. Creating Effective Intergroup Dynamics.

1. The marketing and sales departments of a company know that the organization's Board of Directors expects a major increase in market share, thus they agree to cooperate over the next quarter. Which of the following complexity - resource requirement combinations exist:
   a) High complexity - high resource addition;
   b) Low complexity - low resource addition;
   c) High complexity - low resource addition;
   d) Low complexity - high resource addition.

   b

2. The Scanlon Plan is an example of:
   a) Superordinate group goals and rewards;
   b) Linking roles;
   c) Integrating roles and groups;
   d) Task force.

   a

3. Which of the following is least appropriate for adopting "hierarchy" as a mechanism for integration:
   a) Engineering research group;
   b) A manufacturing plant;
   c) A state police organization;
   d) A retail store.

   a

4. Which of the following would be most appropriate for resolution by the mechanism linking roles:
   a) A manager needs a way to resolve the routine day-to-day conflicts that arise between his sales and service divisions;
   b) A consolidation of two plant sites is going to occur and a group or committee is needed to develop a procedure;

   a

        c)   An employee has become almost impossible to
             deal with.
   5.   Which of the following would be most appropriate
        for resolution by the task force mechanism:
        a)   A manager needs a way to resolve the routine
             day-to-day conflicts that arise between his
             sales and service divisions;
        b)   A consolidation of two plant sites is going to   b
             occur and a group or committee is needed to
             develop a procedure;
        c)   Two departments have major conflicts and
             seemingly cannot cooperate any longer;
        d)   An employee has become almost impossible to deal
             with.
   6.   Which intergroup issues are likely to be appropriate
        for resolution by integrating roles or groups:
        a)   Interdepartmental conflicts;
        b)   Major capital investment decision;   d
        c)   Authority and control problems;
        d)   All of the above;
        e)   None of the above.
   7.   The local board of realtors want to get one of
        their members elected to the City Council to try
        to prevent a "no-growth" policy from being
        developed. This person would serve in what
        boundary-spanning role:
        a)   Ambassador;
        b)   Task Coordinator;   a
        c)   Scout;
        d)   Guard.

PROGRAMMED STUDY SUPPLEMENT

1.   When one group thinks another group's goal   goal
     attainment is detrimental to its own goal   conflict
     attainment, there is _____.

---

2.   The lack of information regarding the future   uncertainty
     creates _____.

---

3.   The degree to which a group can obtain the   substitut-
     services or goods provided by another group   ability
     from alternative sources is known as _____.

4. _____ occur when collaboration is necessary for groups to achieve their goals.

interde-pendent task relations

---

5. _____ refers to the degree to which two or more groups must obtain needed goods or services from a common group.

resource sharing

---

6. _____ are the thoughts and feelings that two or more groups have toward each other.

attitudinal sets

---

7. An approach for obtaining integration or coordination between two or more groups through a common superior is _____.

organiza-tional hierarchy

---

8. _____ occurs when one group makes decisions for or sets the decision-making premises for another group.

uncertainty absorption

---

9. _____ refer to the interactions between mutual decision-making by groups that occur only at the discretion of the groups.

independent task relations

---

10. _____ are the common ends pursued by two or more groups that cannot be attained by each group separately.

superordin-ate group goals

---

11. When groups affect each other occasionally, negligibly, and indirectly, _____ is said to exist.

loose coupling

---

12. _____ is figuring out, to the extent possible, everything that is important to the organization.

planning

---

13. _____ result when one group is able to dominate the behaviors and outputs from interactions with another.

dependent task relations

14. Benefits received by members of two or more groups and determined at least partially by the results of their joint efforts are _____ .

superordin-
ate group
rewards

---

15. _____ are specialized positions that facilitate communication and problem solving between two or more interdependent groups.

linking
roles

---

16. Special groups usually formed to work on temporary issues are called _____ .

task forces

---

17. The _____ is based on employee commitment, participation, and sharing of benefits.

Scanlon
Plan

---

18. _____ link the organization to external groups.

boundary-
spanning
roles

---

19. A(n) _____ is a position filled by a person permanently assigned to assist two or more groups in their relationships with each other.

integrating
role

---

20. _____ is the inability to predict the impact of a future state of the environment on the individual, group, or organization.

effect
uncertainty

---

21. _____ awards employees a proportion of total company profits.

profit
sharing

---

22. _____ means that an individual, group, or organization does not understand how components of the environment might change.

state
uncertainty

---

23. _____ are organizational systems for dividing up the benefits of such things as improved productivity or cost reductions in the form of regular cash bonuses.

gain-
sharing
plans

24. _____ is a lack of knowledge of
    alternatives and/or the inability to
    predict the likely consequences of each.

response
uncertainty

CHAPTER 12

LEADERSHIP

When you read and when you review chapter 12, keep in mind
the learning objectives which have been established by the
authors. Look them over first as a guide to picking out the most
important parts of the chapter, and then think about them as you
are going through the chapter. When you have finished the
chapter, ask yourself whether you have met the objectives.

The authors intend that when you have finished studying this
chapter you should be able to:

* Identify the differences between leaders and
  managers.
* List the skills and sources of power that leaders
  can use to influence subordinates.
* Describe the traits approach to leadership.
* Define the two behavioral leadership dimensions
  found by the Ohio State University Leadership
  Studies.
* Describe Fiedler's contingency model.
* Explain the leadership and contingency variables in
  both Hershey and Blanchard's situational leadership
  model and House's path-goal model.
* Discuss the situational variables in the Vroom and
  Jago model.
* Describe the attributional and charismatic theories
  of leadership.

CHAPTER OUTLINE

After you have read the chapter, complete the following outline.

I.   THE CONCEPT OF LEADERSHIP.

    A.   Leadership is

    B.   The roles of a leader are

        1.

        2.

        3.

        4.

    C.   The roles of a manager are

        1.

        2.

        3.

        4.

II. THE LEADERSHIP PROCESS.

    A.   The relationship between leader and subordinate is

    B.   Effective leadership skills are

        1.

        2.

        3.

        4.

C.   Sources of a leader's power are

    1.   Personal.

        a.

        b.

    2.   Organizational.

        a.

        b.

        c.

III.   LEADERSHIP APPROACHES.

A.   The Traits Model is

    1.   Criticisms of the Traits Models are that

        a.

        b.

        c.

    2.   Traits which are more likely in upper level leaders that in lower level leaders are

        a.

        b.

        c.

        d.

B.   Behavior Models (Ohio State Leadership Studies).

    1.   Consideration is

      a. Consideration is effective where

        (1)

        (2)

        (3)

        (4)

        (5)

2. Initiating structure is

      a. Initiating structure is effective when

        (1)

        (2)

        (3)

        (4)

        (5)

3. The major weakness of the Ohio State Studies is that they

IV. CONTINGENCY MODELS OF LEADERSHIP.

    A. Four common contingency variables are

      1.

      2.

      3.

      4.

    B. Fiedler's Contingency Model specifies that

1. The contingency variables in Fiedler's model are

   a.

   b.

   c.

2. Fiedler identifies a person's leadership style by

3. Problems with Fiedler's Model include

   a.

   b.

4. Organizational implications of Fiedler's models are

   a.

   b.

   c.

C. Hershey and Blanchard's Situational Leadership Model is

   1. Task behavior is

   2. Relationship behavior is

   3. Follower readiness is

   4. Leadership styles are

      a.

      b.

      c.

      d.

5. Organizational implications of the Hershey-Blanchard Model.

    a. The principal appeal of the model is

    b. The principal limitations of the model are

        (1)

        (2)

        (3)

        (4)

D. House's Path-Goal Model suggests that

    1. Types of leader behavior.

        a.

        b.

        c.

        d.

    2. Contingency variables.

        a.

        b.

    3. Effects of different leadership styles.

        a. Supportive style is appropriate when

        b. Directive style is appropriate when

        c. Participative style is appropriate when

        d. Achievement-oriented style is appropriate when

E.   Vroom-Jago Leadership Model indicates

1.   Decisions styles include:

a.   AI:

b.   AII:

c.   CI:

d.   CII:

e.   GII:

2.   The model of decision effectiveness is

a.   Decision quality is

b.   Decision acceptance is

c.   Decision timeliness is

3.   Overall effectiveness of a decision is

4.   Problem attributes of a decision are

a.   QR:

b.   CR:

c.   LI:

d.   ST:

e.   CP:

f.   GC:

g.   CO:

h.   SI:

V.   EMERGING PERSPECTIVES ON LEADERSHIP.

    A.   Attributional Theory of Leadership suggests that

        1.   Leaders' attributional process is

        2.   Employees' attributional process is

        3.   Organizational implications of managers'

            a.   Internal attributions are

            b.   External attributions are

    B.   Charismatic Leadership Theory.

        1.   Charismatic leaders are concerned with

        2.   Charismatic leaders rely on

        3.   Transformational leaders influence employees by

            a.

            b.

            c.

        4.   Transformational leaders are most appropriate when

            a.

            b.

DIRECTED QUESTIONS

I.   Nature of the Leadership Process.

    1. Leaders:
        a) Are people who do the right things;
        b) Are people who do things right;   d
        c) Have the responsibility to manage;
        d) All of the above.
    2. Leadership is the process of:
        a) Creating a vision;
        b) Translating a vision into a reality;   d
        c) Sustaining a vision that has been translated
            into a reality;
        d) All of the above.
    3. People in leadership positions:
        a) Gain economic rewards;
        b) Gain psychological rewards;   d
        c) Receive power or influence over others;
        d) All of the above.
    4. Leaders:
        a) Must enable group members to gain satisfactions
            they could not otherwise obtain;
        b) Receive their authority from a group because   d
            the group has accepted them;
        c) Can affect their own well-being and the well-
            being of others;
        d) All of the above.
    5. When subordinates do something because they believe
        the manager has the right to ask them, they are
        responding to that manager's:
        a) Legitimate power;
        b) Reward power;   a
        c) Expert power;
        d) Referent power;
        e) Coercive power.
    6. Which of the following sources of a leader's power
        is narrowest in scope:
        a) Legitimate power;
        b) Reward power;
        c) Expert power;   c
        d) Referent power;
        e) Coercive power.
    7. When subordinates do something a manager requests
        because they want to be like the manager and want
        to receive the manager's approval, that manager
        can be said to have:
        a) Legitimate power;
        b) Reward power;   d
        c) Expert power;

d)   Referent power;
e)   Coercive power.

8.   Subordinates who do something to avoid punishment
     by the manager are responding to the manager's:
     a)   Legitimate power;
     b)   Reward power;   e
     c)   Expert power;
     d)   Referent power;
     e)   Coercive power.

9.   The power that comes from a manager's ability to
     provide such items as promotions or pay increases
     is known as:
     a)   Legitimate power;
     b)   Reward power;   b
     c)   Expert power;
     d)   Referent power;
     e)   Coercive power.

10. Organizational sources of power:
     a)   Are legitimate, reward, and coercive;
     b)   Are referent and expert;   a
     c)   Lead to higher levels of job satisfaction among
          subordinates than do personal sources;
     d)   Are more likely to lead to high levels of
          performance than are personal power sources.

11. What kind of leadership skill is being exhibited
     when a leader allows followers to share
     satisfaction derived from reaching goals:
     a)   Visionary skills;
     b)   Empowerment skills;   b
     c)   Communication skills;
     d)   Self-understanding.

II. Leadership Approaches.

1.   Picking leaders as managers:
     a)   Is typically best done by utilizing an intuitive
          approach;   d
     b)   Can best be explained by the attribution
          process;
     c)   Is best done by using the traits approach;
     d)   None of the above.

2.   The model based on observed characteristics of a
     large number of successful and unsuccessful leaders
     is the:
     a)   Traits model;   a
     b)   Fiedler's contingency model;
     c)   House's path-goal model;
     d)   Vroom and Yetton's normative model.

3. The model that attempts to tell the manager which
    style of leader behavior is correct by varying the
    degree of subordinate participation in the
    decision-making process is the:
    a) Traits model;   d
    b) Fiedler's contingency model;
    c) House's path-goal model;
    d) Vroom and Yetton's normative model.
4. The model which specifies that a group's performance
    depends upon both the leader's motivational system
    and the degree to which the leader controls and
    influences the system is:
    a) Traits model;   b
    b) Fiedler's contingency model;
    c) House's path-goal model;
    d) Vroom and Yetton's normative model.
5. The model which suggests that a leader must select
    a style most appropriate to the particular situation
    at hand is:
    a) Traits model;   c
    b) Fiedler's contingency model;
    c) House's path-goal model;
    d) Vroom and Yetton's normative model.
6. Which of the following is not one of the reasons
    cited by the authors as why the traits approach is
    inadequate:
    a) No consistent pattern(s) has (have) been found;   b
    b) The traits uncovered are not the correct traits;
    c) It relates physical characteristics to effective
        leadership;
    d) Leadership is too complex to be explained by the
        traits approach.
7. Behavioral models assert that effective leaders:
    a) Are considerate and supportive of group members'
        attempts to achieve personal goals;   d
    b) Focus attribution on the quality and quantity
        of work accomplished;
    c) Work at providing positive reinforcement;
    d) All of the above.
8. The success of behavioral models in explaining
    leader behavior is a result of which of the
    following:
    a) Individual social status within the group;   d
    b) The individual expectations of a certain style
        of supervision;
    c) The individual psychological rewards from
        working with a particular type of leader;
    d) None of the above.
9. "Consideration" is said to be effective in which of
    the following circumstances:

a) The task is complex;
b) Major status differences exist between leader   c
   and followers;
c) Subordinates must learn something new;
d) Subordinates do not want participative
   leadership.

10. "Initiating structure" is most effective in which
    of the following circumstances:
    a) The task is routine;
    b) Subordinates depend on the leader for   b
       information and direction;
    c) A small number of people report to the leader;
    d) Subordinates are dissatisfied with the task.

11. The major weakness of the Ohio State University
    research was:
    a) The limited attention it gave to the effects
       of the situation on leadership style;
    b) The fact that it paid no attention to   a
       relationship between leader and subordinates;
    c) The fact that it focused on the situation
       surrounding the relationships;
    d) All of the above.

12. Which of the following is not a group characteristic
    that affects leadership:
    a) Structure;
    b) Task;   d
    c) Norms;
    d) Rules and regulations.

III. Contingency Models of Leadership.

1. In Fiedler's contingency model, the degree to which
   the work performed by subordinates is routine or
   non-routine is the degree of:
   a) Group atmosphere;
   b) Task structure;   b
   c) Position power;
   d) Decision quality.

2. In Fiedler's contingency model, the measure of a
   leader's acceptance by the group is known as:
   a) Group atmosphere;
   b) Task structure;   a
   c) Position power;
   d) Decision quality.

3. A high-LPC person is one who:
   a) Is a task-motivated leader;
   b) Focuses on initiating structure;   c
   c) Is a relationship-motivated leader;
   d) Classifies the least preferred co-worker in
      negative terms.

4. Fiedler classifies the most favorable situation for
   a leader as:
   a)   One in which the leader has a high LPC score;
   b)   One in which group atmosphere is poor, position   d
        power weak, and tasks unstructured;
   c)   One in which group atmosphere is positive,
        position power strong, and tasks unstructured;
   d)   One in which group atmosphere is positive,
        position power strong, and tasks structured.
5. High-LPC leaders:
   a)   Perform more effectively than low-LPC leaders
        in the least favorable situations;
   b)   Perform more effectively than low-LPC leaders   c
        in the most favorable situations;
   c)   Perform most effectively in moderately favorable
        situations;
   d)   None of the above.
6. According to Fiedler:
   a)   Both high- and low-LPC's perform well under some
        conditions but not under others;
   b)   Leaders' performance depends both on their   d
        motivational bases and on the situation;
   c)   Leaders can do something about their situations;
   d)   All of the above;
   e)   None of the above.
7. House's path-goal model says that:
   a)   There is no one best way to lead;
   b)   A leader must select a style most appropriate   d
        to the situation;
   c)   A leader should improve subordinates' job
        satisfaction to improve their performance;
   d)   All of the above;
   e)   None of the above.
8. House's model refers to the consideration of
   subordinate needs as:
   a)   Supportive leadership;
   b)   Directive leadership;   a
   c)   Participative leadership;
   d)   Achievement-oriented leadership.
9. House's model refers to setting goals and pursuing
   performance as:
   a)   Supportive leadership;
   b)   Directive leadership;   d
   c)   Participative leadership;
   d)   Achievement-oriented leadership.
10. House's model refers to guiding, scheduling, and
    coordinating subordinates' work as:
    a)   Supportive leadership;
    b)   Directive leadership;   b
    c)   Participative leadership;
    d)   Achievement-oriented leadership.

11. According to House, a non-routine task has which
    of the following characteristics:
    a) Employees do parts of the job rather than the
        whole job;
    b) Employees receive substantial amounts of infor-   b
        mation about how well they perform the task;
    c) Employees make few decisions about scheduling
        and means for accomplishing the task;
    d) None of the above.

12. According to House, participative leadership would be
    appropriate when:
    a) The task is tedious, boring, routine, and
        unpleasant;
    b) The task is highly unstructured, complex, and   c
        non-routine;
    c) The task is ambiguous and ego-involving, and the
        subordinates have self-esteem needs;
    d) None of the above.

13. Which of the following statements is true according
    to House?
    a) Workers who perform tedious tasks report higher
        job satisfaction with directive leadership;
    b) Achievement-oriented leadership has little   c
        effect on subordinates' performance and job
        satisfaction when their tasks are routine;
    c) Subordinates who perform unstructured tasks
        are more productive and satisfied when their
        leader uses a more directive style;
    d) All of the above;
    e) None of the above.

14. Regarding participative leadership, House says:
    a) It increases subordinates' efforts if they
        are performing unstructured tasks;
    b) Subordinates learn more and feel more   d
        optimistic about success if they participate
        in decision-making about tasks, goals, plans,
        and procedures;
    c) Participative leadership has little effect on
        subordinates' performance if they have a
        structured task and a clear understanding of
        their job;
    d) All of the above;
    e) None of the above.

15. Regarding the Vroom and Jago model:
    a) Various degrees of participation are
        appropriate in various situations;
    b) One level of participation is appropriate   a
        across all situations;

   c) Like the Fiedler model, it rejects the notion
      that a leader can change his/her style enough
      to fit into different situations;
   d) None of the above.
16. In the Vroom-Jago Model, the degree to which
    subordinate commitment is generated by a decision
    process is known as:
   a) Decision quality;
   b) Decision effectiveness;   c
   c) Decision acceptance;
   d) Decision dependence.
17. According to Vroom-Jago, decision effectiveness
    is especially important if:
   a) There is insufficient time for the leader to
      make a decision;
   b) Subordinate development is critical;   e
   c) It is independent of overall effectiveness;
   d) All of the above;
   e) None of the above.
18. According to Vroom and Jago, a decision situation
    in which management's primary concern is that
    there is so little room for error is one faced
    with a high:
   a) Commitment probability;
   b) Problem structure;   d
   c) Subordinate conflict;
   d) Quality requirement.
19. Commitment probability refers to the question of:
   a) Conflict among subordinates over preferred
      solutions;
   b) Any problems in which subordinates are   c
      uncommitted;
   c) Subordinates' commitment when the manager
      alone makes the decision;
   d) None of the above.
20. The contingency variables group atmosphere, task
    structure, and leader position power are
    associated with:
   a) Vroom and Jago;
   b) House;   c
   c) Fiedler;
   d) None of the above.
21. The contingency variables decision quality and
    decision acceptance are associated with:
   a) Vroom and Jago;
   b) House;   a
   c) Fiedler;
   d) None of the above.
22. The leader effectiveness criteria subordinate job
    satisfaction and job performance are associated
    with:

       a)   Vroom and Jago;
       b)   House;   **b**
       c)   Fiedler;
       d)   None of the above.

23. The Hershey-Blanchard Model takes into account:
       a)   Task behavior;
       b)   Relationship behavior;   **d**
       c)   Follower readiness;
       d)   All of the above;
       e)   a and b.

24. In the Hershey-Blanchard Model, which style works best when subordinates are able but lack confidence:
       a)   Telling;
       b)   Selling;   **c**
       c)   Participative;
       d)   Delegating.

25. In the Hershey-Blanchard Model, which style works best when subordinates are unable and unwilling to perform:
       a)   Telling;
       b)   Selling;   **a**
       c)   Participative;
       d)   Delegating.

IV.   Emerging Perspectives on Leadership.

1. The Attributional Theory of Leadership is based on which of the following dimensions of behavior:
       a)   Distinctiveness;
       b)   Consensus;   **e**
       c)   Consistency;
       d)   Validity;
       e)   a, b, and c.

2. Leaders try to change an employee's behavior only when which of the following attribution is made:
       a)   External;
       b)   Internal;   **b**
       c)   Self-serving;
       d)   Environmental;
       e)   Interpersonal.

3. Which type of leaders concern themselves with referent and personal sources of power:
       a)   Attributional;
       b)   Charismatic;   **c**
       c)   Transformational;
       d)   Distinctive.

4. Charismatic leaders:
       a)   Base their power on their position;

b)   Behave unconventionally;   b
c)   Have goals consistent with the status quo;
d)   Articulate goals weakly.

APPLIED QUESTIONS

I.   The Leadership Process.

1.   A new department is formed at work. You are
     designated as supervisor. Are you the leader?
     a)   Yes;
     b)   No;   d
     c)   Depends on whether you can get the people to
          obey your orders;
     d)   Depends on whether people want to do as you ask.
2.   Which of the following best satisfies the
     prerequisites for leadership:
     a)   The supervisor who "delivers" on the goals
          set forth for her by upper management;
     b)   A new supervisor prefers to allow her
          subordinates to make departmental decisions,   a
          but will make decisions herself when forced
          to do so;
     c)   A manager has organizational authority to
          require subordinates to comply with his orders;
     d)   None of the above.
3.   Which of the following is <u>not</u> illustrative of the
     leadership process:
     a)   The manager's subordinates like him and so say
          they will do what he wants, but they do not see
          any advantage from doing so;
     b)   The manager has the authority to require   d
          subordinates to do certain things, although
          he does not believe that either he or his
          subordinates will derive any benefits in
          doing so;
     c)   An individual agrees to accept a managerial
          role if and only if the additional compensation
          is substantial and continuing, as he does not
          anticipate any non-economic rewards from
          performing the duties;
     d)   None of the above are illustrative of the
          leadership process.
4.   A manager who is an excellent "idea person" but
     does not have the human resource management skills
     to get her ideas implemented, hires an assistant
     who excels at human resource management. Which
     leadership skill is she exhibiting:

a) Empowerment;
b) Communication;
c) Self-understanding;   c
d) Visionary.

II. Sources of a Leader's Power.

1. An organization chart depicts which source of power:
   a) Legitimate;
   b) Referent;   a
   c) Expert;
   d) None of the above.
2. Which of the following sources of power may, e.g.,
   prevent workers from engaging in excessive social
   behavior at work, but is likely to do so without
   encouraging the desired alternative behavior:
   a) Coercive;
   b) Referent;   a
   c) Reward;
   d) Expert.
3. The manager who is known to be good to work for
   because of the training you will get from her has
   which source of power:
   a) Coercive;
   b) Referent;   d
   c) Reward;
   d) Expert.

III. The Traits Approach to Leadership.

1. Which of the following is <u>not</u> consistent with the
   traits identified as those associated with
   successful leaders;
   a) The individual scores high or various tests which
      claim to measure I.Q.;
   b) The individual is not a specialist, but has   d
      a wide range of interests;
   c) The individual has a high energy level and an
      exceptional need to succeed;
   d) The individual prefers to work with a select few
      others under stable conditions and circumstances.
2. Which of the following is <u>not</u> a legitimate
   criticism of the traits approach:
   a) Physical characteristics do not enable one to
      predict an individual's success as a leader;
   b) Personality traits are difficult or impossible   b
      to measure or identify;

    c) The concept of leadership is too complex to be
       explained simply by personality characteristics;
    d) None of the above.

IV. Behavioral Models of Leadership.

  1. Which of the following are associated with
     behavioral explanations of successful leadership:
     a) A manager emphasizes to her subordinates the
       fact that their work must meet inspection
       standards;
     b) A manager makes sure that she provides enough   d
       personal attention to her subordinates to
       ensure that they know she cares about how
       they are progressing;
     c) A manager keeps his subordinates' attention
       attuned to the output levels that are expected
       of them;
     d) All of the above;
     e) None of the above.
  2. In which of the following would consideration leader
     behavior be most likely to have a positive impact
     on productivity and job satisfaction:
     a) An engineer doing research for new product
       development;
     b) A group of 8 accounting clerks, where the   b
       leader is an accounting clerk who has been
       appointed lead clerk;
     c) A 60-person College of Business faculty;
     d) A symphony orchestra.
  3. In which of the following would initiating structure
     leader behavior be most likely to have a positive
     impact on productivity and job satisfaction:
     a) Where the employees are under an incentive plan
       with exceptionally high output levels required
       to break in to the incentive pay range;
     b) A group of 5 janitors, with one acting as lead   a
       janitor;
     c) The manager is not trained in the technical
       aspects of the work being done in his department;
     d) The subordinates basically dislike their work.

V. Fiedler's Contingency Model.

  1. A situation in which the leader exercises tight
     control over group processes can be described as:
     a) Poor group atmosphere;
     b) Positive group atmosphere;   a
     c) High task structure;

d)   Low task structure;
e)   None of the above.

2.   Which of the following is an example of a job
     having high task structure:
     a)   Research engineer;
     b)   Troubleshooter;   d
     c)   Ombudsman;
     d)   Hospital admissions clerk;
     e)   None of the above.

3.   Which of the following would likely have the <u>least</u>
     position power:
     a)   Police chief;
     b)   College honorary fraternity president;   b
     c)   Retail store department head;
     d)   Restaurant manager.

4.   You think of yourself as particularly competent
     in the technical side of your manager's job, but
     you are less comfortable with that part of your
     job which requires you to relate to people. Which
     of the following situations would be <u>least</u> suited
     for your approach:
     a)   Group atmosphere positive, leader position
          power strong, and tasks structured;
     b)   Group atmosphere positive, leader position   c
          power weak, and tasks structured;
     c)   Group atmosphere poor, leader position power
          weak, and tasks structured;
     d)   Group atmosphere poor, leader position power
          weak, tasks unstructured.

5.   You have always been able to achieve your goals as
     a manager by getting along with your subordinates
     and having them go that "extra mile" for you.
     Which of the following situations would <u>least</u>
     utilize your approach:
     a)   Tasks are structured, the group dislikes the
          leader, and the leader must show concern for
          subordinates;
     b)   Tasks are unstructured, the group likes the   c
          leader, and the leader is dependent on the
          group's willingness to work toward goal
          attainment;
     c)   Tasks are structured, the atmosphere is
          positive, and leader position power is strong;
     d)   None of the above.

6.   A task-oriented manager who reports to you is
     poorly. Which of the following is possible,
     according to Fiedler:
     a)   That manager could be a good manager in another
          situation;

b) The current situation in which that manager   d
    exists could be changed so as to improve his
    effectiveness;
c) The manager's effectiveness could be improved
    by changing his motivational state;
d) All of the above;
e) None of the above.

VI. House's Path-Goal Model.

1. According to House, if you have a directive
    leadership style, you would be most effective when:
    a) Subordinates need guidance and clarification
        concerning the path to take to get the job done;
    b) Subordinates are accustomed to contributing   a
        ideas toward problem solution;
    c) Subordinates want to assume responsibility for
        attaining challenging goals;
    d) None of the above.
2. If you are a supportive leader, which of the
    following subordinate characteristics would be
    least compatible with your approach:
    a) High need for belongingness;
    b) High need for affiliation;   c
    c) High need for self-actualization;
    d) All of the above tend to be incompatible.
3. Which of the following is consistent with House's
    model:
    a) It is not useful to send managers to training
        sessions in the hopes they will be able to
        adopt different styles of leadership;
    b) A manager must determine whether task   c
        accomplishment or relationships are most
        in need of attention, because they cannot
        both be attended to at the same time;
    c) A manager must know how to use each style of
        leadership and when to use it;
    d) All of the above;
    e) None of the above.
4. House's model suggests that:
    a) Assembly-line workers would prefer a directive
        leadership style from their supervisors;
    b) Engineers would prefer a supportive   e
        leadership style from their supervisors;
    c) Counter clerks at a fast-food store would
        prefer an achievement-oriented leadership
        style from their supervisors;
    d) All of the above;
    e) None of the above.

VII. Vroom and Jago Model.

   1.   A manager wants to introduce additional automation into the workplace. Which of the following is likely to be the greatest obstacle in the way of that manager if he makes the decision alone:
      a)   Subordinate information;
      b)   Problem structure;   d
      c)   Quality requirement;
      d)   Goal congruence.

   2.   In which of the following cases would a participative style of management be most appropriate:
      a)   Problems frequently need high quality solutions;
      b)   The organization is committed to developing   b
           managerial skills among subordinates;
      c)   The tasks involved are highly technical and require substantial specialized training;
      d)   Subordinates are in general disagreement among themselves as to what the actions should be.

   3.   In the Vroom-Jago model, management training can be used to:
      a)   Help managers learn to diagnose situations;
      b)   Help managers learn to adopt different   d
           leadership styles;
      c)   Help managers choose which style goes best with which situation;
      d)   All of the above.

VIII.   Hershey-Blanchard Model.

   1.   Management has decided to install a strong participative decision-making approach. Subordinates have relied totally on standard operating procedures in the past and have never been allowed to offer their opinions. They don't trust this new program and so are behaving with great reserve. What components of the model are at issue here:
      a)   Task behavior;   d
      b)   Relationship behavior;
      c)   Follower readiness;
      d)   All of the above;
      e)   a and c.

   2.   Frank's principal leadership style is "telling." What behavior does he <u>omit</u>:
      a)   Relationship;   a
      b)   Directive;

c) Task;
d) a and b.

3. This model does <u>not</u> deal directly with which of
the following variables influencing choice of
leadership style:
a) Leader's personality;   a
b) Follower's ability;
c) Follower's willingness;
d) Follower's readiness.

IX. Emerging Perspectives of Leadership.

1. Cindy approaches her work with extreme slowness
regardless of the difficulty of the task or the
urgency of the time requirement. Is this behavior:
a) High distinctiveness;   a
b) High consensus;
c) Low consistency;
d) Low distinctiveness.

2. The coach was highly successful at another school.
His first year at the new school the team won most
of its games and proclaimed him a great coach.
This year, the team won 2 and lost 9. Now team
members say he is a terrible coach. This is:
a) Distinctiveness;   b
b) Self-serving bias;
c) Consensus;
d) Consistency.

3. The new plant manager's primary expertise is that
he is always able to get things done within the
existing system. Is he:
a) A noncharismatic leader;   a
b) A charismatic leader.

PROGRAMMED STUDY SUPPLEMENT

1. A _____ in an organization is one who is   leader
given authority and responsibility to
accomplish the goals of an organization and
who is held accountable for the results.

---

2. _____ is power that comes from the   legitimate
manager's position in the organization.   power

3. The _____ of leadership is based on observed characteristics of a large number of successful and unsuccessful leaders.

traits model

4. The _____ resulted in the identification of consideration and initiating structure as dimensions of leader behavior.

Ohio State University leadership studies

5. _____ specifies that group performance is contingent on both leader's motivational system and degree to which the leader controls and influences the situation.

Fielder's contingency model

6. A high degree of _____ indicates psychological closeness between the leader and subordinates.

considera-tion

7. The manager whose subordinates do something because they admire him is said to have _____.

referent power

8. _____ measures a leader's perception of group acceptance.

group atmosphere

9. The extent to which leaders are likely to define and structure their roles and those of their subordinates toward accomplishing group goals is known as _____.

initiating structure

10. Fiedler uses his _____ instrument to measure leadership style.

LPC

11. _____ is based on the amount of relationship and task behavior that leader provides in a situation.

Hershey and Blanchard

12. The extent to which a task performed by subordinates is routine or non-routine is the degree of _____.

task structure

13. The manager who has _____ may find that subordinates do things out of a belief that she knows what needs to be done.

expert power

---

14. _____ states that a leader shall try to enhance subordinates' satisfaction with their jobs and increase their job performance.

House's path-goal model

---

15. _____ involves setting goals and seeking performance.

achievement oriented leadership

---

16. _____ is effective when subordinates are willing but somewhat unable to carry out their task.

selling style

---

17. _____ is the process of influencing group activities toward the achievement of goals.

leadership

---

18. Managers' ability to provide workers something they value in return for their performance use constitutes _____.

reward power

---

19. _____ includes consulting with subordinates and evaluating their opinions and suggestions when making decisions.

participative leadership

---

20. One problem with _____ is that it does not encourage desired behavior.

coercive power

---

21. A theory of leadership that attempts to tell the manager which style of leadership to use by varying the degree of subordinates' participation in the decision-making process is represented by _____.

Vroom and Jago model

---

22. The type of leader behavior (identified by House) that is similar to the Ohio State model's "consideration" is _____.

supportive leadership

23. In Fiedler's construct, _____ is the extent to which a leader possesses reward, coercive, and legitimate power.

position power

---

24. The type of leader behavior (identified by House) that is similar to the Ohio State model's "initiating structure" is _____.

directive leadership

---

25. _____ means that the leader allows the followers to share satisfactions derived from reaching goals.

empowerment

---

26. _____ is a self-taught process that teaches the individual how to match his/her LPC level with the situation.

leader match

---

27. _____ is influenced by decision effectiveness, time requirements, and the need for subordinates' development.

overall effectiveness

---

28. _____ depends on decision quality, acceptance, and timeliness

decision acceptance

---

29. Suggestion that a leader's judgment about his/her employees is influenced by the leader's views as to the causes of the employees' performance is associated with the _____.

attribution theory of leadership

---

30. _____ use dominance, self-confidence, a need for influence, and a conviction of moral righteousness to increase their leadership effectiveness.

charismatic leaders

---

31. _____ rely on referent and personal sources of power.

transformational leaders

---

32. A person who directs the work of employees and is responsible for results is a _____.

manager

33. Subordinates' ability and willingness to   follower
    perform the task is called _____.   readiness

---

34. _____ provides little task or   delegating
    relationship behaviors because subordinates   style
    made more decisions.

---

35. _____ is similar to "consideration"   supportive
    in the Ohio State Model.   behavior

---

36. _____ is similar to "initiating   directive
    structure" in the Ohio State Model.   behavior

CHAPTER 13

INTERPERSONAL COMMUNICATION

LEARNING OBJECTIVES

When you read and when you review Chapter 13, keep in mind the learning objectives which have been established by the authors. Look them over first as a guide to picking out the most important parts of the chapter and then think about them as you are going through the chapter. When you have finished the chapter, ask yourself whether you have met the objectives.

The authors intend that when you have finished studying this chapter you should be able to:

* Explain the elements of the interpersonal communication process and their relationships to one another.
* Discuss how interpersonal communications can vary across cultures.
* Describe the degree of richness of various media in sending and transmitting messages.
* Evaluate the effects and implications of different types of communication networks.
* Describe the changing role of information technologies in the communication process.
* Explain the importance of communication openness.
* Improve your effectiveness in giving feedback, engaging in self-disclosure, and listening to others.
* Give examples of five types of nonverbal communication.

CHAPTER OUTLINE

After you have read the chapter, complete the following outline.

I.   BASIC COMMUNICATION PROCESS.

    A.   Bypassing:

    B.   Interpersonal Communication:

    C.   Sender:

    D.   Receiver:

    E.   Transmitter:

    F.   Receptors:

    G.   Media richness:

    H.   Data:

    I.   Messages:

    J.   Channels:

    J.   Noise:

    L.   Meanings:

    M.   Encoding:

    N.   Decoding:

    O.   Feedback:

II. INTERPERSONAL COMMUNICATION NETWORKS.

    A. An interpersonal communication network is

        1. Focuses on

    B. Types of networkS.

        1. Manager's networks include

           a.

           b.

           c.

        2. Basic communication networks.

           a.

           b.

           c.

           d.

           e.

    C. Effects of different networks are assessed by four
       criteria:

        1.

        2.

        3.

        4.

    D. Organizational Implications.

        1. Why understand types of networks?

        2. Which networks should be used for:

a. Simple problems?

b. Complex problems?

c. Problems requiring little group member interdependence?

d. Problems requiring high group member interdependence?

3. Implications of networks for day-to-day communications are

a.

b.

c.

E. Role of information technologies is

1. Examples of information technologies include

a. E-Mail:

b. Voice Mail:

c. Telecommuting:

2. Primary advantages of new information technologies are

3. Problems to address in new information technologies include

a.

b.

c.

d.

III. COMMUNICATION OPENNESS.

    A. Openness Continuum.

        1. Openness means that the message transmission and reception are

            a.

            b.

            c.

        2. Open message transmission and reception are linked to

            a.

            b.

            c.

        3. Meta-communication refers to

    B. Situational risk factors affecting the degree of openness are

        1.

        2.

        3.

    C. Giving feedback is

        1. Principles of effective feedback under open communications:

            a.

            b.

            c.

      d.

      e.

      f.

2. Types of interpersonal feedback are

      a.

      b.

      c.

      d.

D. Appropriate self-disclosure.

  1. Self-disclosure is

      a. Non-disclosing individuals may

      b. Total-disclosing individuals may

  2. How can organizational level complicate self-disclosure?

E. Active listening is necessary to

  1. Guidelines for increasing listening skills include

      a.

      b.

      c.

      d.

      e.

      f.

      g.

F. What is the relationship between open communication and ethical behavior?

IV. NONVERBAL COMMUNICATION.

A. Nonverbal communication includes

B. Nonverbal cues include

1.

2.

3.

4.

5.

C. Verbal and nonverbal cues can be related by

1.

2.

3.

4.

D. Principles relating organizational status and nonverbal cues are

1.

2.

3.

E. Gender differences in nonverbal cues include

1.

2.

3.

4.

DIRECTED QUESTIONS

I.   The Basic Communications Process.

1.   Information richness is:
   a)   The input of a communication channel;
   b)   The transmission and reception of facts;
   c)   The potential information-carrying capacity of data;
   d)   The means by which messages travel.   c

2.   Which of the following is <u>not</u> an active part of interpersonal communication:
   a)   Words;
   b)   Emotions;
   c)   Listening;
   d)   All are active parts.   d

3.   Which one of the following information media is highest in richness of information transfer:
   a)   Face-to-face discussion;
   b)   Telephone conversations;
   c)   Formal written documents;
   d)   Informal written documents.   a

4.   Which one of the following information media is lowest in richness of information transfer:
   a)   Face-to-face discussion;
   b)   Telephone conversations;
   c)   Informal written documents;
   d)   All are action parts.   c

5.   Accurate interpersonal communication occurs when:
   a)   The sender transmits the message accurately;
   b)   The receiver listens to and interprets the message transmitted;
   c)   Ideas, facts, opinions, attitudes, and feelings are involved;
   d)   The message intended by the sender is the same as interpreted by the receiver.   d

6.   In interpersonal communication between two people the sender is:
   a)   The one who speaks first;
   b)   The one who receives the message and then responds;
   c)   Whichever person is transmitting at any given time;
   d)   None of the above.   c

7. The communication goals of senders and receivers:
    a) Are irrelevant so long as transmission is
        accurate;
    b) Must be the same in order for accurate
        communication to occur;
    c) Are more likely to distort the process if they
        primarily involve objective facts;   d
    d) Are more likely to distort the process if they
        primarily involve attitudes and values.

8. Receptors:
    a) May include one or more of the five senses;
    b) Include the means available for sending
        messages;   a
    c) Are primarily under control of the sender;
    d) All of the above.

9. Messages:
    a) Include the data and any accompanying coded
        symbols;
    b) Are the meanings that are created by the sender
        and the receiver;   d
    c) May have interpreted meanings that differ
        from those intended by the sender;
    d) All of the above.

10. Channels:
    a) Are the ways in which messages move from sender
        to receiver;
    b) Are interferences with the intended meanings of
        messages;   a
    c) Give particular meaning to the data;
    d) Are the coded symbols that give meaning to
        data.

11. Something which interferes with the intended
    message in the channel is known as:
    a) Noise;
    b) Encoding;   a
    c) Receptor error;
    d) Channel.

12. "Meaning":
    a) Must be translated into messages so that they
        can be transmitted;
    b) Represents an individual's ideas, facts,
        attitudes, opinions, and feelings;   d
    c) Is unlikely to be shared by sender and receiver
        if they share nothing else in common;
    d) All of the above.

13. The sender's translation of meaning into messages
    that can be transmitted is known as:
    a) Encoding;
    b) Decoding;   a
    c) Feedback;
    d) None of the above.

14. The receiver's translation of received messages
    into interpreted meanings is known as:
    a)   Encoding;
    b)   Decoding;
    c)   Feedback;   b
    d)   None of the above.

15. What the authors have termed the "ideal state" is:
    a)   When the decoded message equals the encoded
         message;
    b)   Most likely to occur when the message content
         is primarily unemotional;   d
    c)   Total accuracy of interpersonal communication;
    d)   All of the above.

16. The receiver's response to a message is known as:
    a)   Decoding;
    b)   Feedback;   b
    c)   Encoding;
    d)   Meaning.

17. Feedback:
    a)   Immediately follows encoding;
    b)   Establishes the meaning that the sender
         intended;   c
    c)   Establishes communication as a two-way process;
    d)   Is part of the decoding process.

II. Interpersonal Communication Networks.

1. Communication networks:
    a)   Focus on the individuals in interpersonal
         communication;
    b)   Focus on whether the message was received as
         intended by the sender;   c
    c)   Focus on communication relationships among
         individuals;
    d)   Focus on lateral communication patterns.

2. Which of the following does not affect
    communication networks:
    a)   Group size;
    b)   The match between intended messages and
         messages received;   b
    c)   Relative status of group members;
    d)   Rules and procedures.

3. Which of the following is a useful role of
    communication networks:
    a)   Helping to understand power and control
         relationships in organizations;
    b)   Determining whether communication should be
         lateral or vertical;   a

    c) Evaluating the differences between intended
       messages and messages received;
    d) Determining with whom managers must
       communicate.

4. Complex problems may be most effectively handled
   through:
    a) Centralized communication networks;
    b) Open communication networks;   b
    c) Supervisor-to-subordinate communication
       networks;
    d) None of the above.

5. A complex problem may be effectively handled
   through one of the more centralized communication
   networks if:
    a) There is little member interdependence;
    b) The problem is primarily a "human" problem;   a
    c) There are numerous alternatives to be
       evaluated;
    d) Multiple goals and objectives are to be
       pursued.

6. When an all-channel network appears called-for:
    a) The implied labor costs are likely to be high;
    b) Centralized networks are likely to be
       ineffective;   d
    c) Any simple problems that exist within the group
       will be inefficiently handled if the all-
       channel network is used exclusively;
    d) All the above are true statements.

7. Customers and regulatory agencies are part of what
   of what network:
    a) Vertical;
    b) Lateral;   d
    c) Internal;
    d) External.

8. Which type of network rates highest in terms of
   leadership predictability:
    a) Star;
    b) Y;   a
    c) Chain;
    d) Circle;
    e) All-channel.

9. Which type of network rates highest in terms of
   average group satisfaction:
    a) Star;
    b) Y;   e
    c) Chain;
    d) Circle;
    e) All-channel.

10. A disadvantage that can occur with the use of
    the increasing range of information technologies
    is:

a) Expense;
b) Loss of the richest medium of communication;   e
c) Erosion of delegation;
d) All of the above;
e) b and c.

III. Communication Openness.

1. Meta-communication:
    a) Occurs on the direct level;
    b) Occurs on the hidden level;   b
    c) Are intended to fully reveal meaning;
    d) All of the above.
2. Factors affecting trust in communication are:
    a) History;
    b) Adversarialism;   d
    c) Power and status;
    d) All of the above;
    e) a and c.
3. Giving feedback:
    a) Should be general rather than specific;
    b) Should include the full message in one session,
       however long and complex;
    c) Should be done immediately in cases wherein   d
       it is noticed that the receiver is angry;
    d) Must include checking to see if the receiver
       has understood and accepted;
    e) All of the above.
4. Feedback can appropriately include:
    a) Supportiveness;
    b) Corrective measures;   e
    c) Hidden messages;
    d) All of the above;
    e) a and b.
5. Which of the following is <u>not</u> a factor leading to
    increased listening skills:
    a) Being able to resist "noise";
    b) Pausing between decoding and responding;   c
    c) Rates of speech exceed rates of thought;
    d) Listening to what one has a reason to listen.
6. Which is <u>not</u> true regarding self-disclosure:
    a) Easiest if one has a healthy personality;
    b) Trust is required;   d
    c) High formal power dampens the self-disclosure
       received from others;
    d) Total self-disclosure is necessary in order
       to be a good manager.
7. Open communication is likely to result in:
    a) Hidden agendas;
    b) High level of direct communication;   b

    c)   Low level of direct communication;
    d)   Efforts to conceal;
    e)   All of the above.

IV. Nonverbal Communication.

1. Which of the following is <u>not</u> a form of nonverbal communication:
    a)   Facial expressions;
    b)   Gestures;   d
    c)   Environmental characteristics;
    d)   All of the above are forms of nonverbal communication.

2. Nonverbal communications:
    a)   Are less influential than verbal communications;
    b)   Convey only unintended messages;   c
    c)   Can influence the process and outcome of verbal communication;
    d)   Include only human nonword responses.

3. Shaking one's fist at someone while speaking angrily to them is an example of:
    a)   Nonverbal contradiction;
    b)   Nonverbal substitution;   d
    c)   Nonverbal repetition;
    d)   Nonverbal underlining.

4. You have just discovered that you made an error on your work and you slap your forehead. This is:
    a)   Nonverbal contradiction;
    b)   Nonverbal substitution;   b
    c)   Nonverbal repetition;
    d)   Nonverbal underlining.

5. Yawning while someone speaks to you at great length about something that is of no interest to you is an example of:
    a)   Paralanguage;
    b)   Proxemics;   a
    c)   Environmental characteristics;
    d)   Time-related behavior.

6. Taking the seat at the head of the table is an example of:
    a)   Paralanguage;
    b)   Proxemics;   b
    c)   Environmental characteristics;
    d)   Time-related behavior.

7. An example of "environment" as a form of nonverbal communication is:
    a)   The temperature;
    b)   Cultural differences in time perception;   c

    c)   The physical arrangement of a manager's office;
    d)   The fact that women tend to "take up less space."

8. Which of the following is <u>not</u> one of the principles relating to the concept of "territory":
    a)   Persons of higher status have more and better territory;
    b)   The territory of higher-status people is better protected than that of lower-status people;   d
    c)   The higher the status of people, the easier they find it to invade the territory of lower status people;
    d)   The higher the status of people, the more likely they are to stake out a "territory" in a room.

9. Gender differences in nonverbal cues include:
    a)   Women are more likely to use "touching" as a means of communication;
    b)   Women maintain less eye contact than do men;   c
    c)   People tend to approach women more closely than men;
    d)   All of the above.

APPLIED QUESTIONS

I. Face-To-Face Communication At Work.

1. As a manager, you are faced with an important and complex problem, and a need to settle it as quickly as possible. You need to communicate with the three managers who report to you in a way that can transmit the most information the most efficiently. Which medium of communication would you select:
    a)   A computer print-out;
    b)   A "To all first-level supervisors" memo;   d
    c)   Individual memos;
    d)   Meet and speak directly with them.

2. Which of the following communication media would involve most immediate feedback:
    a)   A computer print-out;
    b)   A "To all first-level supervisors" memo;   d
    c)   Individual memos;
    d)   Meet and speak directly with them.

II. The Basic Communication Process.

1. In which of the following situations would the
   probability of distortion and misunderstanding be
   greatest:
   a) A manager announces to his employees that the
      company has decided there will be no wage
      increase this year;
   b) A labor representative presents his side's wage   b
      demands to an arbitrator after negotiations
      have broken down with the company;
   c) A college economics professor addresses a group
      of steel industry executives and explains why a
      free trade economy would benefit all parties in
      the long run;
   d) A college instructor explains to a class the
      fact that his grading scale allows for fewer
      A's and B's than can be obtained from other
      professors.
2. Which of the following is a transmitter:
   a) The paper on which a union team writes its wage
      demands;
   b) The wage demand statement that is written on
      the paper;   a
   c) The union representative who writes the wage
      demand statement;
   d) The management representative who receives the
      statement.
3. The specific data on the amounts and conditions of
   the wage demand constitute the:
   a) Message;
   b) Transmitter;   a
   c) Channel;
   d) None of the above.
4. A design engineer sends a note to a production
   manager explaining how certain changes should be
   made on a particular item being produced. The
   manager is unable to understand some of the
   technical terms. This is a likely result of a
   problem in which of the following:
   a) Encoding;
   b) Proxemics;   a
   c) Receptors;
   d) Transmitters.
5. At what point in the communication process does the
   process move outside the control of the sender:
   a) After the sender establishes the meaning;
   b) After the meaning is encoded into a message;   c
   c) After the message is transmitted;
   d) After the receiver decodes the message.

6. For which of the following would the "ideal state"
    of communication be most easily attainable?
    a) The qualifications of a candidate for political
        office;
    b) An explanation of why the U.S. trade policy
        should be revised;   c
    c) The decisions of a federal court;
    d) The explanation of why an employee's
        performance has been rated "poor."

III. Interpersonal Communication Networks.

1. For which of the following would a larger percent
    of the total communications likely be lateral
    rather than vertical:
    a) A shop foreman;
    b) A marine drill sergeant;
    c) A professional baseball player;   c
    d) None of the above would be likely to have many
        lateral communication patterns.
2. Which of the following is <u>not</u> a "network" topic:
    a) The message as encoded by "A" is not in a form
        that can be accurately interpreted by "B" or
        "C";
    b) There are so many people who need information
        from "A" that something always seems to go
        wrong;
    c) "A's" oral report in the committee meeting left
        out some vital information because "A" did not   a
        want to expose everything to her boss (who was
        present);
    d) In the department meetings, everyone is asked
        for their inputs but only the supervisors
        actually offer their inputs.
3. One of the reasons that a simple communication
    network can be very effective for a supervisor
    communicating with subordinates in an outside sales
    situation is:
    a) There are relatively few employees with whom
        to communicate;
    b) The supervisor rarely has anything to   d
        communicate to the subordinates;
    c) The subordinates rarely have anything to
        communicate to the supervisor;
    d) There is little interdependence among the
        subordinates.
4. A situation exists in which the work itself is such
    that there is a great deal of interdependence among
    the workers. An incentive plan has been installed

that has created a great deal of competition within the work group. Which of the following may best explain why an all-channel communication network might not generate peak effectiveness:

a) A single network pattern shall not be used in all situations;

b) Inadequate sharing of information is likely to exist;   b

c) All-channel networks generate excessive competition;

d) The tasks may be too complex.

5. I first have to get my boss' O.K. Then I need to get approval from the people in the other departments who will be affected. Finally, I'll have to get a permit from the City. What communication networks are involved:

a) Vertical;   d

b) Lateral;

c) External;

d) All of the above;

e) a and b.

6. My boss won't let me go directly to other people. I have to route all questions through her, and all answers must come back through her. What communication network pattern is this:

a) Star;   a

b) Y;

c) Chain;

d) Cycle;

e) All-channel.

7. What is the level of leadership predictability in the above instance:

a) Very high;

b) High;   a

c) Moderate;

d) Low;

e) Very low.

IV. Communication Openness.

1. I have a plan but I'm not going to reveal it until I can get some idea of what people think. I'll just give some vague hints and see if I can get any reactions. This is:

a) Open communication;   e

b) No communication;

c) Self-disclosure;

d) Poor listening;

e) Meta-communication.

2. Which of the following is a high risk situational factor insofar as open communication is concerned:
   a) We know each other like a book;
   b) This is the first chance I've had to speak directly with my boss' boss;
   c) I know now how far I can go with this guy;
   d) a and b;
   e) b and c.

   e

3. Which of the following comments does <u>not</u> follow the proper guidelines for offering feedback:
   a) The statement, "I am not pleased with your attitude";
   b) The supervisor gives the employee feedback and then asks that employee to repeat the feedback before moving on to the next topic;
   c) The supervisor says, "I know you can't help it if you don't get the parts on time, but you should tell me when that happens so that we can adjust our schedules."

   a

4. A supervisor has a subordinate whose performance has been on the line between "satisfactory" and "unsatisfactory." This has been going on for a long time. The supervisor is getting exasperated, but has never said anything to the subordinate. Finally, the employee totally fouls up an assignment. Which of the following should the supervisor <u>avoid</u> doing:
   a) Providing feedback focusing entirely on this final event;
   b) Providing feedback focusing on the final event, but adding a description of all those prior events that have been frustrating;
   c) Providing feedback about what the employee needs to do to avoid repetition of the event that precipitated the discussion;
   d) All of the above are appropriate.

   b

5. The individual at work who is unwilling to let anyone get to know them and to know how they really feel about their lives and their jobs may:
   a) Be characterized as a "nondisclosing individual";
   b) Have difficulty developing and maintaining a healthy personality;
   c) Cause problems in situations wherein discussion and sharing of employees' work-related problems is important;
   d) All of the above.

   d

6. Reluctance to engage in self-disclosure at work is often caused (partly or wholly) by the fact that:
   a) Others control the rewards we get;
   b) Supervisors are not perceived as trustworthy;

    c) Supervisors are not approachable;   d
    d) All of the above.

7. Which of the following is <u>not</u> a necessary condition for good listening:
    a) The rate of the sender's speech and the rate of the receiver's thought should be approximately the same;
    b) Judgement should be suspended initially;   a
    c) Distractions should be avoided where possible;
    d) Receivers should pause before responding to senders.

V. Nonverbal Communication.

1. Which of the following would be the <u>least</u> useful form of nonverbal communication for showing employees that you wish to play down differences in formal position power:
    a) Time;
    b) Proxemics;   d
    c) Body motion;
    d) Physical characteristics.

2. Which of the following does the text consider as an example of gender differences in nonverbal cues:
    a) Eye contact by men is greater than by women;
    b) Men control less territorial space than do women;   c
    c) Men have greater protection of their territorial space than do women;
    d) All of the above.

PROGRAMMED STUDY SUPPLEMENT

1. _____ leads to erroneous expectations   bypassing
between people regarding near-term behavior
each other.

---

2. A medium's capacity for carrying multiple cues   media
and providing rapid feedback is its _____.   richness

---

3. The output of a communication channel is the   data
_____ it provides.

4. _____ are the means available for sending messages.

transmitters

5. A computer-based system that enables participating individuals to exchange and store messages through their computers is called _____.

E-Mail

6. Sight, hearing, touch, smell, and taste are people's _____ for incoming messages.

receptors

7. The data transmitted and the coded symbols which give meanings to the data together comprise _____.

messages

8. _____ is a computer-based messaging system accessed by telephone.

voice mail

9. Means by which messages travel from sender to receiver are called _____.

channels

10. _____ are ideas, facts, opinions, attitudes, and feelings regarding a particular message.

meanings

11. _____ refers to the practice of working at home while linked to the office or plant through some type of computer or terminal

telecommuting

12. The process of translating received messages into interpreted meanings is called _____.

decoding

13. Interference with the intended message in the channel is called _____.

noise

14. _____ refers to the assumptions, inferences, and interpretations made by the parties that form the basis of overt messages.

meta-communication

15. _____ is a process that integrates   listening
     received inputs in a search for meaning.

---

16. _____ includes the nonword human   nonverbal
     responses and the perceived characteristic   communi-
     of the environment through which verbal   cation
     and nonverbal messages are transmitted.

---

17. Transmission of ideas, facts, opinions,   interper-
     attitudes and feelings in such a way as to   sonal
     produce a response is through _____ .   communi-
                                                             cation

---

18. _____ is the sender's translating   encoding
     meanings into messages that can be transmitted.

---

19. The receiver's response to the message sent   feedback
     by the sender is _____ .

---

20. A(n) _____ is the set of individuals   inter-
     linked together by communications relation-   personal
     ships.   communi-
                                                             cation
                                                             network

---

21. Opening or revealing oneself to others is   self-
     known as _____ .   disclosure

CHAPTER 14

CONFLICT AND NEGOTIATION

<u>**LEARNING OBJECTIVES**</u>

When you read and when you review Chapter 14, keep in mind the learning objectives which have been established by the authors. Look them over first as a guide to picking out the most important parts of the chapter, and then think about them as you are going through the chapter. When you have finished the chapter, ask yourself whether you have met the objectives.

The authors intend that when you have finished studying this chapter you should be able to:

* Define the basic forms of conflict within the organizations.
* Describe the negative, positive, and balanced views of conflict.
* Explain the major levels of conflict within organizations.
* Identify five interpersonal conflict-handling styles and state the conditions under which each may be effective.
* Explain the basics of negotiations.
* Describe the unilateral and interactive negotiation strategies as well as conditions under which each may be effective.
* Describe five structural methods for managing conflicts.

CHAPTER OUTLINE

After you have read the chapter, complete the following outline.

I.   INTRODUCTION TO CONFLICT.

      A.   Basic forms of conflict.

          1.   Goal conflict:

          2.   Cognitive conflict:

          3.   Affective conflict:

          4.   Procedural conflict:

      B.   Views of conflict.

          1.   Positive view:

          2.   Negative view:

          3.   Balanced view:

      C.   Levels of conflict.

          1.   Intrapersonal conflict occurs when

               a.   Basic types of intrapersonal conflict are

                  (1)

                  (2)

                  (3)

b. Cognitive dissonance is

(1) Dissonance could be reduced by

(a)

(b)

2. Interpersonal conflict occurs when

a. Role conflict is

b. A role is

c. A role set is

(1) Types of role conflict that may occur as a result of incompatible messages and pressures from the role set are

(a)

(b)

(c)

(d)

d. Role ambiguity is

(1) Behaviors typically resulting from role ambiguity include:

(a)

(b)

(c)

3.   Intragroup conflict occurs when

4.   Intergroup conflict occurs when

    a.   Special types of intergroup conflict are

    (1)

    (2)

    (3)

II.   INTERPERSONAL STYLES IN CONFLICT MANAGEMENT.

    A.   The avoiding style is

        1.   Circumstances under which this style may be appropriate are

        a.

        b.

        c.

        d.

B.   The forcing style is

   1.   Circumstances under which this style may be
        appropriate are

        a.

        b.

        c.

C.   The accommodating style is

   1.   Circumstances under which this style may be
        appropriate are

        a.

        b.

        c.

        d.

D.   The collaborative style is

   1.   Circumstances under which this style may be
        appropriate are

        a.

        b.

        c.

    d.

E. The compromising style is

    1. Circumstances under which this style may be
        appropriate are

        a.

        b.

        c.

F. The significance of these styles to organizations
    revolves around the fact that collaboration tends to be
    characteristic of

    1.

    2.

III. NEGOTIATIONS IN CONFLICT MANAGEMENT.

    A. Basic types of negotiations.

        1. Distributive negotiations are

        2. Integrative negotiations are

        3. Attitudinal structuring is

        4. Intraorganizational negotiations are

B.   The SBS model is

C.   Unilateral strategies.

   1.   Factors affecting the selection of a unilateral
        strategy are

        a.

        b.

   2.   Strategy options are

        a.   C1:

        b.   S1:

        c.   P1:

        d.   A1:

D.   Interactive strategies.

   1.   Factors affecting the selection of an interactive
        strategy are

        a.

        b.

   2.   Strategy options are

        a.   C2:

    b. S2:

    c. P2:

    d. A2:

    e. A3:

E. Framework of negotiation strategies.

  1. In the SBS Model, outcome priorities are

  2. Three core outcome conditions influence the choice of interactive strategies.

    a.

    b.

    c.

F. Factors within the negotiation phases.

  1. SBS Model views tactics in two ways.

    a.

    b.

  2. Most negotiations go through four phases.

    a.

    b.

    c.

    d.

3. Types of tactics to be selected are

    a.

    b.

    c.

G. Third party facilitators are best used when

  1. Skills of facilitators.

    a.

    b.

    c.

  2. Five functions of facilitators.

    a.

    b.

    c.

    d.

e.

IV.   STRUCTURAL METHODS IN CONFLICT MANAGEMENT.

   A.   Dominance through position:

   B.   Decoupling:

   C.   Buffering with inventory:

   D.   Linking pin:

   E.   Integrating department:

DIRECTED QUESTIONS

I.   Introduction to Conflict.

   1.   A situation in which desired end states or
        preferred outcomes appear to be incompatible is
        known as:
        a)   Goal conflict;
        b)   Cognitive conflict;
        c)   Affective conflict;
        d)   Approach-avoidance conflict.
   2.   A situation in which ideas or thoughts are
        perceived as incompatible is known as:
        a)   Goal conflict;
        b)   Cognitive conflict;
        c)   Affective conflict;
        d)   Approach-avoidance conflict.
   3.   Which of the following is correct:
        a)   Creation of conflict often leads to
             constructive problem solving;

a

b

   b)   Resolution of conflict often leads to   d
        construction problem solving;
   c)   Goal conflict can reflect positive conditions;
   d)   All of the above.
4. Which of the following is correct:
    a)   Competition that leads to goal conflict can
         be beneficial;
    b)   Competition is ill-advised when high quality   d
         is a primary goal;
    c)   Conflict may direct resources away from goal
         attainment;
    d)   All of the above.
5. Conflict between three foremen on three different
    production lines is:
    a)   Vertical conflict;
    b)   Horizontal conflict;   b
    c)   Line-staff conflict;
    d)   Role conflict.
6. Which of the following is said to be a factor in
    causing line-staff conflict:
    a)   Differences in the personal characteristics of
         line vs staff managers;
    b)   Differences in the attitudes and values of   d
         line vs staff managers;
    c)   Line managers' assertions that staff managers
         infringe on their authority;
    d)   All of the above.
7. Receipt of incompatible messages about what you
    are expected to do in your position may create:
    a)   Vertical conflict;
    b)   Horizontal conflict;   d
    c)   Line-staff conflict;
    d)   Role conflict.
8. Expectations, perceptions, and evaluations
    regarding a person's role and activities comprise a:
    a)   Role;
    b)   Role set;   b
    c)   Role episode;
    d)   Role model.
9. When messages and pressures which the focal person
    receives from one person oppose messages and
    pressures received from one or more other persons,
    the result may be:
    a)   Interrole conflict;
    b)   Person-role conflict;   c
    c)   Intersender role conflict;
    d)   Role ambiguity.

10. A lack of clear, consistent information about the required activities and tasks of the job may create a condition known as:
   a) Interrole conflict;
   b) Person-role conflict;
   c) Intersender role conflict;
   d) Role ambiguity.

   d

II. Levels and Styles of Conflict.

   1. A situation in which an individual has a choice of two or more alternatives with positive outcomes would be an example of which of the following types of conflicts:
      a) Intergroup;
      b) Intragroup;
      c) Interpersonal;
      d) Intrapersonal.

      d

   2. Which of the following conditions can be said to exist when individuals recognize inconsistencies in their own thoughts, values, or behaviors:
      a) Approach-approach conflict;
      b) Approach-avoidance conflict;
      c) Avoidance-avoidance conflict;
      d) Cognitive dissonance.

      d

   3. When inconsistencies in our thoughts, values, or behaviors become sufficiently stressful, we are usually motivated to:
      a) Reduce the consonance;
      b) Ignore information;
      c) Change our thoughts, values, or behaviors;
      d) All of the above.

      c

   4. The greater the conflict between alternatives before the decision:
      a) The less the post-decision dissonance because the alternatives have been considered more carefully;
      b) The less the post-decision dissonance because it is recognized that the accepted alternative has negative elements;

      c

      c) The more the post-decision dissonance because it is recognized but the rejected decision has positive elements;
      d) All of the above.

   5. Certain irrational personality-based mechanisms create inner conflicts which frequently result in behavior that lead to conflicts with others. Such conditions are known as:

a)   Neurotic tendencies;
b)   Cognitive dissonance;   a
c)   Vertical conflict;
d)   None of the above.

6.   Neurotic tendencies:
a)   Cause managers to over-emphasize formal
     controls;
b)   Cause managers to de-emphasize formal   c
     controls;
c)   Cause some managers to over-emphasize formal
     controls and others to de-emphasize formal
     controls;
d)   Are found in rather high degrees in most
     managers.

7.   Which of the following statements regarding
     cooperation is correct:
a)   When the situation involves a series of
     decisions, cooperation tends to be high at
     first and then decline;
b)   A person is more likely to cooperate if the   c
     other person is consistently cooperative from
     the start than if the other person starts out
     competitively and then switches to cooperation;
c)   Feedback and communication usually increase
     the probability of cooperation;
d)   All of the above.

III. Interpersonal Styles in Conflict Management.

1.   A conflict-handling style that is unassertive and
     uncooperative is referred to as:
a)   Avoidance style;
b)   Forcing style;   a
c)   Accommodating style;
d)   Collaborative style.

2.   A conflict-handling style that is assertive and
     uncooperative is referred to as:
a)   Avoidance style;
b)   Forcing style;   b
c)   Accommodating style;
d)   Collaborative style.

3.   A conflict-handling style that is strongly
     cooperative and assertive is referred to as:
a)   Forcing style;
b)   Accommodating style;   c
c)   Collaborative style;
d)   Compromising style.

4. A conflict-handling style that typically involves
    negotiation and a series of concessions but tends
    <u>not</u> to maximize joint satisfaction is referred
    to as:
    a) Forcing style;
    b) Accommodating style;
    c) Collaborative style;   d
    d) Compromising style.
5. The authors indicate that one of the following
    styles is more characteristic of successful than
    of less successful managers and of high performing
    than of lesser performing organizations:
    a) Forcing style;
    b) Accommodating style;   c
    c) Collaborative style.
6. When might an "avoiding" style of conflict
    management be appropriate:
    a) The situation requires quick action;
    b) Harmony is important;   d
    c) There is a potential for mutual benefit;
    d) The issue is a very minor one.
7. When might a "forcing" style be appropriate:
    a) The issue is unpopular;
    b) Conflicts are based on personality;   a
    c) There is a parity of power;
    d) There is insufficient information.

IV. Negotiations in Conflict Management.

1. Traditional win-lose negotiations are:
    a) Distributive negotiations;
    b) Integrative negotiations;   a
    c) Attitudinal structuring;
    d) Intraorganizational negotiations.
2. Trying to establish the desired relationships in
    negotiations is:
    a) Distributive negotiations;
    b) Integrative negotiations;   c
    c) Attitudinal structuring;
    d) Intraorganizational negotiations.
3. Joint benefit outcomes are the basis for:
    a) Distributive negotiations;
    b) Integrative negotiations;   b
    c) Attitudinal structuring;
    d) Intraorganizational negotiations.
4. If both relationship and substantive outcome are
    important, which is the best:

a) Trusting collaboration;
b) Firm competition;   a
c) Active avoidance;
d) Open subordination.
5. If substantive interests are important but
relationships are not, which is the best:
a) Trusting collaboration;
b) Firm competition;   b
c) Active avoidance;
d) Open subordination.
6. Which of the following assumes that substantive
outcome is of little importance:
a) Principled collaboration;
b) Focused subordination;   b
c) Soft competition;
d) Passive avoidance;
e) Responsive avoidance.
7. Which of the following assumes that the other
party will reciprocate to a disclosure of
information:
a) Principled collaboration;
b) Focused subordination;   a
c) Soft competition;
d) Passive avoidance;
e) Responsive avoidance.
8. Which strategy is <u>not</u> appropriate for outcome
condition three:
a) Trusting collaboration; ·
b) Soft collaboration;   e
c) Firm competition;
d) Responsive avoidance;
e) c and d.
9. Key functions of a third party facilitator's role
include:
a) Eliminate tension;
b) Develop one party as dominant;   c
c) Ensure mutual motivation;
d) All of above.

V.   Structural Methods of Conflict Management.

1. When a manager issues a directive and assumes
that such will resolve a conflict, the method of
conflict management being used is:
a) Dominance through position;
b) Decoupling;   a
c) Buffering with inventory;

      d)   Linking pin;

      e)   Integrating department.

2.   One problem associated with use of the dominance method is that:

      a)   Managers may not want to resolve the conflict;

      b)   It cannot be used to settle interdepartmental conflicts;   c

      c)   It does little to prevent conflict from occurring again;

      d)   All of the above.

3.   One problem associated with the decoupling method is that:

      a)   Once conflict has begun, decoupling cannot occur;

      b)   Decoupling is likely to intensify the conflict;   c

      c)   Decoupling may increase costs because of duplication;

      d)   All of the above.

4.   A conflict management method that utilizes change in organizational design is:

      a)   Dominance through position;

      b)   Decoupling;   b

      c)   Buffering with inventory;

      d)   Linking pin.

5.   A method that seeks to reduce conflict by avoiding work flow interruptions is:

      a)   Dominance through position;

      b)   Decoupling;

      c)   Buffering with inventory;   c

      d)   Linking pin;

      e)   Integrating department.

6.   When one part of an organization has formal authority to direct the activities of other parts and to resolve conflicts that might arise among them, the organization has adopted which of the following methods of conflict management:

      a)   Dominance through position;

      b)   Decoupling;   e

      c)   Buffering with inventory;

      d)   Linking pin;

      e)   Integrating department.

7.   The linking pin method of conflict management requires that the individual who serves as the linking pin:

      a)   Understand the operations of both departments.

      b)   Is perceived by both departments as someone who can be trusted;   d

c)   Is a strong advocate of collaboration and
     compromise;
d)   All of the above.
8. A conflict management method that assigns an
    individual to help integrate departments with
    overlapping activities is called:
    a)   Dominance through position;
    b)   Decoupling;   d
    c)   Buffering with inventory;
    d)   Linking pin;
    e)   Integrating department.

APPLIED QUESTIONS

I.   Conflict--Its Positive and Its Negative Forces.

1.   A supervisor attends a training program which has a
     major focus on attaining positive supervisor-
     subordinate relationships, but receives no support
     from his organization when trying to follow the
     principles emphasized in the program. Which of the
     following is most descriptive of that situation:
     a)   Goal conflict;
     b)   Cognitive conflict;   b
     c)   Affective conflict;
     d)   Intragroup conflict.
2.   A college professor who is doing an outstanding
     job sees himself approach mid-career without
     having begun to establish the financial security
     he seeks. He is committed to his work but he is
     frustrated at what he believes to be a low
     probability of ever attaining financial security.
     Which of the following is most descriptive of that
     situation:
     a)   Goal conflict;
     b)   Cognitive conflict;   a
     c)   Affective conflict;
     d)   Intragroup conflict.
3.   Which of the following conditions would not be one
     in which there might be negative effects from
     introducing conflict or allowing conflict to
     continue:
     a)   High product quality is a primary
          organizational goal;
     b)   A short-run need for increased quantity;   b

     c)   There is a substantial disagreement over definition and appropriateness of organizational goals;

     d)   The production process requires strong interdependency among workers.

II.   Levels, Sources of Conflict and Styles of Management.

1.   A high-performing technical employee is given the opportunity to move into a managerial position. The employee likes the technical aspects of the current job but knows that long-term advancement is greater in the management job. This sets up what kind of conflict:
    a)   Role;
    b)   Approach-approach;   b
    c)   Avoidance-avoidance;
    d)   Approach-avoidance.

2.   If you go to the big game tonight, you may fail tomorrow's quiz. Which kind of conflict is involved in this case:
    a)   Role;
    b)   Approach-approach;   c
    c)   Avoidance-avoidance;
    d)   Approach-avoidance.

3.   Which of the following best describes a situation wherein cognitive dissonance exists:
    a)   You want to accept a job which you have just been offered, but you do not want to do the amount of travelling that would be required;
    b)   You have a tendency to do a lot of your   d
subordinates' work because you really do not trust them;
    c)   Your basic style is to ignore disagreements when you see them occurring;
    d)   You have always had a strong anti-union philosophy but things at work now look like your rights can only be protected if the employees deal collectively with the employer.

4.   You are frustrated because your boss has developed such tight controls over all phases of the work that no one can display any amount of initiative, creativity or decision-making potential. Which of the following is most likely responsible for the behavior of your boss:
    a)   Neurotic tendencies;
    b)   Interpersonal conflict;   a

    c)   An avoidance style of conflict-handling;
    d)   Intergroup conflict.

5. When interpersonal problems emerge, your boss
    brings everyone together to work out problems.
    He will go along with any solution selected, so
    long as it is at all reasonable. This style of
    handling interpersonal conflict can be described
    as:
    a)   Avoidance;
    b)   Force;   c
    c)   Accommodation;
    d)   None of the above.

6. When a conflict exists between persons, your boss
    will make certain that the solution adopted is one
    consistent with the outcome that she desires,
    without regard to whether a resolution more
    acceptable to the parties may have been possible.
    Her style of handling interpersonal conflict can
    be described as:
    a)   Avoidance;
    b)   Force;   b
    c)   Accommodation;
    d)   None of the above.

7. A manager knows that conflict exists within the
    group of employees which she supervises. She
    asks each group member to make a list of all those
    problems which they have encountered with other
    group members. The reason that this list alone
    is not enough to allow resolution of the
    intragroup conflict is that:
    a)   Other processes within the group influence the
        causes or resolution of intragroup conflict;
    b)   Intragroup conflict involves more than the   d
        simple aggregate of all interpersonal
        conflicts;
    c)   Intragroup conflict involves more than the
        simple aggregate of all intrapersonal
        conflicts;
    d)   All of the above.

8. A department head has divided his employees into
    teams and has organized a competition among them
    as to which will generate the most output over
    the next thirty days. Which of the following
    statements regarding this event is correct:
    a)   The losing group may become demoralized and
        thus less productive;
    b)   The losing group may become determined to win   e
        the next round of competition and thus become
        more productive;

c)   The winning group may become complacent and thus less productive;

d)   The winning group may be stimulated to make certain it wins the next round and thus become more productive;

e)   All of the above;

f)   None of the above.

9.   "The boss pushes us to work harder and harder. He says we ought to do it 'for the company.' I'm tired of being pushed around. I'm really getting to the point where I may quit." This statement is an example of:

a)   Vertical conflict;

b)   Horizontal conflict;   a

c)   Role conflict;

d)   Role ambiguity.

10. "The boss told me that my job was to question all the invoices I receive. Then, today, I got in trouble with her because someone else complained to her that I had asked them to explain an expenditure." This person is experiencing:

a)   Vertical conflict;

b)   Horizontal conflict;   d

c)   Line-staff conflict;

d)   Role conflict.

11. "I've been on this job for a long time now, and I still don't really know what they expect of me. I can't get a straight answer from anyone." This statement indicates the person is experiencing:

a)   Person-role conflict;

b)   Horizontal conflict;   c

c)   Role ambiguity;

d)   Role conflict.

12. Management engages in hostility and public ridicule toward the union during negotiations, until finally the union members strike. This is an example of:

a)   Cognitive dissonance;

b)   Avoidance-avoidance conflict;   c

c)   Intergroup conflict;

d)   All of the above.

13. The Sales Department of a firm continually sells more product than the Production people can make, and they sell new product lines before they make it out of New Design into Production. This is an example of:

a)   Horizontal conflict;

b)   Vertical conflict;   a

c)   Role ambiguity;
d)   Decoupling.

III. Negotiations in Conflict Management.

1.   The Steelworkers' Union and a steel company
     negotiate over base wage rates. This is:
     a)   Distributive negotiations;
     b)   Integrative negotiations;   a
     c)   Attitudinal structuring;
     d)   Intraorganizational negotiations.
2.   One party to the negotiations shows up early,
     adjusts the temperature in the room to a
     comfortable level, and cordially greets the other
     party upon its arrival. This is:
     a)   Distributive negotiations;
     b)   Integrative negotiations;   c
     c)   Attitudinal structuring;
     d)   Intraorganizational negotiations.
3.   The union meets to iron out the question of which
     benefits it will pursue. The older members want
     a different set than do the younger members. What
     is happening at the meeting:
     a)   Distributive negotiations;
     b)   Integrative negotiations;   d
     c)   Attitudinal structuring;
     d)   Intraorganizational negotiations.
4.   "Looking at it from our own point of view only,
     we're going to have to go into this to win. We
     can't worry about what they're going to do or
     what they'll think of us afterwards." Which of
     the following strategies is implied in the above
     statement:
     a)   Open subordination;   c
     b)   Soft competition;
     c)   Firm competition;
     d)   Open subordination;
     e)   Principled collaboration.
5.   "I think this is going to go fine. But, I'm going
     to clarify the procedure at the outset." Which of
     the following is implied:
     a)   Open subordination;   e
     b)   Soft competition;
     c)   Firm competition;
     d)   Open subordination;
     e)   Principled collaboration.
6.   Conceding to the other party's demands is which
     negotiation tactic:

      a) Collaborative;
      b) Competitive;
      c) Subordinative.

  c

7. Conceding to the other party's demands is part of which negotiation phase:
      a) Search;
      b) Stating of demands and offers;
      c) Narrowing of differences;
      d) Final bargaining.

  c

IV. Structural Methods in Conflict Management.

1. The source of much of the conflict within an organization is the fact that employees just go off in whatever direction they choose. Each person does what he/she feels like doing. The work never gets done and then everyone blames everyone else. An appropriate way to resolve such conflict might be:
      a) Dominance through position;
      b) Decoupling;
      c) Buffering with inventory;
      d) Linking pin;
      e) Integrating department.

  a

2. The establishment of an individual as "Marketing-Manufacturing Liaison" to try to get those two functions to work together better is an example of:
      a) Dominance through position;
      b) Decoupling;
      c) Buffering with inventory;
      d) Linking pin;
      e) Integrating department.

  d

3. Formerly, all production work was done in one unit, all assembly in another, and all packing and shipping in another. Now, because of steps taken to resolve certain conflicts that were disruptive to productivity, the full range of activities for each item produced by the company are done in separate divisions of the company. Which of the following methods was used to manage the conflict:
      a) Dominance through position;
      b) Decoupling;
      c) Buffering with inventory;
      d) Linking pin;
      e) Integrating department.

  b

4. A collective bargaining session begins with
    management trying to show the union that the
    company hopes for a cooperative set of
    negotiations. Management is engaging in:
    a) Distributive negotiations;
    b) Mediation;   c
    c) Attitudinal structuring;
    d) Unfair labor practices.

PROGRAMMED STUDY SUPPLEMENT

1.	_____ refers to any situation in which incompatible goals, cognitions, or emotions lead to opposition or antagonistic interaction.	conflict
2.	_____ is a situation in which individuals have a choice between two or more alternatives with positive outcomes.	approach-approach conflict
3.	A situation in which desired end states or preferred outcomes appear to be incompatible is known as _____.	goal conflict
4.	Behavior that is assertive and uncooperative, reflecting a win-lose approach is a part of the _____.	forcing style
5.	When role pressures associated with membership in one group are incompatible with pressures stemming from membership in other groups, there is _____.	interrole conflict
6.	The conflict-handling style that is cooperative but not assertive is the _____.	accommo-dating style
7.	A give-and-take approach to conflict-handling, usually involving negotiation and concessions is known as the _____.	compro-mise style

8. _____ is a situation in which individuals must choose between two or more alternatives with negative outcomes.

avoidance-avoidance conflict

9. When a person's own attitudes, values, or beliefs are incompatible with that person's role requirements, there is _____.

person-role conflict

10. Incompatible feelings or emotions constitute _____.

affective conflict

11. A situation in which ideas or thoughts are perceived as incompatible is known as _____.

cognitive conflict

12. _____ is a situation in which individuals must decide whether to do something that has both positive and negative outcomes.

approach-avoidance conflict

13. _____ exists when individuals recognize inconsistencies in their own thoughts, attitudes, values and/or behaviors.

cognitive dissonance

14. Two or more individuals who perceive themselves as having opposing goals, attitudes, values, and/or behaviors experience _____.

interpersonal conflict

15. The term _____ refers to behavior that is strongly cooperative and assertive in its approach to conflict-handling.

collaborative style

16. _____ is a process in which two or more parties, having both common and conflicting interests, discuss proposals concerning specific terms of a possible agreement.

negotiation

17. _____ occurs within an individual and often involves some form of goal conflict or cognitive conflict.

intra-personal conflict

---

18. _____ means that messages and pressures from one role sender oppose those from one or more other senders.

inter-sender role conflict

---

19. Disagreement over which process to use to resolve a conflict is _____.

procedural conflict

---

20. _____ is the focal person's perception of a lack of clear, consistent information about the required activities and tasks of the job.

role ambiguity

---

21. Behavior that is unassertive and uncooperative is _____ conflict handling.

avoiding style

---

22. The group of role senders for the focal person constitute a _____.

role set

---

23. When different messages and pressures from a single member of the role set are incompatible, there is _____.

intra-sender role conflict

---

24. _____ refers to clashes among some or all of the individual group members.

intra-group conflict

---

25. _____ refers to opposition and clashes between two or more groups.

inter-group conflict

---

26. _____ is the procedure by which parties seek to establish the desired tone and relationship in negotiation.

attitud-inal structu-ring

27. A _____ is the cluster of tasks that others expect a person to perform in his or her position.

role

---

28. _____ occurs when a focal person perceives incompatible messages and pressures from the role senders.

role conflict

---

29. _____ are typical win-lose, fixed-sum situations.

distributive negotiations

---

30. _____ concentrate on joint problem-solving and search for solutions through which both parties can gain.

integrative negotiations

---

31. _____ is to settle conflict between two or more groups inside a firm.

intraorganizational negotiations

---

32. An individual assigned to help integrate two departments that have overlapping tasks is called a _____.

linking pin

---

33. _____ is designed to avoid unnecessary conflict, reduce or resolve existing conflict, and sometimes introduce or increase conflict.

conflict management

CHAPTER 15

ORGANIZATIONAL CULTURE

LEARNING OBJECTIVES

When you read and when you review Chapter 15, keep in mind
the learning objectives which have been established by the
authors. Look them over first as a guide to picking out the most
important parts of the chapter, and then think about them as you
are going through the chapter. When you have finished the
chapter, ask yourself whether you have met the objectives.

The authors intend that when you have finished studying this
chapter you should be able to:

* Explain the concept of organizational culture.
* Describe how organizational cultures are developed,
  maintained, and changed.
* Understand the possible relationships between
  organizational culture and performance.
* Discuss the implications of organizational culture
  for ethical behavior in organizations.
* Explain the importance of effectively managing
  cultural diversity.
* Describe the process of organizational socialization
  and explain its relationship to organizational
  culture.

CHAPTER OUTLINE

After you have read the chapter, complete the following outline.

I.   CHARACTERISTICS AND DYNAMICS OF ORGANIZATIONAL CULTURE.

    A.   Organizational culture is

        1.   The components of organizational culture are

            a.

            b.

            c.

            d.

            e.

            f.

        2.   Cultural symbols are

        3.   Cultural heroes are

        4.   Organizational rites and ceremonies are

        5.   Cultural values are

    B.   Developing organizational culture.

        1.   Problems of external adaptation and survival are

            a.

   b.

   c.

   d.

   e.

2. Problems of internal integration are

    a.

    b.

    c.

    d.

    e.

C. Maintaining organizational culture is primarily
    accomplished through

    1.

    2.

    3.

    4.

5.

6.

D. Changing organizational culture can be done by

1. Multiple cultures are sometimes known as

II. PERFORMANCE AND CULTURE.

A. Strong cultures are likely to be associated with good performance because

1.

2.

B. Characteristics of the high performance-high commitment culture are

1.

2.

3.

4.

5.

C. Performance-related effects of organizational culture appear to be that

1.

2.

3.

4.

5.

III. ETHICAL BEHAVIOR AND ORGANIZATIONAL CULTURE.

A. The ethical component of an organizational culture is composed of

B. Principled organizational dissent is

1. Whistle-blowing is

C. The creation of organizational cultures that encourage ethical behavior should include

1.

2.

3.

4.

IV.   MANAGING CULTURAL DIVERSITY.

    A.   Acculturation is

    B.   Guidelines for managing cultural diversity include

        1.

        2.

        3.

        4.

        5.

        6.

        7.

V.   ORGANIZATIONAL SOCIALIZATION.

    A.   Socialization is

    B.   Steps in the process of socialization are

        1.

        2.

        3.

        4.

5.

6.

7.

C.   Outcomes of socialization.

   1.   What are the positive outcomes of successful
        socialization?

   2.   What are some dilemmas created by successful
        socialization?

DIRECTED QUESTIONS

I.   Characteristics and Dynamics of Organizational Culture.

   1.   Which of the following is an example of a norm that
        might evolve in a work group:
        a)   Employee perceptions of an organization's
             culture;
        b)   The rituals that emerge regarding deference   d
             and demeanor;
        c)   A firm's "price leadership" policy;
        d)   A belief that there should be a "fair day's
             work for a fair day's pay."
   2.   An organization's shared philosophies, ideologies,
        values, beliefs, assumptions, expectations,
        attitudes, and norms constitute its:
        a)   Climate;
        b)   Philosophy;   d
        c)   Dominant values;
        d)   Culture.
   3.   Beliefs and expectations shared by organizational
        members generate:

a)   Products and services;
b)   Behaviors;   d
c)   Emotions;
d)   All of the above.
4.   Which of the following statements is accurate:
a)   Organizational behaviors are strongly shaped
by norms;
b)   Norms determine the shared beliefs,   a
expectations, and actions of an organization's
numbers;
c)   The behaviors of individuals and groups within
an organization determine its norms;
d)   All of the above.
5.   Highly effective cultures are characterized by:
a)   Managerial roles performed in ways desired by
the organization;
b)   An internal environment that is flexible enough   a
to allow employees to set their own definitions
of desired performance;
c)   Human resource programs that bring in employees
compatible with a wide range of organizational
cultures;
d)   All of the above.
6.   Cultural symbols are:
a)   Gestures, pictures, or other physical objects;
b)   People who possess characteristics highly   a
valued by the culture;
c)   Planned activities or rituals that leave
important cultural meaning;
d)   All of the above.
7.   The deepest level, or the core, of culture:
a)   Cultural symbols;
b)   Cultural heroes;   d
c)   Organizational rites;
d)   Cultural values.

II.   Developing Organizational Culture.

1.   Problems of external adaptation and survival
include:
a)   Rewards and punishments;
b)   Power and status;   c
c)   Mission and strategy;
d)   Group boundaries.
2.   Problems of internal integration include:
a)   Effective work relationships among members;
b)   Culture of the larger society;   a

   c)   Dominant values of national cultures;
   d)   All of the above.
3. Which of the following is a true statement regarding influences on the origins of organizational culture:
   a)   The culture of the society in which the organization operates influences the culture of the organization itself;
   b)   The culture of an organization at any point in time largely reflects the assumptions and ideas of its founder(s);   a
   c)   Internal integration has to do with an organization's efforts to find its niche and cope with its constantly changing environment;
   d)   All of the above.
4. Power distance refers to:
   a)   Extent to which individuals feel threatened by unstable situations and try to avoid them;
   b)   Maintaining organizational culture;   c
   c)   Extent to which society encourages unequal distributions of power among people;
   d)   All of the above.
5. The <u>basic</u> mechanism for maintaining organizational culture is:
   a)   The processes and behaviors to which the managers pay the most attention;
   b)   Recruitment, selection, and retention of individuals who fit;   b
   c)   Managerial role modeling, teaching, and coaching;
   d)   Criteria for rewards and status.
6. When employees attempt to perform their duties in a fashion similar to that in which their superiors carry out their responsibilities, which specific reinforcement mechanism is in force:
   a)   Reaction to critical incidents and crises;
   b)   Role modelling, teaching, and coaching;   b
   c)   Criteria for allocation of rewards and status;
   d)   Criteria for recruitment and selection.
7. Which of the following statements concerning reinforcement of a culture by allocation of rewards and status is accurate:
   a)   Allocation of rewards and status is one of the most effective ways of reinforcing organizational culture;
   b)   Organizations almost universally are highly effective in their use of this reinforcement mechanism;   a

    c) Organizations are highly consistent in their allocation of rewards and status;
    d) All of the above.

8. Changes in organizational culture:
    a) Can be generated through the same mechanisms that are used to maintain cultures;
    b) Accompany almost all comprehensive organizational changes;   d
    c) Can be generated through techniques used to change organizational behavior;
    d) All of the above.

9. An organizational culture characterized by high risk taking behavior with quick feedback regarding action is:
    a) Process culture;   d
    b) Bet-your-company culture;
    c) Work hard-play hard culture;
    d) Tough guy, macho culture.

10. Which of the following is <u>not</u> a way to manage cultural change successfully:
    a) Understand the old culture first;
    b) Eliminate subcultures;   b
    c) Provide support for employees with ideas for a better culture;
    d) "Live" the new culture.

III. Performance and Organizational Culture.

1. With regard to the relationship between strong organizational culture and high performance:
    a) Strong culture can help establish commitment;
    b) Firms with participative management have been found to have successful cultures;   d
    c) Strong culture serves as a control mechanism to channel employee behaviors toward desired behaviors;
    d) All of the above.

2. High degrees of participative management:
    a) Are often cited as characteristic of successful culture;
    b) Can be adapted to all work settings if appropriate change mechanisms are utilized;   a
    c) Can be developed out of a traditional management setting with relative ease;
    d) All of the above.

3. Characteristics of high performance-high commitment work culture include:

a) Centralization of information and decision-making;
b) Employees primarily focused on their own function or department;
c) Technology controls employee behavior;
d) Shared sense of purpose;
e) All of the above.

d

4. Regarding the performance-related effects of organizational culture:
   a) Knowing the culture helps employees understand the organization;
   b) Culture serves to establish commitment to corporate philosophy and values;
   c) Culture serves as a control mechanism;
   d) Certain organizational cultures are related to greater organizational effectiveness;
   e) All of the above.

e

IV. Ethical Behavior and Organizational Culture.

1. Which of the following is true with respect to ethical behavior and organizational culture:
   a) Organizational culture can affect ethical behavior;
   b) Principled organizational dissent is the effort by individuals to protest the status quo on ethical grounds;
   c) Both of the above.

b

2. Which of the following can be suggested for creating organizational cultures that encourage ethical behavior:
   a) Discourage input regarding values and practices;
   b) Opt for a stronger culture;
   c) Explore methods to provide for diversity and dissent;
   d) All of the above.

c

3. Principled organizational dissent:
   a) Is based on ethical grounds;
   b) Is a protest of the status quo;
   c) Is a protest of some organizational practice or policy;
   d) All of the above.

d

4. Whistle-blowing:
   a) Is secretly blowing the whistle inside an organization;
   b) Is publicly blowing the whistle outside an organization;

e

      c) Is secretly blowing the whistle outside an
           organization;
      d) Is publicly blowing the whistle inside an
           organization;
      e) All of the above.

V.   Managing Cultural Diversity.

    1. Acculturation refers to:
      a) Resolution of differences between a dominant
           culture and minority or subcultures;
      b) Cultural change;   a
      c) Eliminating subcultures;
      d) All of the above.
    2. Guidelines for managing cultural diversity include:
      a) Be tolerant of racial and/or sexist remarks
           until acculturation occurs;
      b) Prevent the topic of diversity from becoming a
           topic of open discussion;   c
      c) Explore and understand employee background
           differences;
      d) All of the above.

VI. Organizational Socialization.

    1. The process of socialization:
      a) Includes measurement of operational results and
           rewarding individual performance;
      b) May create conflict by requiring individuals   a
           to make personal sacrifices to fulfill their
           membership roles;
      c) Includes all aspects of "learning" a new job
           and environment except the specific skills and
           knowledge required to do the job itself;
      d) All of the above.
    2. Socialization includes:
      a) Learning organizational values, rules, and
           procedures;
      b) Developing social and working relationships;   d
      c) Sets of early experiences wherein the
           individual is highly unlikely to achieve goals
           that are set;
      d) All of the above.
    3. To which of the following areas is a strong
       socialization most likely to have a negative
       impact:

a) Job satisfaction;
b) Organizational change;   b
c) Commitment to the organization;
d) Internalized values.

4. Which of the following outcomes is solely a
   function of successful socialization:
   a) High performance;
   b) High work motivation;   d
   c) Role clarity;
   d) None of the above.

APPLIED QUESTIONS

I. The Concept of Organizational Culture.

1. Which of the following best illustrates an aspect
   of an organizational culture:
   a) A goal of capturing 23% of the market for the
      product which the company produces;
   b) An expectation that everyone in the company   b
      is a "professional" and will expend whatever
      effort is necessary to get the job done;
   c) A belief in the free enterprise system;
   d) An expectation that the economy will improve,
      and markets for the company's product will
      therefore improve.

2. Shared beliefs and expectations:
   a) Are partly responsible for the goods and
      services which firms produce;
   b) Influence how employees behave at work;   d
   c) Affect employees' emotions;
   d) All of the above.

II. Characteristics and Dynamics of Organizational Culture.

1. Which of the following might be taken as an
   indicator of a highly effective organizational
   culture:
   a) Managers are left alone to do those things
      which they individually believe will be best
      for them and best for the organization;
   b) Hiring decisions are made at the lowest   c
      level possible, so that "stereotyping" and
      "cloning" are least likely to occur;

    c) Managers place a great deal of emphasis on communication, in an attempt to make certain everyone has all the information and organizational cues necessary to carry out the mission of the organization as seen by top management;

    d) All of the above.

2. According to the text, IBM's success is attributed primarily to its:
   a) Organizational norms;
   b) Dominant values;   b
   c) Rules as laid out for its newcomers;
   d) Flexible culture.

3. Which of the following would be included as part of organizational culture:
   a) An understanding that all supervisors at or above the level of Division Chief are to be addressed formally;
   b) Avoiding at almost any cost the laying off of   d
      employees;
   c) The remodelling of an office area to allow for an informal atmosphere conducive to open communication;
   d) All of the above.

4. A banquet at which top performers are given awards and descriptions of their performances are described is a:
   a) Rite of passage;   d
   b) Rite of degradation;
   c) Rite of enhancement;
   d) Rite of integration.

III. Developing Organizational Culture.

1. When organizations merge, one early problem that has to be dealt with is clarification of whatever differences there may be in language (terms, jargon, etc.). This is an example of:
   a) Ways in which organizational culture is formed;
   b) Problems of internal integration;   d
   c) Establishing and maintaining effective working relationships among the members of the organization;
   d) All of the above.

2. A firm is struggling to identify its direction, attempting to settle on the segment of the market which would offer the best choice for its survival. This is an example of a firm dealing with:

   a)   The problem of external adaptation and
        survival;
   b)   The search to find its niche;
   c)   Formation of organizational culture;
   d)   All of the above.

   d

3. Which of the following would <u>not</u> serve to maintain
    organizational culture?
    a)   "I really like my boss. He dresses the way he
         wants. He doesn't feel like he has to play
         follow-the-leader and dress like everyone
         else."
    b)   "If you're going to get along here, you'd
         better get your cost control reports done
         right. I know a lot of places say that, but
         they really mean it here. All the bosses go
         over them in detail."
    c)   "You don't have to worry about flak from
         outside. If you do your job, management will
         back you up all the way. They really support
         their people here."
    d)   All of the above serve to maintain
         organizational culture.

   a

4. Which of the following is typical of U.S.
    organizations:
    a)   Implicit control mechanisms;
    b)   Explicit control mechanisms;
    c)   Slow evaluation and promotion;
    d)   Nonspecialized career paths.

   b

5. Which of the following would be the most destructive
    to maintaining organizational culture:
    a)   "Be careful. Around here if it's the employee
         -vs- the customer, the employee loses every
         time."
    b)   "Where I worked before, they really took care
         of their management staff. Here, you don't
         even get a parking space until you're at the
         VP level."
    c)   "Sure, they say it's the employees that count,
         but there's no evidence that they mean it."
    d)   "They don't care about the employee here.
         They'll come right out and tell you that the
         bottom line is production."

   c

6. The executive team has decided that it wants to
    send the workforce a clear message that the
    culture of the organization is changing. Which
    of the following actions would provide the
    clearest statement of a sharp change:

   a)   Employees are told that they will all be
        required to get with their supervisors and
        work up a personal development plan;
   b)   Group meetings at which employees are told of   c
        the financial difficulties facing the firm
        are held;
   c)   A manager whom everyone knows has not pulled
        his own weight for years is placed on early
        retirement against his wishes;
   d)   Employees are told that cutbacks in the
        workforce will become necessary if earnings
        continue to decline.
7.   At this organization, there are extensive sets of
     rules, procedures, and directions that employees
     must follow. Employees know that "doing things
     right" is at least as important as "doing the right
     things." This organization has a:
     a)   Tough guy, macho culture;   d
     b)   Work hard-play hard culture;
     c)   Bet-your-company culture;
     d)   Process culture.

IV.   Performance and Organizational Culture.

   1.   Which of the following would likely be facilitated
        by having a strong organizational culture:
        a)   A firm's desire that its employees behave in
             a way consistent with its philosophy of serving
             the customer;
        b)   A firm's desire that employees care about the   d
             quality of their work;
        c)   A firm's intent that employees always know what
             they are expected to do;
        d)   All of the above;
        e)   None of the above.
   2.   Participative management includes employee
        participation in such matters as:
        a)   Trying to determine the best ways to change the
             product mix to offset some problems brought
             about by structural demand shifts;
        b)   Establishing production targets for next   d
             quarter;
        c)   Choosing from among alternative ways of meeting
             next quarter's targets;
        d)   All of the above;
        e)   None of the above.

3. Which of the following needs to be revised to facilitate a high performance-high commitment organization:
    a) Job rotation as a developmental approach;
    b) Pay for learning as a part of the compensation program;
    c) A "star" communication pattern;
    d) All of the above;
    e) None of the above.

                                                                    c

V. Ethical Behavior and Organizational Culture.

1. A manager "fails" in her job because she refuses to engage in illegal practices, even though she knows that "everyone does it. Which of the following describes her situation:
    a) Opting for a strong culture;
    b) Principled organizational dissent;
    c) Ineffective organizational culture;
    d) All of the above.

                                                                    b

2. Which of the following would be <u>least</u> effective in terms of developing ethical behavior:
    a) Knowing that you would be suspended from work if caught falsifying your expense account;
    b) Receiving public praise from a high-ranking manager;
    c) Observing what you perceived as highly ethical behavior by top management in the organization;
    d) A written corporate code of ethics.

                                                                    d

3. Which of the following is principle organizational dissent:
    a) A worker refuses to work overtime because she does not wish to work more than forty hours per week;
    b) A worker refuses to handle parts not made by a unionized firm;
    c) A worker refuses a promotion because he does not want a supervisory position;
    d) A worker refuses to look the other way when the organization takes some safety short-cuts;
    e) All of the above.

                                                                    d

4. Which of the following people are "whistle blowing" regarding an unethical practice of the organization? The one who:
    a) Confides in a friend regarding the practice;
    b) Calls the newspaper regarding the practice;
    c) Tells her boss that if the company does not change its practices she'll break the story;

                                                                    e

    d)   Quits rather than following the practice;
    e)   All of the above.

VI. Managing Cultural Diversity.

    1.   Which of the following is appropriate as a part of a program to better manage cultural diversity:
       a)   Employee surveys;
       b)   Unilateral decrees to obey fair employment regulations;   d
       c)   Management training and development;
       d)   All of the above.
    2.   Benefits of better management of cultural diversity can include:
       a)   More centralized decision making;
       b)   Simpler, more uniform marketing strategies;   c
       c)   Greater creativity and innovation;
       d)   All of the above.

VII. Organizational Socialization.

    1.   Giving a new MBA an initial assignment of more work than can reasonably be accomplished in a given period can appropriately be used to:
       a)   Promote openness toward acceptance of the firm's norms and values;
       b)   Provide appropriate role models;   a
       c)   Assist the newcomer in developing a proven track record;
       d)   Test proper choice of entry-level candidates.
    2.   Successful socialization:
       a)   Will help develop commitment to the organization;
       b)   Will result in high job satisfaction;   d
       c)   Will bring about high job involvement;
       d)   All of the above;
       e)   None of the above.

PROGRAMMED STUDY SUPPLEMENT

1.   Problems of _____ have to do with how the organization will find its place in and cope with its constantly changing external environment.   external adaptation and survival

2.	_____ is a pattern of beliefs and expectations shared by organizational members.	organizational culture
3.	A high degree of _____ is often cited as a characteristic of successful cultures.	participative management
4.	_____ is used to teach new employees "the ropes" about their new jobs.	organizational socialization
5.	_____ refers to such items as rewards and punishment, group boundaries, and common language.	internal integration
6.	_____ is the effort by individuals in the organization to protest the status quo on ethical grounds.	principled organizational dissent
7.	The firing of a manager is an example of an _____ that gets interpreted by employees as a reflection of organizational culture.	organizational rite
8.	_____ possess characteristics highly valued by the culture and thus serve as role models for the culture.	cultural heroes
9.	The deepest level, or the core, of culture is _____.	cultural values
10.	Words, gestures, and pictures or other physical objects that carry particular meaning within a culture are _____.	cultural symbols
11.	Multiple cultures in organizations are sometimes called _____.	subcultures

12. A _____ is protective of individual
    security and does not emphasize individual
    accountability.

    maternal-
    ism
    culture

---

13. A _____ holds individuals responsible
    for their behavior.

    accounta-
    bility
    culture

---

14. An organizational culture designed to foster
    productivity and high levels of employee
    involvement is called a _____.

    high per-
    formance-
    high
    commitment
    work
    culture

---

15. Methods by which culture differences between
    dominant cultures and minority cultures are
    resolved and managed constitute _____.

    accultura-
    tion

CHAPTER 16

POWER AND POLITICAL BEHAVIOR

<u>**LEARNING OBJECTIVES**</u>

When you read and when you review Chapter 16, keep in mind the learning objectives which have been established by the authors. Look them over first as a guide to picking out the most important parts of the chapter and then think about them as you are going through the chapter. When you have finished the chapter, ask yourself whether you have met the objectives.

The authors intend that when you have finished studying this chapter you should be able to:

* Explain the concepts of organizational power and organizational politics.
* Identify five interpersonal sources of power.
* Describe four major categories of structural and situational sources of power.
* Discuss effective and ineffective uses of power.
* Diagnose the personal and situational factors that contribute to the occurrence of political behavior.
* Explain why political behavior is not necessarily undesirable.
* Identify some personality dimensions that are related to political behavior.

CHAPTER OUTLINE

After you have read the chapter, complete the following outline.

I.   THE NATURE OF POWER.

    A.   Power is

    B.   Authority is

II. INTERPERSONAL SOURCES OF POWER.

    A.   Rewards power is

    B.   Coercive power is

    C.   Legitimate power is

    D.   Expert power is

    E.   Referent power is

III. STRUCTURAL AND SITUATIONAL SOURCES OF POWER.

    A.   Structural sources.

        1.   Centrality:

        2.   Criticality:

        3.   Flexibility:

4.   Visibility:

5.   Relevance:

B.   Situational sources.

    1.   Knowledge as power means

    2.   Resources as power means

    3.   Decision making as power means

    4.   Networks as power means

        a.   Examples of connecting links are

           (1)

           (2)

           (3)

C.   Power of lower-level employees.

    1.   What are the sources of the power of lower-level employees?

IV.   INFLUENCE STRATEGIES: THE EFFECTIVE USE OF POWER.

   A.   What factors influence the selection of an influence strategy?

B.   The "exchange process" in power relationships is

C.   Characteristics of people who are successful at exercising power and influence.

    1.

    2.

    3.

    4.

    5.

D.   Suggestions for establishing influence in an organization.

    1.

    2.

    3.

    4.

    5.

V.   POLITICAL BEHAVIOR.

A.   People engage in political behavior to

B.   Organizational politics is

C.   Are the effects of political behavior positive or negative?

D.   Occurrence of political behavior.

   1.   Political behavior is most likely to occur when

      a.

      b.

   2.   Strategies for avoiding political behavior.

      a.

      b.

      c.

      d.

VI.   POLITICAL BEHAVIOR AND PERSONALITY.

   A.   The need for power is

      1.   How is the need for power related to being an effective manager?

   B.   Machiavellianism is characterized by

      1.

      2.

3.

C. How is locus of control related to political behavior?

D. How is risk-seeking propensity related to political behavior?

DIRECTED QUESTIONS

I. The Nature of Power.

1. The concept of power:
    a) Applies only when more than one person is involved;
    b) Is a static relationship;
    c) Is synonymous with the concept of authority;   a
    d) All of the above.

2. Power:
    a) Is narrower in scope than authority and applies to a smaller percentage of behaviors in an organization;
    b) Is legitimated through acceptance by employees   c
        as being right and proper;
    c) Will change as situations and individuals change;
    d) All of the above.

3. The term "power" can be used in reference to:
    a) Individuals;
    b) Groups;   d
    c) Organizations;
    d) All of the above.

II. Interpersonal Sources of Power.

1. A supervisor's ability to promote a subordinate is an example of:
    a) Coercive power;
    b) Expert power;   c
    c) Reward power;

d) Referent power;
e) Legitimate power.

2. A supervisor's ability to insert a letter of
    reprimand in a subordinate's file is an example of:
    a) Coercive power;
    b) Expert power;   a
    c) Reward power;
    d) Referent power;
    e) Legitimate power.

3. A zone of indifference is the range within which
    employees allow a manager:
    a) Coercive power;
    b) Expert power;   e
    c) Reward power;
    d) Referent power;
    e) Legitimate power.

4. A manager's ability to influence a subordinate
    because that subordinate admires the manager's
    supervisory competency is an example of:
    a) Coercive power;
    b) Expert power;   b
    c) Reward power;
    d) Referent power;
    e) Legitimate power.

5. The source of interpersonal power which is least
    related to job circumstances is:
    a) Coercive power;
    b) Expert power;   d
    c) Reward power;
    d) Referent power;
    e) Legitimate power.

6. The "organizational" category of interpersonal
    power sources includes:
    a) Knowledge;
    b) Reward;   b
    c) Expertise;
    d) All of the above.

7. Regarding the relationships among interpersonal
    power sources:
    a) Managers' power to influence is complex and
        depends on a variety of sources;
    b) The way managers use one type of power can   d
        affect the effectiveness of power from other
        sources;
    c) Sources of power are interdependent;
    d) All of the above.

III. Structural and Situational Sources of Power.

1. Structural and situational sources of power:
   a) Result from division of labor and departmentalization;
   b) Include knowledge, resource, and decision-making power sources;
   c) Result from organizational design and access to critical organizational features;
   d) All of the above.

d

2. The effect that computers are having on power by making access to and use of information more widespread is an example of:
   a) Knowledge as power;
   b) Resources as power;
   c) Decision-making as power;
   d) None of the above.

a

3. The phrase "he who has the gold makes the rules," is an expression of:
   a) Knowledge as power;
   b) Resources as power;
   c) Decision-making as power;
   d) None of the above.

b

4. Being able to influence organizational objectives, alternatives considered, or outcomes being projected is an example of:
   a) Knowledge as power;
   b) Resources as power;
   c) Decision-making as power;
   d) None of the above.

c

5. Structural and situational power depend partly on managers' ability to get cooperation in carrying out tasks--i.e., on:
   a) Knowledge as power;
   b) Resources as power;
   c) Decision-making as power;
   d) Connecting links as power.

d

6. The ability of lower-level employees to influence behavior is most likely to stem from which source of power:
   a) Reward;
   b) Coercive;
   c) Legitimate;
   d) Structural or situational.

d

IV. The Effective Use of Power.

1. Ineffective use of power may have negative implications for:

a) The individual;
b) The organization;   c
c) Both a and b;
d) Neither a nor b.

2. A manager who attempts to draw on expertise in an
    area in which he/she is not an expert commits
    which of the following errors:
    a) Failure to seek the managerial positions that   a
        allow the development and use of power;
    b) Failure to temper power-oriented behavior;
    c) Failure to understand which power source is
        most appropriate for a given situation.

3. A manager who becomes known as "power hungry"
    commits which of the following errors:
    a) Failure to seek the managerial positions that
        allow the development and use of power;
    b) Failure to temper power-oriented behavior;   b
    c) Failure to understand which power source is
        most appropriate for a given situation.

4. A strategy of assertiveness is most likely to be
    used when:
    a) Attempting to gain personal objectives;
    b) Past experience indicates a high probability   c
        of success;
    c) Attempting to gain organizational objectives;
    d) Seeking benefits from a superior.

5. A strategy of reason is most likely to be used
    when:
    a) Objectives are of benefit to the person;
    b) Expectations for success are high;   b
    c) Organizational power is low;
    d) Seeking benefits from a superior.

6. The use of a direct forceful approach is:
    a) Reason;
    b) Bargaining;   d
    c) Coalition;
    d) Assertiveness.

7. Which of the following is not good advice for
    establishing influence in an organization:
    a) Pick a single influence strategy and stick
        with it;   a
    b) Develop a reputation as an expert;
    c) Develop a network of resource persons;
    d) All the above are good advice.

V. Political Behavior.

    1. Political behavior:
        a) Is more likely when there is little
            competition for scarce resources;

b)   Can be eliminated in most organizations;   c
c)   Is more likely when goals are unclear than
      when goals are clear;
d)   Would not occur if everyone had information
      about the situation surrounding that behavior.
2.   Which of the following is not a strategy for
     reducing the likelihood of political behavior:
     a)   Increasing the resources available;
     b)   Recruitment of people with similar goals and   d
           beliefs;
     c)   Socialization to promote similarity of goals
           and beliefs;
     d)   Making decisions appear more important than
           they actually are.
3.   Which of the following does not represent the
     consensus from research on political behavior:
     a)   It can have positive effects on individuals
           and organizations;
     b)   It can have negative effects on individuals   d
           and organizations;
     c)   People expect it to be greater at top
           management levels;
     d)   People expect it to be greater at lower and
           middle management levels.
4.   Which of the following is not an area generally
     ranked as among the most political organizational
     decisions:
     a)   Interdepartmental coordination;
     b)   Disciplinary penalties;   b
     c)   Delegation of authority;
     d)   Promotions and transfers.

VI.   Political Behavior and Personality.

1.   A manager's need for power may not lead to
     effective management if:
     a)   It is strong;
     b)   It emphasizes institutional power;   c
     c)   It emphasizes personal power;
     d)   All of the above.
2.   Which of the following statements is not consistent
     with Machiavellianism:
     a)   The best way to handle people is to tell
           them what they want to hear;
     b)   Do not completely trust anyone;   d
     c)   Never reveal the real reasons behind your
           actions unless it is useful for you to do so;
     d)   If you flatter important people they will
           have the advantage over you.

3. Locus of control is related to political behavior in the following way:
   a) High internals are likely to exhibit more political behavior than high externals;
   b) High externals are likely to exhibit more political behavior than high internals;
   c) Those who believe that fate or chance primarily determine events are most likely to engage in political behavior;
   d) None of the above.

   a

4. Risk-seeking propensity is related to political behavior in the following way:
   a) Political behavior can be negative;
   b) Risk seekers more willing to engage in political behavior than are risk avoiders;
   c) To engage in political behavior advocating one position may create risk because it may be interpreted as opposing another position;
   d) All of the above.

   d

APPLIED QUESTIONS

I. Organizational Power and Organizational Politics.

1. By studying an organization chart, one can see:
   a) All those who have equal power;
   b) Each individual's power relative to all other individuals;
   c) Formal lines of authority;
   d) All of the above.

   c

2. To understand the organizational power that any individual has, it is first necessary to know about:
   a) Others with whom the individual interacts;
   b) Situations in which the individual is involved;
   c) Changes that are occurring in the individual and situations involving the individual;
   d) All of the above.

   d

3. A manager wishes to effect a change without drawing attention to one major implication that change may have. Attempts to do this:
   a) Involve organizational politics;
   b) Are likely to result in a decision without considering all of the relevant information;
   c) May include subterfuge;
   d) All of the above.

   d

4. A manager believes that he could be in trouble if those around him begin engaging in political behavior to acquire power to use against him and

so he adopts strategies which he believes will
reduce that behavior. Which of the following
strategies would he be <u>least</u> likely to adopt:
   a) Surround himself with people with a wide range
      of backgrounds and beliefs;
   b) Try to reduce the critical nature of some   a
      important decisions;
   c) Increase the resources available for people to
      work with;
   d) None (i.e., all are likely).

II. Structural, Situational, and Interpersonal Sources of
    Power.

   1. A manager calls all her subordinates to her office
       to describe the new merit pay system and to explain
       that she will be the one who recommends the amounts
       of the merit awards. In doing so, she draws from
       which of the following power sources:
       a) Reward;
       b) Coercive;   a
       c) Legitimate;
       d) Expert;
       e) Referent.
   2. A manager who is known as a "great person to work
       for" because all his people seem to get promoted
       into good jobs, is likely to be able to draw on
       what source of power to influence subordinates'
       behavior:
       a) Reward;
       b) Coercive;   a
       c) Legitimate;
       d) Expert;
       e) Referent.
   3. Heavy reliance on coercive power is likely to have
       most adverse effect in which of the following power
       bases:
       a) Reward;
       b) Legitimate;   d
       c) Expert;
       d) Referent.
   4. By releasing no more data to a line manager than
       he/she absolutely must have to operate at the time,
       a budget officer may be attempting to influence
       behavior through what power source:
       a) Legitimate;
       b) Referent;   d
       c) Decision-making;
       d) Knowledge.

5. Top managers frequently have one or two individuals
    they rely on as "sounding boards" for their ideas.
    Those individuals tend to have which of the
    following kinds of power:
    a) Legitimate;
    b) Referent;   c
    c) Decision-making;
    d) Coercive.

6. "Empire-building" is a form of acquiring which of
    the following kinds of power:
    a) Expert;
    b) Knowledge;   d
    c) Decision-making;
    d) Resources.

7. If a lower-level employee wants to be able to
    exercise some influence over those above her, she
    would be best advised to seek to acquire power
    from which of the following sources:
    a) Reward;
    b) Coercion;   c
    c) Expert;
    d) Legitimate.

8. A frequently-heard piece of advice is to get to
    know your boss' secretary well. The most
    compelling reason for this is probably the
    acquisition of which base power:
    a) Legitimate;
    b) Information;   b
    c) Reward;
    d) Coercion.

9. Organizational factors which contribute to power
    include:
    a) A large number of rules inherent in the job;
    b) High task variety;   b
    c) Low contact with senior officials;
    d) Many established routines involved in the job.

III. Effective Uses of Power.

1. Which of the following is consistent with the
    characteristics of effective use of power:
    a) A manager attempts to draw on the expert base
        of power by acting outside the zone of
        indifference;
    b) An individual manages to avoid risky   e
        managerial positions;
    c) A manager identifies his strongest power
        source and sticks with it;
    d) All of the above;
    e) None of the above.

2. An employee who in the past has not been highly
    successful in influencing his/her supervisor might
    best use which of the following strategies to
    achieve an organizational objective:
    a) Friendliness;
    b) Reason;   c
    c) Assertiveness;
    d) All of the above.

3. An employee trying to influence a supervisor to
    approve a leave of absence might best use which
    of the following strategies:
    a) Assertiveness;
    b) Reason;   c
    c) Friendliness;
    d) Higher authority.

4. An employee has had numerous new ideas accepted
    by her supervisor and is trying to influence the
    supervisor to accept another new idea. Which of
    the following strategies would be most appropriate:
    a) Assertiveness;
    b) Reason;   b
    c) Friendliness;
    d) All of the above.

5. A manager noted that each time his secretary
    brought him some items she'd just baked, it would
    be followed within a day or so by a request for a
    special favor. This technique is known as:
    a) Bargaining;   c
    b) Reason;
    c) Ingratiation;
    d) Sanction.

6. "My boss was totally opposed to the idea of
    flextime. He thought I just wanted to play more
    golf. Then I got people to talk to him who had
    all sorts of reasons why they wanted flextime."
    This person is engaged in:
    a) Assertiveness;   d
    b) Reason;
    c) Bargaining;
    d) Coalition.

IV. Is Political Behavior Necessarily Undesirable?

1. What is the probability that political behavior
    will occur in an organization:
    a) Less than a 50% chance;
    b) About a 50% chance;   d
    c) More than likely;
    d) Inevitable.

2. Which of the following is a potentially positive
    effect of political behavior:
    a) A greater range of alternatives is likely
        to be considered;
    b) More points of view may be heard;   d
    c) More intensive analysis may be undertaken;
    d) All of the above.
3. Which of the following is a potential negative
    effect of political behavior:
    a) Distraction from organizational goals;
    b) Individual power and position enhancement;   a
    c) More analysis in decision-making;
    d) All of the above.
4. A budget manager is to attend an important meeting
    at which he will unveil a set of new budgetary
    limits. The day before the meeting anyone calling
    the budget manager's office is told that he is out
    of the office and unavailable for the day. This
    manager may be attempting to draw from which use
    of power:
    a) Knowledge;
    b) Resources;   a
    c) Referent;
    d) Coercive.

V. Factors Contributing to the Occurrence of Political
    Behavior.

    1. An employee gives up trying to favorably influence
        his supervisor because he feels that no matter
        what he does things will be stacked against him.
        This may be a result of which of the following
        personal traits:
        a) High internal locus of control;
        b) High external locus of control;   b
        c) Low need for power;
        d) Machiavellianism.
    2. A supervisor has a long-service, competent employee
        who should be a great source of help to him in his
        department. It has not worked out that way because
        the employee never really speaks frankly or openly
        with him. Which of the following personal traits
        would be most likely to lead to that sort of
        behavior by the employee:
        a) High internal locus of control;
        b) High external locus of control;   d
        c) Low need for power;
        d) Machiavellianism.

3. In the above question (#2), if it were known that
    the supervisor was one who held grudges, was
    retaliatory, and the like, then another personal
    trait which might explain the behavior of the
    employee is:
    a)   High need for power;
    b)   High external locus of control;   c
    c)   Low risk-seeking propensity;
    d)   All of the above.

4. A manager is able to control a group of difficult
    employees. They will do almost anything he asks.
    This manager is transferred and his successor--who
    is a fully competent manager--has an extremely
    difficult time with these employees. The departing
    manager may have:
    a)   Emphasized institutional power;
    b)   Emphasized personal power;   b
    c)   Been Machiavellian;
    d)   Been a low risk-seeker.

5. As an experienced manager who has just been
    transferred to a new department you analyze the
    situation and determine that the major issues
    facing you are: the need to reprimand an employee
    who is violating safety standards; the need to
    have someone to fill a position that has been
    vacant for a long time; the need to delegate more
    authority to the supervisors who report to you;
    and the need to more fully communicate and enforce
    the sick leave policy. Which is most likely to
    generate political behavior within the department:
    a)   Reprimanding the safety violator;
    b)   Filling the vacant position;   c
    c)   Delegating authority;
    d)   Dealing with the sick leave policy.

6. Which of the following is most likely to contribute
    to the occurrence of political behavior:
    a)   Full information to assist in decision making;
    b)   Shortage of critical resources;   b
    c)   Inability of individuals or groups to affect
         the decision-making process;
    d)   A homogeneous/stable environment.

PROGRAMMED STUDY SUPPLEMENT

1.   _____ refers to the ability of   expert
     managers to influence their subordinates'   power
     behavior because of the managers' perceived
     skills, talents, or knowledge.

2. _____ involves the actions that people engage in to acquire, develop, and use power to obtain the outcomes they want when there is uncertainty or disagreement about choice.

organizational politics

---

3. The range of activities within which employees will accept certain directives without consciously questioning the manager's power is called a _____.

zone of indifference

---

4. _____ is a manager's ability to influence subordinates' behavior because of their personal liking of or admiration for the manager.

referent power

---

5. _____ consists of your attempts to influence others to behave in ways that best serve your needs.

political behavior

---

6. Since there at times may be negative outcomes for those who engage in political activity in organizations, those with low _____ are less likely to do so than are those more willing to take the chance.

risk-seeking propensity

---

7. _____ is a manager's ability to influence subordinates' behavior because of the position held in the organization.

legitimate power

---

8. People with a high internal _____ are more likely to be willing to engage in political behavior than those who are less likely to believe that they can "make a difference."

locus of control

---

9. _____ is a manager's ability to influence subordinates' behavior by applying negative sanctions for undesired behavior.

coercive power

---

10. _____ may exist for anyone who has the ability to affect any part of the decision-making process.

decision-making as power

11. _____ is the name given to behavior characterized by the use of deceit and opportunism in interpersonal relationships.

Machiavellianism

12. _____ is a manager's ability to influence subordinates' behavior by applying positive sanctions for desirable behavior.

reward power

13. The old saying, "he who has the gold makes the rules" sums up the concept of _____.

resources as power

14. The basic desire to influence and lead others and to be in control of one's own world is called the _____.

need for power

15. People who can control information are in a position to utilize _____.

knowledge as power

16. "Power" that is legitimated through its acceptance by employees as being right or proper is _____.

authority

17. The ability to influence others and affect their behavior is called _____.

power

18. The concept of _____ implies that various affiliations, both inside and outside the organization, represent sources of power.

networks of power

19. The knowledge, know-how, and skill that exists in an organization is known as its _____.

intellectual capital

20. The _____ is based on the "law of reciprocity."

exchange process

CHAPTER 17

JOB DESIGN

LEARNING OBJECTIVES

When you read and when you review Chapter 17, keep in mind the learning objectives which have been established by the authors. Look them over first as a guide to picking out the most important parts of the chapter, and then think about them as you are going through the chapter. When you have finished the chapter, ask yourself whether you have met the objectives.

The authors intend that when you have finished studying this chapter you should be able to:

* Describe five approaches to job design and state the differences between them.
* Explain the linkages between technological factors and job design.
* Understand and diagnose the problems caused by poorly designed jobs.
* Describe the job characteristics enrichment model and explain how it may increase performance, motivation, and satisfaction.
* Explain how the sociotechnical systems model attempts to integrate the needs and goals of employees with those of the organization.

CHAPTER OUTLINE

After you have read the chapter, complete the following outline.

I.   NATURE OF JOB DESIGN.

   A.   Job design is

   B.   Impact of job design means

   C.   Complexity of job design involves

      1.

      2.

      3.

II. JOB DESIGN APPROACHES.

   A.   Job rotation is

      1.   The impact and complexity of job rotation is

      2.   Job rotation is most beneficial when
         a.

         b.

   B.   Job engineering is

      1.   The purposes of job engineering are

      a.

      b.

      c.

      d.

C. Job enlargement is

    1. What does job enlargement do?

    2. Some employees may resist job enlargement because

      a.

      b.

D. Job enrichment is

E. Sociotechnical systems approach is to match

    1.

    2.

    3.

III. JOB DESIGN AND TECHNOLOGY.

    A. Work-flow uncertainty is

   B.   Task uncertainty is

   C.   Task interdependence is

      1.   Types of task interdependence.

         a.

         b.

         c.

IV.   JOB CHARACTERISTICS ENRICHMENT MODEL.

   A.   Core job characteristics.

      1.

      2.

      3.

      4.

      5.

   B.   Individual differences that influence the way employees
        respond to enriched jobs.

      1.

      2.

3.

C.   Job diagnosis methods.

  1.   Structural clues method focuses on five structural
       factors.

       a.

       b.

       c.

       d.

       e.

  2.   Survey method.

       a.   One survey method is the Job Diagnostic Survey.
            How does it work?

D.   Techniques used to implement a job-enrichment program.

  1.   Vertical loading is

       a.   Elements of vertical loading include

            (1)

            (2)

            (3)

2. Natural work groups are

    a. Possible criteria for forming natural work groups are

        (1)

        (2)

        (3)

        (4)

        (5)

3. Client relationship enrich jobs by

4. Product ownership enriches jobs by

5. Direct feedback enriches jobs by

E. How do job design, technology, and the job characteristics enrichment model tie together?

F. Social information processing.

    1. What role does social information play in employees' perceptions of their jobs?

2.   Basic tenets of the social information processing model.

   a.

   b.

   c.

   d.

V.   SOCIOTECHNICAL SYSTEMS MODEL.

A.   The primary emphasis of the model is

B.   The three parts of the model are

   1.

   2.

   3.

C.   The social system includes

   1.

   2.

   3.

   4.

   5.

   D.   The technological system includes

        1.

        2.

        3.

        4.

        5.

        6.

   E.   The moderators are

        1.

        2.

        3.

   F.   The extent to which an organization operates along the
        lines of sociotechnical systems design can be evaluated
        by looking at its

        1.

        2.

        3.

        4.

        5.

        6.

   G.   Organizational significance.

        1.   The most basic issue to consider in designing jobs
             is

DIRECTED QUESTIONS

I.   Nature of Job Design.

    1. Managers should know how to design and redesign
        jobs because:
        a) The ideal state should always be attained;
        b) They should be able to determine whether   c
            improvements in employee-job-organization
            relationships would be beneficial;
        c) Tasks and the best means for performing them
            change over time;
        d) All of the above.
    2. Job design:
        a) Involves task interdependencies and excludes
            interpersonal relationships;
        b) Focuses on the formal rather than the   d
            informal specification of tasks;
        c) Focus on the content factors rather than on
            the contextual faction of the job;
        d) Takes into account employee as well as
            organizational needs and goals.
    3. Time and motion studies are associated with:
        a) Job engineering;
        b) Job enlargement;   a
        c) Job rotation;
        d) Job enrichment.
    4. Job engineering focuses on:
        a) Specialization of labor and efficiency;
        b) The time required to do a task;   d
        c) The efficiency of motion required to perform
            tasks;
        d) All of the above.
    5. Job engineering:
        a) Is sometimes criticized for creating boring
            jobs;
        b) Is an important approach because it can   d
            generate immediate cost savings;
        c) Dates back to Frederick W. Taylor;
        d) All of the above.
    6. Which of the following approaches to job design
        is not likely to create, extend, or increase boredom:
        a) Job rotation;
        b) Job enrichment;   b
        c) Job engineering;
        d) Job enlargement.
    7. Which of the following does not involve altering the
        tasks of a job:

    a)   Job rotation;
    b)   Job enrichment;
    c)   Job engineering;
    d)   Job enlargement.

  a

8. Herzberg's two-factor theory of motivation emphasized:
    a)   Job rotation;
    b)   Job enrichment;
    c)   Job engineering;
    d)   Job enlargement.

  b

9. Which of the following utilizes vertical loading:
    a)   Job rotation;
    b)   Job enrichment;
    c)   Job engineering;
    d)   Job enlargement.

  b

10. Job rotation is of most benefit under which of the following conditions:
    a)   Where all tasks are similar and routine;
    b)   Where it can be isolated from a larger redesign system underway;
    c)   Where it is used as a training technique;
    d)   Where it is closely related to job enlargement.

  c

11. The job enrichment approach originated:
    a)   At AT&T in the 1960's;
    b)   At Texas Instruments in the 1970's;
    c)   At IBM in the 1940's;
    d)   With Herzberg in the 1950's.

  c

12. Which of the following is not involved in the implementation of a job enrichment approach:
    a)   Client relationships;
    b)   Self-scheduling;
    c)   Low work-flow uncertainty;
    d)   Product ownership.

  c

13. The sociotechnical system focuses on all but which of the following:
    a)   Tasks that are independent of each other;
    b)   Clusters of tasks as bases for forming natural work groups;
    c)   Specific tasks to be performed by each member of the work group;
    d)   Matches of technology, people, and organizational needs.

  a

14. The "complexity" of the various approaches to job design means:
    a)   The extent to which a job design approach is likely to be linked to factors beyond the immediate job;
    b)   The extent to which a job design approach is likely to require individuals with diverse skills;

  e

    c) The extent to which a job design approach is likely to require changes in many factors;

    d) a and b;

    e) b and c.

II. Technology and Job Design.

1. Which of the following are components of what the authors define as "technology":
    a) Production techniques;
    b) Knowledge;
    c) People's actions;
    d) All of the above.

        d

2. Knowledge of when inputs will be received for processing is known as:
    a) Low work-flow uncertainty;
    b) High task uncertainty;
    c) Low task interdependence;
    d) None of the above.

        a

3. Knowledge about how to perform one's job is known as:
    a) Work-flow uncertainty;
    b) Task uncertainty;
    c) Task interdependence;
    d) None of the above.

        b

4. Low task uncertainty means the employee has:
    a) Little freedom to decide which, when, or where tasks will be performed;
    b) Great freedom to decide which, when, or where tasks will be performed;
    c) Relatively complete prespecified knowledge about how to go about producing the desired outputs;
    d) Relatively little prespecified knowledge about how to go about producing the desired outputs.

        c

5. High work-flow uncertainty means the employee has:
    a) Little freedom to decide which, when, or where tasks will be performed;
    b) Great freedom to decide which, when, or where tasks will be performed;
    c) Relatively complete prespecified knowledge about how to go about producing the desired outputs;
    d) Relatively little prespecified knowledge about how to go about producing the desired outputs.

        b

6. Job enrichment generally involves:
    a) Increasing the task uncertainty and/or the work-flow uncertainty;

    b)   Decreasing the task uncertainty and/or the   **a**
work-flow uncertainty;
    c)   Increasing the task uncertainty and decreasing
the work-flow uncertainty;
    d)   Decreasing the task uncertainty and increasing
the work-flow uncertainty.

7.   The type of task interdependence in which one
employee must complete certain tasks before other
employees can perform their tasks:
    a)   Pooled;
    b)   Sequential;   **b**
    c)   Reciprocal.

8.   Increases in pooled interdependence:
    a)   Decreases the amount of required job
integration;
    b)   Increases the amount of required job   **a**
integration;
    c)   Increases the amount of sequential
interdependence;
    d)   Increases the amount of reciprocal
interdependence.

9.   Decreases in the amount of job integration:
    a)   Require increases in the amount of task
uncertainty and/or work flow uncertainty;
    b)   Require decreases in the amount of task   **a**
uncertainty and/or work flow uncertainty;
    c)   Require decreases in the amount of task
uncertainty and/or increases in work flow
uncertainty;
    d)   Require increases in the amount of task
uncertainty and/or decreases in work flow
uncertainty.

10. The social information processing model states that:
    a)   The individual's social environment may
provide cues that help characterize the work
environment;
    b)   The social environment may provide information   **c**
that will help rank the importance of the
different dimensions of a job;
    c)   Both of the above;
    d)   Neither of the above.

III. Job Characteristics Enrichment Model.

1.   Which of the following is <u>not</u> one of the job
characteristics that are critical for job
enrichment efforts:
    a)   Job feedback;

b)   Task significance;   d
c)   Autonomy;
d)   Satisfaction with contextual factors.
2.   Job characteristics:
a)   Affect individuals' strength of growth needs;
b)   Affect individuals' psychological states;   b
c)   Are the criteria for forming natural work
groups;
d)   Are the core of the sociotechnical system model.
3.   Regarding the psychological states of feedback,
experience of personal responsibility, and
meaningfulness:
a)   At least one must be present for maximum
task-based motivation;
b)   All three must be present for maximum task-   b
based motivation;
c)   These states affect the five core job
characteristics;
d)   These states affect the "individual differences"
discussed by the authors.
4.   Increases in which of the following job
characteristics are most likely to increase the
employee's level of experiencing personal
responsibility:
a)   Skill variety;
b)   Task significance;   c
c)   Autonomy;
d)   Job feedback.
5.   Increases in which of the following job
characteristics are most likely to increase the
extent to which the employee experiences
meaningfulness of work:
a)   Skill variety;
b)   Autonomy;   a
c)   Job feedback;
d)   None of the above.
6.   Which of the following might be likely to respond
negatively to attempts at job enrichment:
a)   Employees not competent to perform;
b)   Employees who wish to perform well but   d
realize that they are not;
c)   Individuals who score low on growth need
strength;
d)   All of the above;
e)   None of the above.
7.   Which of the following is <u>not</u> a contextual factor
(of a job):
a)   Technical supervision;
b)   Interpersonal relationships;   d

    c)   Company policy;
    d)   Low-skill task components.

8. The structural clues method of job diagnosis:
    a)   Assumes that employees can respond accurately and objectively about characteristics of their jobs;
    b)   Checks for situational factors often associated with deficiencies in job design;   b
    c)   Calculates a "motivating potential score";
    d)   None of the above.

9. Which of the following structural elements tends to reduce or dilute task identity:
    a)   The existence of troubleshooters;
    b)   The existence of communications or customer relations units;   d
    c)   The existence of labor pools;
    d)   All of the above;
    e)   None of the above.

10. Overly narrow spans of control may tend to reduce:
    a)   Task identity;
    b)   Task significance;
    c)   Autonomy;   c
    d)   Feedback.

11. Vertical loading is:
    a)   Formation of natural work groups;
    b)   Putting one type business on top of another;   c
    c)   Giving employees responsibilities that had previously been managerial responsibilities;
    d)   Expanding the variety of tasks to be performed by an individual.

12. Which of the following is **not** a basis for the formation of natural work groups:
    a)   Geography;
    b)   Task significance;   b
    c)   Organizational type;
    d)   Customer groups.

13. All of the criteria for forming natural work groups tend to:
    a)   Increase pooled interdependence and decrease sequential and reciprocal interdependence;
    b)   Decrease pooled interdependence and increase sequential and reciprocal interdependence;   a
    c)   Both of the above;
    d)   None of the above.

14. Vertical loading tends to:
    a)   Increase task uncertainty and work-flow uncertainty;
    b)   Decrease task uncertainty and work-flow uncertainty;   a

    c)   Increase task uncertainty and decrease work-
       flow uncertainty;

    d)   Decrease task uncertainty and increase work-
       flow uncertainty.

15. Vertical loading sometimes has the tendency to:

    a)   Increase pooled interdependence and decrease
       sequential and reciprocal interdependence;

    b)   Decrease pooled interdependence and increase   a
       sequential and reciprocal interdependence;

    c)   Both of the above;

    d)   None of the above.

IV. Sociotechnical System Model.

1. Which of the following is <u>not</u> a characteristic
   of the sociotechnical system approach:

    a)   Focuses on clustering together jobs with high
       reciprocal or sequential interdependence;

    b)   Increases the pooled interdependence between   c
       work groups;

    c)   Increases the pooled interdependence between
       individual jobs;

    d)   Designs work roles to integrate people with
       technology.

2. The sociotechnical systems model:

    a)   Focuses on vertical job loading to the cluster
       of jobs within the group;

    b)   Focuses on vertical job loading to each
       individual job;

    c)   Works better in changing an existing way of   a
       operation than in designing jobs for an
       entirely new plant;

    d)   All of the above.

3. The social system in the sociotechnical model
   includes which of the following:

    a)   Human factors influencing how individuals
       perform their tasks;

    b)   Human factors influencing how groups perform   d
       their tasks;

    c)   Individuals' attitudes toward their work;

    d)   All of the above.

4. The technological dimensions of the sociotechnical
   model vary according to:

    a)   Type of production process;

    b)   Physical work setting;   d

    c)   Complexity of the production process;

    d)   All of the above;

    e)   None of the above.

5. Which of the following is <u>not</u> categorized as a "moderator" in the sociotechnical system:
    a) Work roles;
    b) The time pressures inherent in the production   b
        process;
    c) Work team and/or organizational goals;
    d) Skills and abilities of the employees.
6. Goals, as moderators, serve to:
    a) Define the work relationships between workers
        and technological requirements of the work;
    b) Set the structure of the work so that workers   c
        have only to work within a pre-established
        structure;
    c) Set the boundaries within which workers can
        structure their work;
    d) Establish sets of expected behaviors for
        employees.
7. Which of the following approaches would a manager
    interested only in productivity and efficiency be
    <u>least</u> likely to select:
    a) Job engineering;
    b) Job rotation;   c
    c) Sociotechnical model;
    d) Job enlargement.
8. Which key principle of sociotechnical systems
    design involves the extent to which employees are
    dedicated to accomplishing organizational goals:
    a) Cooperation;   b
    b) Commitment/energy;
    c) Joint optimization;
    d) Innovativeness.
9. Which key principle of sociotechnical systems
    design involves the extent to which the
    organization is designed to use both its social
    and its technical resources efficiently:
    a) Cooperation;   c
    b) Commitment/energy;
    c) Joint optimization;
    d) Innovativeness.

APPLIED QUESTIONS

I. Nature of Job Design.

   1. The job design method most likely to cause workers
       to say they feel like robots is:

a) Job rotation;
b) Job enlargement;   c
c) Job engineering;
d) Job enrichment.

2. Which approach would be concerned with identifying
the appropriate clerical jobs to be automated:
a) Job rotation;
b) Job enlargement;   c
c) Job engineering;
d) Job enrichment.

3. Which approach to job design is being used when a
worker's job is changed from the ordering of
electronic parts to the ordering of both electronic
and electro-mechanical parts:
a) Job rotation;
b) Job enlargement;   b
c) Job engineering;
d) Job enrichment.

4. Which approach to job design is being used when a
worker's job is changed from sweeping floors and
cleaning rest rooms to sweeping floors and cleaning
rest rooms plus ordering and inventorying the
necessary cleaning supplies:
a) Job rotation;
b) Job enlargement;   d
c) Job engineering;
d) Job enrichment.

5. A computer chip company treated its employees very
impersonally when its orders were up and business
was booming, emphasizing only productivity and
efficiency. Now, when times are tougher, it is
having difficulty in getting employees to pitch
in and help. A change to which of the following
approaches would be most likely to result in
greater employee involvement:
a) Job rotation;
b) Job enlargement;   c
c) Sociotechnical system;
d) Job engineering.

II. The Linkage Between Technology and Job Design.

1. Which of the following jobs would generally have
the greatest work flow uncertainty:
a) Santa Claus;
b) Waiter;   d
c) Teacher;
d) Trouble shooter.

2. Which of the following jobs would generally have
    the least task uncertainty:
    a)   Research scientist;
    b)   Trouble shooter;   c
    c)   Dentist;
    d)   Inventor.

3. Which of the following approaches to job design
    would be most likely to result in high task
    uncertainty and high work flow uncertainty:
    a)   Job engineering;
    b)   Job enrichment;   b
    c)   Job enlargement;
    d)   Job rotation.

4. Which of the following is the best example of a
    setting wherein pooled task interdependence exists:
    a)   A School of Business within a university;
    b)   The different stops or stations along the   a
         line at fall semester registration;
    c)   A brain-storming session;
    d)   A professional golfer.

5. Which of the following is the best example of a
    setting wherein sequential task interdependence
    exists:
    a)   A School of Business within a university;
    b)   The different stops or stations along the   b
         line at fall semester registration;
    c)   A brain-storming session;
    d)   A professional golfer.

6. Which of the following helps explain why two
    employers performing the same tasks with the same
    job characteristics under different managers
    might respond differently to the objective
    characteristics of their jobs:
    a)   The Job Diagnostic Survey;
    b)   Artificial intelligence;   c
    c)   Social information processing model;
    d)   The job feedback model.

III. Job Characteristics Enrichment.

1. A change which would likely increase the sense of
    meaningfulness that an employee feels about
    his/her work would be:
    a)   Adding a task which requires the worker to
         learn something new in order to perform that
         task;

   b)   Adding a set of tasks which requires the   d
        worker to be responsible for a large portion
        of an entire unit of output;
   c)   Shifting the worker to a product line which
        he/she feels consumers value more highly;
   d)   All of the above.

2.   A change which would be likely to increase the
     sense of personal responsibility that a worker
     feels would be:
   a)   Providing more direct feedback from the
        worker's superiors;
   b)   Convincing the worker of the importance that   c
        his/her output has for others;
   c)   Leaving it with the employee to determine how
        tasks are to be performed and in what sequence;
   d)   All of the above.

3.   Under which of the following conditions is job
     enrichment most likely to succeed:
   a)   The addition of new tasks that require skills
        and abilities several levels above those of
        the current employees;
   b)   Employees are seeking salary increases and   c
        are very dissatisfied with the low-paying
        status of their current jobs;
   c)   Employees with strong growth needs;
   d)   All of the above.

IV.   Diagnosing Job Design Problems.

   1.   Which of the following statements offers a clue
        that job enrichment might be appropriate:
      a)   "I don't know if this will be OK or not
           because I don't really know what happens to
           the order next";
      b)   "I wish she'd get off our back and let us do   d
           our work. She hovers right over us all
           the time";
      c)   "I don't really know what this little part
           does. I just make'em";
      d)   All of the above;
      e)   None of the above.

   2.   Which of the following is an example of vertical
        loading:
      a)   The employee is allowed to "sign off" on his
           own work, documenting when it is completed;

    b)   The employee is allowed to do claim adjustments   a
          from customers in any industry, as opposed to
          the single industry assigned in the past;
    c)   The employee moves between different jobs every
          three months;
    d)   All of the above;
    e)   None of the above.

3. Which of the following is <u>not</u> a basis for natural
    work group formation:
    a)   Random selection;
    b)   Grouping by work function;   a
    c)   Selection by industry or region serviced;
    d)   All of the above are natural work groups.

V.   Sociotechnical System Model.

1. Volvo's Kalmar plant represents:
    a)   An attempt at increasing task identity;
    b)   A job design experiment;   d
    c)   A management process change;
    d)   All of the above.

2. The definition of a worker's job and of how the
    holder of that job relates to other workers and
    the technological requirements of the tasks:
    a)   Is a characteristic of the technological
          system;
    b)   Is an aspect of the social system;   d
    c)   Moderates the relationship between the social
          system and the technological system;
    d)   All of the above.

3. An employer decides against computerizing his
    operation at a particular point in time because
    he does not think his current work force can
    handle the technical demands that would be imposed.
    Which element of the sociotechnical system is
    being described here:
    a)   Social system;
    b)   Technological system;
    c)   Moderators;   c
    d)   None of the above.

4. An "employee advisory committee" whose purpose is
    to react to the impact and feasibility of certain
    engineering changes before those changes are
    formally adopted is consistent with which of key
    principles of sociotechnical systems design:
    a)   Cooperation;   c
    b)   Commitment/energy;

c)   Joint optimization;
d)   Innovativeness.

PROGRAMMED STUDY SUPPLEMENT

1.   _____ is the formal and informal   job
     specification of tasks that are performed by   design
     employees.

---

2.   The _____ approach to job design   socio-
     focuses simultaneously on attempts to   technical
     integrate the technical system and human   system
     system.

---

3.   The _____ of a job would give the   vertical
     job-holder responsibilities formerly held only   loading
     by management or staff specialists.

---

4.   _____ is primarily concerned with   job
     the time required to do each task, the   engineer-
     efficiency of motion needed to perform it,   ing
     and the appropriate levels of automation.

---

5.   The degree to which decision-making and   task
     cooperation between employees or groups is   interde-
     necessary in order for them to perform their   pendence
     jobs is called _____.

---

6.   The _____ is used to measure   job diag-
     perceptions of the amounts of the fine core   nostic
     job characteristics in a job.   survey

---

7.   The self-scheduling of work that typically is   flextime
     a part of a job enrichment approach can be
     facilitated by the use of _____.

8. The approach to job design that attempts to add variety and interest to the job by expanding the number of different tasks performed is known as _____ .

job enlarge-ment

---

9. _____ occurs when outputs from one individual become inputs for the other, and vice versa.

recipro-cal interde-pendence

---

10. _____ is a measure of the extent to which a worker perceives his/her job as having an impact on the lives of others.

task signif-icance

---

11. _____ attempts to add variety and reduce boredom by continuously moving workers from job to job.

job rotation

---

12. Freedom, independence, and discretion constitute the amounts of _____ that one has in a job.

autonomy

---

13. The actions, knowledge, techniques, and physical implements used to transform inputs into outputs are known collectively as _____ .

technology

---

14. The degree to which a job involves completion of a "whole" piece of work is known as _____ .

task identity

---

15. _____ adds to employees' jobs tasks that allow them to assume more accountability and responsibility for planning, organizing, controlling, and evaluating their own work.

job enrich-ment

---

16. The _____ is the degree to which an individual desires the opportunity for self-direction, learning, and personal accomplishments at work.

growth need strength

17. The information that the job itself gives you about how well you have done is known as _____ .

    job feedback

18. _____ is the term given to the amount of knowledge an employee has about how to perform job tasks.

    task uncertainty

19. _____ is degree to which a job requires a range of personal competencies and abilities.

    skill variety

20. Task relations wherein each employee is not required to interact with others to complete their tasks are known as _____ .

    pooled interdependence

21. The _____ says that job enrichment is an increase in the amounts of skill variety, task identity, task significance, autonomy, and feedback found in a job.

    job characteristics enrichment model

22. The _____ for a job gives an indication of the likely outcome of a job enrichment redesign of that job.

    motivating potential score

23. When one employee must complete certain tasks before other employees can complete their tasks, the task relationship is called _____ .

    sequential interdependence

24. The _____ of job design designs work roles to integrate people with technology and to optimize relationships between the technological and the social systems.

    sociotechnical system model

25. The amount of knowledge that an employee has of when inputs will be received for process is termed _____ .

    work-flow uncertainty

26. Comments, observations, and similar cues from
    people whose views are considered important
    is _____.

    social
    informa-
    tion

---

27. The _____ assumes that people's
    perceptions of job characteristics may be
    influenced by social information.

    social
    informa-
    tion
    processing
    model

CHAPTER 18

ORGANIZATION DESIGN

When you read and when you review Chapter 18, keep in mind the learning objectives which have been established by the authors. Look them over first as a guide to picking out the most important parts of the chapter and then think about them as you are going through the chapter. When you have finished the chapter, ask yourself whether you have met the objectives.

The authors intend that when you have finished studying this chapter you should be able to:

* Explain the influence of environmental forces, strategic choices, and technological factors on the design of organizations.
* Evaluate the extent to which an organization is organic or mechanistic.
* Diagnose interdepartmental relations through the use of three key variables.
* Identify the bases of departmentalization and circumstances under which each may be effective.
* Describe the multidivisional structure and multinational corporation as complex organization designs.
* Describe the network organization and explain how it overcomes the limitations of other designs.
* Discuss the influence of organization design on employee and organizational effectiveness.

CHAPTER OUTLINE

After you have read the chapter, complete the following outline.

I.   THREE FACTORS IN DESIGN.

    A.   Environmental forces.

        1.   Two sets of forces are

            a.

            b.

        2.   Task environment and structure.

            a.   The task environment is

            b.   Environmental characteristics are

                (1)

                (2)

        3.   Types of task environments.

            a.

            b.

            c.

            d.

    B.   Strategic choices.

        1.

        2.

3.

C.   Technological factors.

1.   Work-flow uncertainty:

2.   Task uncertainty:

3.   Task interdependence:

a.   Pooled interdependence:

b.   Sequential interdependence:

c.   Reciprocal interdependence:

II.   MECHANISTIC -VS- ORGANIC SYSTEMS.

A.   A mechanistic system is

B.   An organic system is

C.   Hierarchy of authority is

1.   Centralization is

D.   Division of labor means

E.   Rules are

F.   Procedures are

      G.   Impersonality is

III. INTERDEPARTMENTAL RELATIONS.

      A.   What influence do the following variables have on interdepartmental relations?

          1.   Differentiation:

          2.   Integration:

          3.   Uncertainty:

      B.   Organizational Significance.

          1.

          2.

          3.

IV. FUNCTIONAL DEPARTMENTALIZATION.

      A.   Functional departmentalization is

      B.   Line and staff functions.

          1.   Line functions are

          2.   Staff functions are

C. Chain of command.

    1. Scalar chain of command means

    2. Unity of command means

D. Span of control refers to

E. Organizational significance.

    1. The primary advantage of a functional design is

    2. The disadvantages are

      a.

      b.

V. PRODUCT DEPARTMENTALIZATION.

A. Product departmentalization is

    1. How do product design organizations usually evolve?

B. A multidivisional structure is

    1. Why would an organization adopt a multidivisional structure?

C. Organizational significance.

1. The primary advantage of product departmentalization is

2. The disadvantages are

a.

b.

VI. OTHER BASES OF DEPARTMENTALIZATION.

A. Place departmentalization is

1. Organizational significance.

a. Advantage of place departmentalization.

b. Disadvantage of place departmentalization.

B. Matrix departmentalization is

1. Role relationships in a matrix design are

a.

b.

c.

2. Stages of evolution.

a.

b.

c.

d.

3. Conditions under which matrix design is appropriate.

a.

b.

c.

C. Multinational corporations attempt to balance

VII. NETWORK ORGANIZATION.

A. Network organization is

B. Key characteristics of a network organization are

1.

2.

3.

4.

          5.

          6.

          7.

          8.

     C.   External networking is done to establish

          1.   The six "I's" of creating successful partnership.

               a.

               b.

               c.

               d.

               e.

               f.

DIRECTED QUESTIONS

I.   Three Factors in Design.

     1.   Which of the following is a purpose of
          organization design:
          a)   To eliminate or reduce uncertainty;
          b)   To ensure that authority and responsibility   c
               are loosely defined so that managers can
               remain flexible in performing their tasks;
          c)   To help link together technology, tasks, and
               people;
          d)   All of the above.
     2.   Which of the following is <u>not</u> one of the key
          contingencies impacting organization design:
          a)   Division of labor;
          b)   Environmental forces;   a

    c)   Strategic choices;
    d)   Technological factors.

3.   A situation in which some uncertainty exists but managers can assign probabilities to the effects of various alternatives would be an example of:
    a)   Homogeneous/stable environment;
    b)   Heterogenous/stable environment;   b
    c)   Homogeneous/unstable environment;
    d)   Heterogeneous/unstable environment.

4.   A situation in which standardized rules and procedures are insufficient for handling the numerous uncertainties that exist would be a:
    a)   Homogenous/stable environment;
    b)   Heterogeneous/stable environment;   d
    c)   Homogenous/unstable environment;
    d)   Heterogenous/unstable environment.

5.   The strategic choice between centralization and decentralization:
    a)   Affects resource allocation to support units;
    b)   Will affect the number of levels in the   d
        hierarchy;
    c)   Is partly a matter of philosophy;
    d)   All of the above;
    e)   None of the above.

6.   Technological factors influence organization design:
    a)   As work-flow and task uncertainties and task interdependencies vary;
    b)   In terms of delegation of authority and   d
        responsibility to departments;
    c)   In terms of the need for formal integrating mechanisms among departments;
    d)   All of the above;
    e)   None of the above.

7.   Work-flow and task uncertainty:
    a)   Can be regulated by the way in which organizational units are designed;
    b)   Allow more departmental discretion when low;   a
    c)   Must be minimized if organizations are to be managed effectively;
    d)   None of the above.

8.   Which of the following exists where each department is relatively autonomous and makes discrete contributions to the organization as a whole:
    a)   Reciprocal interdependence;
    b)   Pooled interdependence;   b
    c)   Absence of interdependence;
    d)   Sequential interdependence.

9.   Which of the following exists where outputs from one department become inputs for another department, and vice versa:

a) Reciprocal interdependence;
b) Pooled interdependence;   a
c) Absence of interdependence;
d) Sequential interdependence.

II. Mechanistic vs. Organic Systems.

1. Which of the following is <u>not</u> a characteristic of bureaucracy:
   a) The absence of hierarchy;
   b) Formally established body of rules;   a
   c) Impersonality;
   d) Career ladders.

2. Which of the following is <u>not</u> a characteristic of a mechanistic system:
   a) Emphasis on the technical competence of individuals, rather than on their position in the hierarchy;
   b) Most effective when the environment is   a
      homogeneous/stable;
   c) Most effective when task and work-flow uncertainties are low;
   d) Generalization of decision making.

3. Which of the following is a characteristic of an organic system:
   a) Permits greater flexibility in coping with uncertainties;
   b) Most effective when the environment is   a
      homogeneous/stable;
   c) Narrowly defined job responsibilities;
   d) Routine technology.

4. Hierarchy of authority:
   a) Means that all major decisions are made at the top levels;
   b) Is found in mechanistic systems but not in d
      organic systems;
   c) Is found as organic systems but not in mechanistic systems;
   d) Specifies the decisions that can be made by employees at each level in the organization.

5. Division of labor:
   a) Is necessary to achieve organizational goals;
   b) Can become counterproductive;   d
   c) Is likely to be more "controlled" in organic systems;
   d) All of the above;
   e) None of the above.

6. Rules:
   a) Are established in organic systems whenever possible;

b)   Are established in mechanistic systems only
     when necessary;   c
c)   Specify acceptable and unacceptable behaviors
     and decisions;
d)   All of the above.
7.   Impersonality:
     a)   Is more characteristic of organic than of
          mechanistic systems;
     b)   Means that individual characteristics are   b
          minimized in decision making;
     c)   Is absent in organic systems, as only personal
          factors are considered in such systems;
     d)   All of the above;
     e)   None of the above.

III. Interdepartmental Relations.

   1.   The extent to which an organization's departments
        vary in structure, people orientations, time
        horizon orientations, and uncertainty is known as:
        a)   Line and staff separation;
        b)   Integration;   c
        c)   Differentiation;
        d)   Departmentalization.
   2.   The degree of cooperation and mutuality among
        departments is known as:
        a)   Line and staff separation;
        b)   Integration;   b
        c)   Differentiation;
        d)   Departmentalization.
   3.   The amount of thinking time necessary in a
        department before trying to implement solutions
        is one factor to consider in assessing which of
        the following:
        a)   Bureaucracy;
        b)   Differentiation;   c
        c)   Uncertainty;
        d)   Differentiation.
   4.   Which of the following statements is true
        regarding the relationship between organization
        design and management:
        a)   Department management is easiest when
             departments are virtually independent of each
             other;
        b)   Increases in uncertainty, differentiation,   a
             and desired integration should be accompanied
             by decreases in the formal mechanisms applied
             to obtain integration;

    c)   Resources required to manage an organization
        are greatest when there is low uncertainty, low
        differentiation, and low required integration;
    d)   All of the above.

IV.   Functional Departmentalization.

1.   Positions and departments are created on the
basis of specialized activities under a:
    a)   Matrix structure;
    b)   Product structure;   c
    c)   Functional structure;
    d)   Mechanistic structure.

2.   Activities that directly affect the principal
work flow in an organization are:
    a)   Staff functions;
    b)   Chain of command activities;   c
    c)   Line functions;
    d)   Span of control activities.

3.   Which of the following is the optimum span of
control:
    a)   5-7;
    b)   8-12;   d
    c)   12-15;
    d)   None of the above.

4.   Authority and responsibility arranged
hierarchically is known as:
    a)   Span of control;
    b)   Unity of command;   c
    c)   Scalar chain of command;
    d)   Matrix structure.

5.   Which of the following is <u>not</u> an advantage of the
functional structure form of organization:
    a)   Promotes skill specialization;
    b)   Encourages short time horizons;   b
    c)   Reduces duplication of scarce resources;
    d)   Enhances career advancement for specialists.

6.   The functional structure:
    a)   Can be effective in any external environment
        as long as range of products, geographic areas
        served, and customer types served are narrow;
    b)   May encourage limited points of view;   d
    c)   Permits clear assignments and identification
        of responsibilities;
    d)   All of the above;
    e)   None of the above.

V.   Product Departmentalization.

   1.   The product structure:
        a)   Has relatively self-contained units;
        b)   Increases the use of pooled interdependence;   d
        c)   Is attractive when each product environment
             is heterogeneous/unstable;
        d)   All of the above;
        e)   None of the above.
   2.   Organizations that adopt the product structure:
        a)   Usually begin with the functional structure;
        b)   Usually retain something of the functional   d
             structure within each product unit;
        c)   Are responding to increasing growth,
             complexity, and change;
        d)   All of the above;
        e)   None of the above.
   3.   Which of the following is not an advantage of the
        product structure:
        a)   Increased departmental cohesion;
        b)   Places multiple role demands on people;   b
        c)   Ensures accountability by department members;
        d)   Allows diversification and expansion of skills
             and training.
   4.   Some advantages of the product structure include:
        a)   Recognizes interdepartmental independence;
        b)   Uses skills and resources more efficiently;   a
        c)   Multiple role demands;
        d)   All of the above.
   5.   The multidivisional structure:
        a)   Is a variation of the functional structure;
        b)   Is used along with a matrix structure;   c
        c)   Is a variation of the product structure;
        d)   None of the above.

VI. Matrix Departmentalization.

   1.   A situation in which some employees report to two
        or more higher level managers:
        a)   Matrix structure;
        b)   Scalar hierarchy;   a
        c)   Line and staff organization;
        d)   Differentiation.
   2.   Matrix structure:
        a)   Usually involves both functional and product
             structures;
        b)   Uses dual authority, information, and   d
             reporting relationships and systems;
        c)   Has lower level managers who report to both
             functional and product managers;

     d) All of the above;
     e) None of the above.

3. Which of the following statements about a matrix structure is correct:
     a) It usually begins with the appointment of a project manager who is accountable for integrating activities and inputs;
     b) It rests on formal reward or position power;   c
     c) It involves much negotiation;
     d) All of the above;
     e) None of the above.

4. Which of the following is <u>not</u> a disadvantage of the matrix structure:
     a) It shifts emphasis back and forth between project and functional aspects of the organization;
     b) It increases role ambiguity and stress;   a
     c) It may reward political skills at the expense of technical skills;
     d) It makes inconsistent demands on employees.

5. The matrix structure is most likely to be effective when:
     a) Attention must be given to both functional and product line concerns;
     b) Managers face simple/stable environments;   a
     c) Resources are abundant;
     d) The time available for implementation is short.

VII. Network Organization.

1. Key characteristics of a network organization include <u>all but</u> one of the following:
     a) Distinctive competence;   c
     b) Goal setting;
     c) Vertical communication focus;
     d) Diverse information technologies.

2. The culture of a network organization is:
     a) Highly stable;
     b) Mechanistic;   c
     c) Open;
     d) Highly internally-oriented.

APPLIED QUESTIONS

I.   Factors Affecting Organization Design.

1.   Which of the following does <u>not</u> appear to be an
     example of a task environment relationship:
     a)   The marketing department and the customers;
     b)   The research/design department and the   c
          scientific community;
     c)   The personnel department and the raw materials
          suppliers;
     d)   The executive group and that group's
          counterparts in the outside business community.

2.   For which of the following is the complexity
     dimension likely to be lowest:
     a)   A research department;
     b)   A planning and forecasting department;   d
     c)   An assembly department;
     d)   A fast foods counter.

3.   Which of the following strategic courses results
     in least increases in complexity and dynamism:
     a)   Coors' decision to produce and market
          nationwide;
     b)   Coors' decision to retain major policy making   b
          and decisions in Colorado;
     c)   Coors' decision to try to appeal to wider
          range of types of consumers;
     d)   Coors' decision to challenge the national
          producers for higher market position.

4.   Two university classes in Labor Relations are
     engaged in a collective bargaining simulation,
     one as the union and one as management. This is
     an example of:
     a)   Pooled interdependence;
     b)   Sequential interdependence;   c
     c)   Reciprocal interdependence.

5.   In which of the following departments is work-flow
     uncertainty likely to be greatest:
     a)   Payroll;
     b)   Training;   d
     c)   Shipping;
     d)   President's office.

6.   Task uncertainty would be highest in which of the
     following situations:
     a)   Where people have not been adequately trained
          to do their job;
     b)   Where the amount of work which would be coming   d
          in could not be predicted far in advance;

c) Where the type of work which would be coming
   in could not be predicted far in advance;
d) Where experience, judgement, and intuition are more
   helpful than formally prescribed procedures.

II. Mechanistic and Organic Characteristics of Organizations.

1. Which of the following is most likely to be an
   organic system:
   a) U.S. Department of Labor;
   b) American Telephone and Telegraph Company;   d
   c) Boy Scouts of America;
   d) Smith's Grocery (of Muleshoe, Texas).
2. Which of the following would best describe an
   organization in which people with high technical
   competence have considerable amounts of influence
   regardless of their formal position:
   a) An organic system;
   b) A mechanistic system;   a
   c) A combination of organic and mechanistic
      systems;
   d) None of the above.
3. A university chooses one candidate over another
   for a job solely because the one has a Ph.D. and
   the other does not. This is an example of:
   a) Procedural specifications;
   b) Division of labor;   c
   c) Impersonality;
   d) Differentiation.

III. Interdepartmental Relations.

1. In which of the following is differentiation
   likely to be greatest:
   a) Research and sales departments;
   b) Research and production departments;   b
   c) Sales and production departments;
   d) Accounting departments.
2. In which of the following is the need for
   integration greatest:
   a) An organization with regional offices that are
      allowed to make their own decisions independent
      of each other;
   b) Between an organization's marketing, planning,   b
      and R&D departments;
   c) Between two plants of an organization where
      one produces parts for assembly at the second;
   d) The above all have approximately the same
      need for integration.

3. Which of the following is most likely to require greatest managerial skill and concentration:
    a) An organization has established a new department to forecast product demand fluctuations that may occur because of technological change;
    b) A firm has re-organized so that each geographical area is in effect a separate corporation;   c
    c) All departments in the organization are loosely structured;
    d) Planning periods for all units in the organization have been revised from 10-year to 5-year periods.

IV. Bases for Departmentalization.

1. A matrix structure violates which of the following:
    a) Span of control;
    b) Departmentalization;   d
    c) Line and staff organization;
    d) Unity of command.
2. A firm is involved in providing a large number of services throughout the United States. Which of the following would probably be the <u>least</u> appropriate organization structure:
    a) Functional;
    b) Product;   a
    c) Matrix;
    d) The above are equally appropriate.
3. For which of the following would the span of control likely be greatest:
    a) An assembly line;
    b) A group of vice-presidents;   a
    c) A team of research scientists;
    d) A group of regional managers.
4. Which of the following problems would the product structure most effectively address:
    a) Need to promote skill specialization;
    b) Need to reduce duplication of scarce resources;   c
    c) Need to diversify and expand skills;
    d) Need to expose specialists to others within the same specialty.
5. A manager with a low level of skill in negotiating and bargaining would be best in which structure:
    a) Functional;
    b) Product;   a
    c) Matrix.

6. A manager who is likely to feel stress in
    conditions of ambiguity would probably have <u>least</u>
    success in which structure:
    a) Functional;
    b) Product;   c
    c) Matrix.

7. An organization that has just determined to get
    "closer to its customers" for the wide range of
    products it produces is appropriate for:
    a) Product structure;   b
    b) Network organization;
    c) Functional structure;
    d) Matrix structure.

PROGRAMMED STUDY SUPPLEMENT

1. The management process of diagnosing and   organiza-
    selecting the structure and formal system of   tion
    communication, authority, and responsibility   design
    aimed at achieving an organization's goals
    is called _____.

---

2. The _____ implies a specification of   hierarchy
    the decisions that can be made by employees   of auth-
    who occupy positions at each level in an   ority
    organization.

---

3. The _____ is a design for managing   network
    complex relationships between people and   organiza-
    departments, divisions, or external entities.   tion

---

4. A mechanistic system is essentially the same   bureauc-
    as a _____.   racy

---

5. A _____ exists when positions and   functional
    departments are created on the basis of   departmen-
    specialized activities.   talization

---

6. As the range of products and services produced   product
    by an organization increases, it becomes more   departmen-
    likely that a _____ will be adopted.   talization

7.   External groups and forces with which the   task
     organization has direct contact and   environ-
     transactions make up its _____.   ment

---

8.   _____ prevails when all major   centrali-
     decisions are made only at the top levels of   zation
     the organization.

---

9.   Support activities which provide service and   staff
     advice to line departments are known as   functions
     _____.

---

10. A(n) _____ uses low-to-moderate   organic
     levels of formal rules and regulations,   system
     decentralized and shared decision making,
     broadly defined job responsibilities, and a
     flexible authority structure with few levels
     in the hierarchy.

---

11. Collaboration and mutual understanding between   integra-
     departments is referred to as _____.   tion

---

12. In a _____, authority and   scalar
     responsibility are arranged hierarchically.   chain of
                                                         command

---

13. Interdepartmental variation in structure   differen-
     levels, time horizon orientation, task   tiation
     environment certainty, and control of people
     is known as _____.

---

14. The various ways of dividing up tasks and   division
     labor to achieve desired goals is called   of labor
     _____.

---

15. Extensive formal rules and regulations,   mechanis-
     centralization of decision making, narrowly   tic
     defined job responsibilities, and rigid   system
     hierarchy of authority are characteristic of
     a(n) _____.

16. _____ is a measure of the extent to which organizations treat members and outsiders without regard to individual characteristics.

impersonality

---

17. _____ refers to the number of people supervised by a manager.

span of control

---

18. _____ are those activities which directly affect principal work-flow in an organization.

line functions

---

19. An organization's formal written statements specifying acceptable and unacceptable behaviors and decisions are its _____.

rules

---

20. The _____ organizes tasks into divisions on the basis of the product or or geographic markets.

multidivisional structure

---

21. The number and similarity of factors in an organization's environment constitute the _____ with which it is faced.

complexity dimension

---

22. The principle that no subordinate should receive orders from more than one supervisor is known as _____.

unity of command

---

23. The predetermined sequence of steps that employees and departments must follow are called _____.

procedures

---

24. The _____ relates to the extent to which the factors in an organization's environment change over time.

dynamism dimension

---

25. A _____ uses dual authority, information, and reporting relationships and systems.

matrix departmentalization

26. The _____ typically often finds itself having to maintain a three-way consideration of organizational perspectives and capabilities among products, functions, and geographic areas.

multi-national corpora-tion

---

27. _____ is a design with relatively self-contained units, each developing, producing, and marketing its own goods and services.

product departmen-talization

---

28. _____ involves the establishment of organization units according to geographic areas.

place departmen-talization

---

29. _____ is what is missing and is needed in order to make sound decisions and perform tasks effectively.

uncertain-ty

CHAPTER 19

ORGANIZATIONAL DECISION MAKING

LEARNING OBJECTIVES

When you read and when you review Chapter 19, keep in mind the learning objectives which have been established by the authors. Look them over first as a guide to picking out the most important parts of the chapter, and then think about them as you are going through the chapter. When you have finished the chapter, ask yourself whether you have met the objectives.

The authors intend that when you have finished studying this chapter you should be able to:

* Discuss the core questions in ethical decision making.
* Outline three basic models of organizational decision making.
* Describe the phases of managerial decision making.
* Explain the human biases in information processing.
* Describe three methods for stimulating creativity in organizational decision making.

CHAPTER OUTLINE

After you have read the chapter, complete the following outline.

I.   ETHICAL DECISION MAKING.

   A.   Ethics deals with

   B.   Ethical intensity is

      1.   It is determined by

         a.

         b.

         c.

         d.

         e.

         f.

   C.   Decision principles.

      1.   The distributive justice principle is

      2.   Suggestions for integrating ethical decision making
           into an organization include

         a.

         b.

c.

d.

e.

f.

D. Who is affected by the ethical aspect of decision making?

  1. Employment-at-will means

    a. Common management errors in the termination process are

      (1)

      (2)

E. Benefits and costs of decisions.

  1. Values are

  2. Utilitarianism is

F. Employee rights.

  1. Employee responsibilities and rights issues.

    a.

        b.

        c.

    2.   Privacy rights are important in

        a.

        b.

        c.

        d.

II.   DECISION MAKING MODELS.

    A.   The rational model assumes

        1.

        2.

        3.

    B.   The bounded rationality model.

        1.   Reflects individuals' tendencies to

            a.

            b.

            c.

        2.   Makes what assumption regarding complete
             information?

        3.   Satisficing is

    C.   The political model is based on the idea that

1.   Decisions are a result of

    a.

    b.

2.   Decision principles include:

    a.   Hedonistic principle:

    b.   Market principle:

    c.   Conventionalist principle:

    d.   Might-equals-right principle:

III. PHASES OF MANAGERIAL DECISION MAKING.

    A.   Problem recognition.

        1.   Impact of structure of problem recognition.

            a.   With structured problems:

            b.   With unstructured problems:

        2.   Conditions increasing the likelihood of incorrect
             problem recognition and formulation.

            a.

            b.

            c.

            d.

  e.

  f.

  g.

B. Problem interpretation is

  1. Inattention may result from

    a.

    b.

    c.

  2. Factors contributing to ineffective problem
      interpretation.

    a.

    b.

    c.

  3. Information processing biases.

    a.

    b.

    c.

    d.

    e.

4.   Organizational learning is

C.   Attention to problems tends to result from

1.

2.

3.

D.   Courses of action.

1.   A quick-action process is appropriate when

a.

b.

c.

2.   A convoluted-action process is appropriate when

a.

b.

c.

d.

E.   What takes place during the aftermath of a decision?

1.   Escalating commitment is

a. One explanation for escalating commitment is

IV. STIMULATING ORGANIZATIONAL CREATIVITY.

A. Organizational creativity is

1. Organizational innovation is

B. Lateral thinking method.

1. What is the difference between lateral thinking and
vertical thinking?

2. Lateral thinking involves techniques for

a.

b.

c.

3. The reversal technique is

4. Cross-fertilization involves

5. An analogy is

6. Random word stimulation is

C. Devil's advocate method is

1. Its basic purpose is

D. Artificial intelligence is

1. Experts systems are

DIRECTED QUESTIONS

I. Ethical Decision Making.

1. Which of the following is <u>not</u> an area in
    which ethical dilemmas are likely to arise:
    a) Managing human resources processes;
    b) Managing external stakeholders;   d
    c) Managing your own personal career;
    d) All are areas of potential ethical dilemma;
    e) None are areas of potential ethical dilemma.
2. Which of the following is a true statement
    regarding ethical decision making:
    a) The more you can keep the identity of those
        affected in general rather than specific
        terms, the more likely an ethical decision;
    b) The more you assume the values of others to be   e
        the same as yours, the more likely an ethical
        decision;
    c) Utilitarianism is not concerned with the
        ethical outcome of a decision;
    d) All are true;
    e) None are true.
3. The distributive justice principle means that:
    a) Everyone should be treated alike;
    b) Different treatment of individuals should   b
        not be based on arbitrarily defined
        characteristics;

   c)   Both a and b;
   d)   Neither a nor b.
4. The degree of importance given to an issue-related
   moral imperative is:
   a)   Utilitarianism;
   b)   Ethical intensity;   b
   c)   Bounded rationality;
   d)   Moral imperative.
5. The feeling of nearness that a decision maker has
   for those affected by a decision is known as the:
   a)   Proximity of the issue;
   b)   Temporal immediacy of the issue;   a
   c)   Social consensus of the issue;
   d)   Probability of effect of the issue.
6. The length of time between the present and the
   start of the consequences of an issue is:
   a)   Proximity of the issue;
   b)   Temporal immediacy of the issue;   b
   c)   Social consensus of the issue;
   d)   Probability of effect of the issue.
7. According to the authors, what management error
   can be found to underlie a significant number of
   terminations that wind up in court:
   a)   Being unclear about actual reasons for
        terminating someone;   d
   b)   Failure to understand employee's perspective
        of "fairness";
   c)   Unawareness of law;
   d)   a and b.
8. Determination of whether the good in an action
   outweighs the bad is:
   a)   Categorical imperative principle;
   b)   Conventionalist principle;   c
   c)   Utilitarian principle;
   d)   Disclosure principle.
9. Examples of issues of privacy rights include:
   a)   Genetic testing;
   b)   Honesty testing;   d
   c)   Drug testing;
   d)   All of the above;
   e)   None of the above.

II. Decision Making Models.

   1. Which decision making model is based on the idea
      that the outcomes of decision making are
      alternatives that have been intentionally chosen
      to bring maximum benefits:

    a)   Rational model;

    b)   Bounded rationality model;   a

    c)   Political model.

2. Which decision making model is based on the idea that organizational decisions reflect individuals' desires to satisfy their own interests:

    a)   Rational model;

    b)   Bounded rationality model;   c

    c)   Political model.

3. Which decision making model suggests that individuals engage in satisficing behavior:

    a)   Rational model;

    b)   Bounded rationality model;   b

    c)   Political model.

4. Satisficing is part of which decision making model:

    a)   Political;

    b)   Rational;   c

    c)   Bounded rationality.

5. Limited search is part of which decision making model:

    a)   Political;

    b)   Rational;   c

    c)   Bounded rationality.

6. Which decision making model draws from the hedonistic, the market, the conventionalist, and the might-makes-right principles:

    a)   Political;

    b)   Rational;   a

    c)   Bounded rationality.

III. Phases of Managerial Decision Making.

1. Managerial decision-making:

    a)   Is an orderly process beginning with recognizing a problem and concluding with evaluating the outcomes of actions to resolve it;

    b)   Requires the ability to shift from one subject   b

         or problem to another;

    c)   Is generally a simple process;

    d)   All of the above.

2. Problem recognition:

    a)   Is more difficult when problems are structured;

    b)   Is more difficult when problems are

         unstructured;   b

    c)   Will result in problem solution;

    d)   Is independent of managers' previous decisions and experiences.

3. Problem interpretation:
   a) Results in attention being given to the problem;
   b) Prioritizes problems;   b
   c) Is a direct outcome of the availability of objective information;
   d) All of the above;
   e) None of the above.

4. Factors affecting problem interpretation include:
   a) Preconceptions;
   b) Filtering;   d
   c) Defensiveness;
   d) All of the above.

5. Specialization affects problem interpretation in which of the following ways:
   a) It may lead to conflict between specialties;
   b) Corrective action is more likely when goals   d
      are unmet;
   c) New information may go unrecognized if it's not clearly within an area of specialization;
   d) All of the above;
   e) None of the above.

6. Organizational learning:
   a) Involves knowledge about action-outcome relationships;
   b) Is the way in which organizational members   a
      learn about the culture of their organization;
   c) Is a result of problem recognition;
   d) Is a result of problem interpretation.

7. Which of the following statements is not correct regarding prioritization of attention to problems:
   a) Prioritization ensures that all problems are dealt with in the desired time frame;
   b) Prioritization is likely to go to those   a
      problems supported by strong pressure from above;
   c) Prioritization is likely to go to those problems supported by the resources necessary to take action;
   d) None of the above are incorrect.

8. A convoluted action process is appropriate when:
   a) The problem is structured;
   b) A single manager has clear authority and   e
      responsibility;
   c) The search for information and alternatives is limited;
   d) All of the above;
   e) None of the above.

9. A quick action process:

    a) Involves tradeoffs and negotiations;

    b) Involves conflicts and political processes;   c

    c) Is appropriate for many more problems than is a convoluted action process;

    d) All of the above;

    e) None of the above.

10. Resolution of unstructured problems:

    a) Can be evaluated by objective measures;

    b) Require actions in the face of risk and   b
        uncertainty;

    c) Can be evaluated soon after a course of action is implemented;

    d) All of the above.

11. Intuition:

    a) Is a result of creativity;

    b) Consists of hunches, insights, thoughts that   b
        spontaneously surface to conscious awareness;

    c) Requires a period of elaboration;

    d) All of the above.

12. Creativity:

    a) Is a less involved process than intuition;

    b) Results in intuition;   c

    c) Requires an incubation phase;

    d) All of the above.

13. Conditions that can increase the likelihood of incorrect problem recognition include which of the following:

    a) Plenty of time is available;

    b) A high quality decision is sought;   d

    c) The problem is a new, unfamiliar one;

    d) Emotions are high.

14. Which of the following might lead to escalating commitment:

    a) Not wanting to admit an error;

    b) Feeling responsible for a negative outcome;   d

    c) A rigid belief in consistency;

    d) All of the above;

    e) None of the above.

15. Which bias exists when vivid, direct experience dominates abstract information:

    a) Selective perception;   b

    b) Concrete information;

    c) Law of small numbers;

    d) Gambler's fallacy.

16. Which bias exists when what people expect to see influences what they do see:

    a) Selective perception;   a

    b) Concrete information;

    c) Law of small numbers;
    d) Gambler's fallacy.

IV. Stimulating Organizational Creativity.

    1. Which of the following is defined as the production
        ideas that are novel and useful to the organization:
        a) Organizational creativity;
        b) Organizational innovation;   a
        c) Lateral thinking;
        d) Reversal;
        e) None of the above.
    2. Which of the following is defined as the logical
        step-by-step process where ideas are developed by
        proceeding on a continuous path from one bit of
        information to another:
        a) Organizational creativity;
        b) Organizational innovation;   e
        c) Lateral thinking;
        d) Reversal;
        e) None of the above.
    3. Which of the following is a statement about how
        objects, persons, or situations are similar to
        one another:
        a) Reversal;   c
        b) Cross-fertilization;
        c) Analogy;
        d) Random word stimulation;
        e) None of the above.
    4. Which of the following involves asking experts from
        other fields how they see the problem from the
        perspective of their own fields:
        a) Reversal;   b
        b) Cross-fertilization;
        c) Analogy;
        d) Random word stimulation;
        e) None of the above.
    5. Which of the following is a method used to point
        out weaknesses in the assumptions underlying a
        proposal, internal inconsistencies in it, and
        problems that could lead to failure if it were
        followed:
        a) Reversal;   e
        b) Cross-fertilization;
        c) Analogy;
        d) Random word stimulation;
        e) None of the above.

6. Which of the following is that subset of artificial intelligence that attempts to achieve high level results in solving problems through computer programs designed to imitate intelligent behavior:
    a)   Reversal;   e
    b)   Cross-fertilization;
    c)   Analogy;
    d)   Random word stimulation;
    e)   None of the above.

APPLIED QUESTIONS

I. Ethical Decision Making.

1. Which of the following is true with respect to ethical decision making:
    a)   Since our laws are meant to ensure ethical behavior, the organization that does not violate the law is behaving ethically;
    b)   A decision that is bound to harm someone,   d
         whichever way it goes, cannot be ethical;
    c)   The 1963 Equal Pay Act is an example of utilitarianism;
    d)   If our two sets of values are different we may legitimately have different interpretations of what behavior is ethical;
    e)   All of the above.
2. Which of the following is <u>not</u> an issue of ethics:
    a)   The specification of the parties' rights in a labor contract;
    b)   Mandatory drug testing in the workplace;   d
    c)   Fair employment regulations;
    d)   All are ethical issues;
    e)   None are ethical issues.
3. The authors provide a list of the major ethical issues facing U.S. business, in rank order of the importance of those issues. This list, then, pertains to:
    a)   Distributive justice;   d
    b)   Moral strength;
    c)   Utilitarianism;
    d)   Ethical intensity.
4. Our concern over who should be laid off in a budget cut at the company where we work is greater than our concern over who should be laid off in a cutback that occurs at a company in another state.

That is known as:
a) The proximity of an ethical issue;
b) The temporal immediacy of an ethical issue;
c) The concentration of effect;
d) None of the above.

a

5. Comparable worth cases rest on:
a) The principle of distributive justice;
b) The temporal immediacy of an issue;
c) The probability of effect of a decision;
d) None of the above.

a

6. Which of the following is most closely related to whistle blowing:
a) Disclosure principle;
b) Conventionalist principle;
c) Means-end principle;
d) Golden rule principle.

c

II. Decision Making Models.

1. A manager must decide on which of piece of equipment to purchase. She buys the first one that she finds that meets the minimum criteria of the engineering specifications. This decision has the features of which model:
a) Rational model;
b) Bounded rationality model;
c) Political model.

b

2. A conference is held to discuss a company-wide project that is underway. There is little progress underway because managers remain locked into what they have done in past, rather than pursuing solutions in new areas. This has features of which model:
a) Rational model;
b) Bounded rationality model;
c) Political model.

b

3. "It is possible that with more time, more money, and more effort we could have done better, but we can live with this." The foregoing statement refers to which decision model:
a) Rational model;
b) Bounded rationality model;
c) Political model.

b

4. "Do it to them before they can do it to you," refers to which decision model:
a) Rational model;
b) Bounded rationality model;
c) Political model.

c

III. Phases of Managerial Decision Making.

1. The fact that a manager may have to interrupt
    dealing with an <u>important</u> problem to respond to an
    <u>urgent</u> problem means that:
    a) Managerial decision making cannot be
        systematically analyzed;
    b) Attempts to prioritize problems generally are   d
        not useful;
    c) The flow of managerial work generally has no
        order;
    d) Managers must have the ability to make frequent
        and sudden shifts in subject matter.

2. You receive a phone call saying that your employee
    who was to meet an important visitor at the airport
    did not show up. This is an example of a(n):
    a) Structured problem;
    b) Unstructured problem;   a
    c) Failure to attend to a problem;
    d) Convoluted action process.

3. In some cases, problems go by unnoticed for
    substantial periods of time, possibly because:
    a) There is incorrect interpretation to the
        problem;
    b) The problem gets insufficient attention;   c
    c) The problem is unstructured;
    d) The wrong course of action is taken.

4. In their book, <u>In Search of Excellence</u>, Peters and
    Waterman claim that the better managed
    organizations "stay close to the customer." This
    means that managers in these companies:
    a) Recognize structured problems better;
    b) Are active listeners who can interpret   b
        problems better;
    c) Devote more attention to problems;
    d) Are more willing to set courses of action.

5. The sharing of information, building of consensus,
    and participative decision making are the Japanese
    firm's ways of:
    a) Specialization;
    b) Organizational learning;   b
    c) Problem recognition;
    d) Taking action.

6. Which of the following problems would likely
    receive the <u>least</u> amount of your immediate time:
    a) Your boss tells you that you must coordinate
        the United Charity Drive so that it will be
        completed in two weeks;

   b)   You know that you need to devote more time to   **b**
training your employees if the overall level
of your departmental performance is to improve
substantially;

   c)   If you get to your boss before your co-workers,
you may be able to get that extra storage space
that has just been vacated;

   d)   Can't say from the above descriptions because
of the problems are of varying levels of
importance.

7. Which of the following is most likely to result in
a convoluted action process:

   a)   Teachers in a school district have finally
pressured the School Board to recognize that
even though economic times are bad,something
has to be done about teachers' salaries;

   b)   Teachers have convinced their School Board   **a**
that they will not return to work after the
upcoming Spring break if a new grievance
process is not developed;

   c)   The School Board has just learned that the
ceiling is likely to collapse in Room 331 of
the junior high school;

   d)   All of the above;

   e)   None of the above.

8. The aftermath phase is _least_ difficult when:

   a)   The problem was unstructured;

   b)   A quick action process was implemented;   **b**

   c)   Action took place in the face of risk and
uncertainty;

   d)   Both intended and unintended results have
occurred.

9. Brainstorming sessions base decision making on:

   a)   Intuition;

   b)   Quick action process;   **c**

   c)   Creativity;

   d)   Convoluted action process.

10. Which one of the following statements is most
likely to contribute to incorrect problem solving:

   a)   "I never saw that happen before."

   b)   "This has to be done just right."   **c**

   c)   "Here's the problem."

   d)   "Let me know when you get this figured out."

11. The basketball coach tells his team, "I know we're
falling behind, but this is the game plan we've
worked on all week and we're going to stick with
it." That is an example of:

   a)   Specialization;

   b)   Escalating commitment;   **b**

c)   Gambler's fallacy;
d)   Goal attributes.
12. "We hired a graduate of the local university a few
    years ago. She was terrible. We've decided never
    to hire anyone else from there." This is:
    a)   Availability bias;   b
    b)   Law of small numbers bias;
    c)   Recency bias;
    d)   Halo effect.

IV. Stimulating Organizational Creativity.

1.   "Let's brainstorm. Just get all ideas we can on
     the table. Then we'll refine, build, and go from
     there." This is:
     a)   Vertical thinking;   b
     b)   Lateral thinking;
     c)   Analogy;
     d)   Devil's advocate.
2.   "Mr. Frick will present his proposal on the design
     for the auditorium. Ms. Frack has read the
     proposal. Her job is to point out all the problems
     with it." This is:
     a)   Vertical thinking;   d
     b)   Lateral thinking;
     c)   Analogy;
     d)   Devil's advocate.

PROGRAMMED STUDY SUPPLEMENT

1.   _____ is a process and set of   manager-
     activities beginning with a recognition or   ial deci-
     awareness of problems and concluding with   sion mak-
     an assessment of the results of the actions.   ing

---

2.   The degree of importance given to an issue-   ethical
     related morale imperative is its _____.   intensity

---

3.   The _____ means that treating individuals   distribu-
     differently should not be based on arbitrarily   tive
     defined characteristics.   justice
                                                       principle

4.	Problems for which there is unclear or inadequate information are called _____.	unstructured problems
5.	_____ are the relatively permanent and deeply held desires of individuals and groups.	values
6.	The process of giving meaning and definition to problems is called _____.	problem interpretation
7.	Easy recall of events may lead to _____.	availability bias
8.	Problem recognition is straight-forward and relatively simple when there are _____.	structured problems
9.	What people expect to see may lead to _____.	selective perception bias
10.	_____ is the process by which knowledge about action-outcome relationships and the environment's effects on these relationships occurs.	organizational learning
11.	In _____ subordinates meet one-on-one with supervisors to set goals and plan actions.	individual focused MBO
12.	Vivid, direct experiences tend to dominate abstract information and may lead to _____.	concrete information bias
13.	If a few cases are incorrectly deemed representative of the larger population,	law of small numbers bias

14. The phase in which outcomes and consequences are evaluated is the _____ phase.

aftermath

15. _____ is a process of continuing or increasing the commitment of resources to a cause of action even though there is a substantial amount of feedback that indicates the action is wrong.

escalating commitment

16. The production of ideas that are novel and useful to the organization is _____.

organizational creativity

17. _____ is the implementation of creative and useful ideas.

organizational innovation

18. The _____ suggests that decision makers desire to be rational, but suffer from cognitive limitations, habits, and perceptual biases.

bounded rationality model

19. _____ means that decision makers look for a course of action that is "good enough" and meets a set of minimal requirements.

satisficing

20. According to the _____, decisions reflect individuals' desires to satisfy their own interests.

political model

21. The _____ of decision making means that the outcomes of decision making are alternatives that have been intentionally chosen to bring maximum benefits.

rational model

22. _____ has to do with ideas of right and wrong in the values and actions of individuals and the institutions of which they are a part.

ethics

23. _____ emphasizes the provision of the "greatest good for the greatest number" in judging the ethics of decision making.

    utilitarianism

24. The _____ proposes a deliberate process for generating new ideas through changes in typical logic patterns for processing and storing information.

    lateral thinking

25. _____ is the process where ideas are developed by proceeding on a continuous path from one bit of information to another.

    vertical thinking

26. Systematic critiques of recommended courses of action are the bases of the _____.

    devil's advocate method

27. Attempts to give computers and software human-like capabilities are the basis of _____.

    artificial intelligence

28. _____ follow specific sets of rules to reach conclusions.

    expert systems

29. The assumption that the right to fire is absolute (for the employer) and creates little cost to either party is the basis for _____.

    employment at will

30. Techniques to determine the existence of inherited genetic changes that might cause a predisposition to certain illness are called _____.

    genetic testing

31. When an unexpected number of similar chance events leads to the belief that a specific other event will occur, _____ exists.

    gambler's fallacy

CHAPTER 20

CAREER PLANNING AND DEVELOPMENT

LEARNING OBJECTIVES

When you read and when you review Chapter 20, keep in mind the learning objectives which have been established by the authors. Look them over first as a guide to picking out the most important parts of the chapter, and then think about them as you are going through the chapter. When you have finished the chapter, ask yourself whether you have met the objectives.

The authors intend that when you have finished studying this chapter, you should be able to:

* Describe the socialization process.
* Define career and describe its components.
* State the factors that influence a person's choices of career and occupation.
* Describe the four career stages that most people go through.
* Identify the central activities and career concerns associated with each career stage.
* Discuss the factors that affect career planning.
* List the problems facing dual-career couples and employees who have been outplaced.

CHAPTER OUTLINE

After you have read the chapter, complete the following outline.

I. ORGANIZATIONAL SOCIALIZATION.

    A. Organizational socialization is

    B. Major stages in the socialization process.

        1. Getting in.

            a. Anticipatory socialization is

            b. What is the purpose of a realistic job preview?

        2. Breaking in.

            a. What happens during the encounter stage?

                (1)

                (2)

            b. What is orientation?

                (1) What are the purposes of orientation programs?

                    (a)

                    (b)

3.   Settling in.

    a.   What happens during change and acquisition?

II.   CAREERS: CHANGES THROUGHOUT LIFE.

  A.   Concept of a career.

    1.   A career is

      a.   Assumptions underlying concept of a career.

        (1)

        (2)

        (3)

        (4)

    2.   Career development is

  B.   Matching organizational and individual needs.

    1.   What determines organizational needs?

    2.   What determines individual needs?

      a.   What is a career plan?

    3.   How does the matching processes determine organizational effectiveness?

    C.   Factors affecting organizational choice.

        1.   Personality factors are

            a:

            b:

        2.   Social background influences include

    D.   Individuals make organizational choices according to

III. CAREER STAGES.

    A.   A career stage is

    B.   Career movement within an organization.

        1.   Vertical career movement is

        2.   Horizontal career movement is

        3.   Inclusion movement is

    C.   Working-life career stages.

        1.   Establishment.

            a.   Challenges upon first entering an organization.

                (1)

                (2)

                (3)

b. Concerns of employees at the establishment stage.

(1)

(2)

(3)

c. Characteristics of successful employees at the establishment stage.

(1)

(2)

(3)

(4)

(5)

(6)

(7)

d. A mentor is

(1) How do employees pick mentors?

(a)

(b)

(c)

(2) What do mentors want in return?

(a)

(b)

(c)

(d)

(3)   How important is it to have a mentor?

2.   Advancement.

a.   Concerns of employees at the advancement stage.

(1)

(2)

(3)

b.   Characteristics of successful employees at the advancement stage.

(1)

(2)

(3)

(4)

(5)

(6)

c.   Golden handcuffs are

3.   Maintenance.

a.   Concerns of employees at the maintenance stage.

(1)

(2)

(3)

b.   Characteristics of successful employees at the maintenance stage.

(1)

(2)

(3)

(4)

(5)

(6)

c.   Paths within the maintenance stage.

(1)

(2)

(3)

(4)

d.   What is the "mid-life crisis"?

4.   Withdrawal.

a.   What is the "maverick" or "internal entrepreneur" role?

b.   Time and energy in this stage can be productively spent in

(1)

(2)

IV. CAREER PLANNING ISSUES.

    A. Effects of career planning.

        1. Typical components of a career planning program.

            a.

            b.

            c.

            d.

        2. What are the positive effects of career planning?

        3. What are the negative effects of career planning?

    B. Dual career couples.

        1. Sources of stress are

        2. Concern in the job selection process are

    C. Major success factors for working women include

        1.

        2.

3.

4.

5.

6.

D.   Outplacement services include

DIRECTED QUESTIONS

I.   Organizational Socialization: The Process of Joining Up.

1.   The "getting in" stage of socialization includes:
   a)   Anticipatory socialization;
   b)   The encounter stage;   a
   c)   Orientation;
   d)   Change and acquisition;
   e)   None of the above.

2.   Providing job applicants with an accurate
   description of the job they will perform is:
   a)   Anticipatory socialization;
   b)   The encounter stage;   e
   c)   Orientation;
   d)   Change and acquisition;
   e)   None of the above.

3.   Orientation occurs during which stage:
   a)   Getting in;
   b)   Breaking in;   b
   c)   Settling in.

4.   In which stage do individuals develop self-images
   and behaviors that are consistent with the culture
   of the organization:
   a)   Getting in;
   b)   Breaking in;   c
   c)   Settling in.

II.   Career: Changes Throughout Life.

1.   Which of the following is a true statement about
   career:

a) The concept of career refers to rapid
   advancement toward a successful career;
b) There are no absolute standards for evaluating   b
   careers;
c) A career consists of the sum total of all
   work for which the individual is paid;
d) None of the above.

2. Career consists of:
   a) Alternatives available to the individual;
   b) Individual choices among alternatives;   d
   c) Individual experiences stemming from choices
      made;
   d) All of the above.

3. Costs and benefits of career development:
   a) Are stable over time within each individual;
   b) Change within individuals over time but not   d
      within organizations;
   c) Change within organizations over time but not
      within individuals;
   d) Change in various ways over time, and both
      parties attempt to manage the fit.

4. Which of the following are matching processes that
   integrate organizational and individual needs:
   a) Recruitment, selection, and training;
   b) Career choice;   d
   c) Planning for staffing;
   d) All of the above.

5. Which of the following is true about matching
   individual and organizational needs:
   a) People's needs and organizations' needs change
      at different rates and thus matching tends not
      to occur;
   b) People's needs and organizations' needs change   c
      at approximately the same rates and thus
      matching is usually possible;
   c) Matching individual and organizational needs
      is complex but is part of what determines
      organizational effectiveness.

III. Career Choices.

1. Holland's theory of personality types:
   a) Is a theory of leadership;
   b) Attempts to predict career aspirations and   b
      choice;
   c) Says that career choice tends to shape one's
      interests;
   d) All of the above.

2. Which of the following personality types does
   Holland associate with the occupation of manager:

    a) Enterprising;
    b) Conventional;
    c) Realistic.

3. Which personality type does Holland say is affected by social background:
    a) Investigative;
    b) Artistic;
    c) Social;
    d) All of the above;
    e) None of the above.

4. Self-esteem influences vocational choice because:
    a) It includes a person's opinions of his/her own ability and overall worth;
    b) It is related to the value which others place on a chosen occupation;
    c) It is related to one's level of success on a job being performed;
    d) All of the above;
    e) None of the above.

5. An individual's interests:
    a) Are determined by his/her occupation;
    b) Tend to cause them to pursue careers that match those interests;
    c) Determine his/her personality;
    d) All of the above;
    e) None of the above.

6. The social background of an individual:
    a) Determines his/her personality type;
    b) Determines his/her interests;
    c) Provides socializing experience and practical constraints which influence career choices;
    d) All of the above.

7. Factors affecting organizational choice (by individuals) include:
    a) The availability of opportunities at any given time;
    b) The information about the available opportunities;
    c) The opinions and attitudes that individuals form about organizations;
    d) All of the above;
    e) None of the above.

IV. Career Stages.

1. A career stage in a person's life is characterized by developmental tasks, concerns, needs, values, and activities which are:
    a) Variable but predictable;
    b) Distinctive but unpredictable;

Answer key (right margin): a · e · d · b · c · d · c

c)   Distinctive and predictable;
d)   None of the above.

2.   Career movements within an organization are:
a)   Vertical;
b)   Horizontal;
c)   Movement toward the center;   d
d)   All of the above;
e)   None of the above.

3.   Vertical career movement:
a)   Stops early in the careers of some people;
b)   Is more limited in "flatter" organizations;   d
c)   May be related to inclusion;
d)   All of the above;
e)   None of the above.

4.   Horizontal career movements:
a)   Involve moving to the inner circle of an
      organization;
b)   Are related to one's knowledge, skills, or   b
      expertise in functional or technical areas;
c)   Are typically upward hierarchical moves;
d)   All of the above.

5.   Inclusion:
a)   Amounts to being "kicked upstairs";
b)   When it occurs, is the most obvious of career   c
      moves;
c)   Is related to the frequency at which one is
      consulted regarding important matters;
d)   All of the above.

6.   The career stage at which the primary relationship
      concern is the peer relationship is known as the:
a)   Advancement stage;
b)   Establishment stage;   a
c)   Withdrawal stage;
d)   Maintenance stage.

7.   The career stage at which the central activity
      concerns are helping, learning, and following
      directions is known as the:
a)   Advancement stage;
b)   Establishment stage;   b
c)   Withdrawal stage;
d)   Maintenance stage.

8.   The career stage at which the central activity
      concerns are training and developing others is
      known as the:
a)   Advancement stage;
b)   Establishment stage;   d
c)   Withdrawal stage;
d)   Maintenance stage.

9.   According to the authors, the career stage at
      which many managers can play an entrepreneurial
      role is the:

   a)   Advancement stage;
   b)   Establishment stage;
   c)   Withdrawal stage;
   d)   Maintenance stage.

c

10. Which of the following is <u>not</u> associated with the establishment career stage:
   a)   Employees must use both formal and informal channels of communication;
   b)   The employee needs to successfully complete routine tasks and to show some initiative;
   c)   The employee needs to establish a mentoring relationship with a supervisor;
   d)   Peer relationships are the most critical interpersonal relationships.

d

11. Which of the following is <u>not</u> associated with the advancement stage:
   a)   Feedback from superiors regarding one's performance is most critical;
   b)   Mid-life crisis is most likely;
   c)   Golden handcuffs are most likely to appear;
   d)   Peer relationships are the most critical interpersonal relationships.

b

12. The maintenance stage is the one in which:
   a)   An employee tends to become a star, a solid citizen, or deadwood;
   b)   Career plateauing may occur;
   c)   Special assignments and mentoring roles become important to those who receive them;
   d)   All of the above;
   e)   None of the above.

d

13. A career plateau means that:
   a)   An employee's performance will probably begin to deteriorate;
   b)   An employee has reached a point where the number of positions at higher levels reduces the probability of further promotions;
   c)   The employee has been labelled a decliner;
   d)   All of the above.

b

14. Mentors consider the following in picking employees to mentor:
   a)   Finding the person pleasant to be around;
   b)   Being impressed with the person's performance;
   c)   Being sought out by the employee;
   d)   All of the above;
   e)   a and b.

d

15. What do mentors seek in return for their efforts:
   a)   That the person work hard;
   b)   That the person be a loyal supporter;
   c)   Recognition for having served as a mentor;
   d)   Sense of accomplishment;
   e)   All of the above.

e

V.   Career Planning Issues.

    1. Career planning is the process of choosing:
        a) Occupations;
        b) Organizations;
        c) Career paths;   d
        d) All of the above;
        e) None of the above.
    2. Which of the following can be a negative effect
        of career planning:
        a) Supervisory roles are clarified;
        b) Career commitments are strengthened;
        c) Employee expectations are raised;   c
        d) None of the above.
    3. Which of the following activities typify those
        included in an organization's career planning
        program:
        a) Career counselling;
        b) Programs for employee self-help;
        c) Information about job opportunities;   d
        d) All of the above.
    4. According to the authors, career planning can
        raise employee expectations and therefore:
        a) Enhance performance;
        b) Strengthen career commitment;
        c) Increase employee anxiety;   d
        d) All of the above;
        e) None of the above.
    5. "Dual careers" means that:
        a) An individual has two careers progressing
            equally;
        b) An individual has made a career change and   c
            is now in his/her second career;
        c) Both the husband and the wife in a family have
            jobs outside the home;
        d) All of the above;
        e) None of the above.
    6. In which of the following family types is the
        woman most likely to work outside the home:
        a) Semi-traditional couple;
        b) Typical dual career couple;
        c) Egalitarian couple;   d
        d) All of the above;
        e) None of the above.
    7. More employers are moving into programs to relieve
        the child-care problems of their employees,
        because:
        a) The typical child-care center is run at a
            profit and management wants to share in that
            profit;

b) It is projected that nearly 4/5 of the
    employed women will at some time be pregnant
    during their work careers;   b

c) The salary reduction programs previously used
    are not working out;

d) All of the above;

e) None of the above.

8. Relocation problems:
    a) Are generally becoming more complex;

    b) Are tougher to deal with in the dual career   d
        household than in the traditional couple
        household;

    c) Require employers to know about labor market
        conditions in the occupation/industry/
        geographic area into which the spouse is
        contemplating moving;

    d) All of the above;

    e) None of the above.

9. Pressures felt by women advancing into managerial
    positions include:
    a) The job itself;

    b) Scarcity of role models or mentors;   d

    c) The stress of role reversal between home and the
        office;

    d) All of the above.

10. According to outplacement counsellors, job-losers
    who bounce back most quickly are those who:
    a) Take the first job they can find in order to
        get back on their feet;

    b) Define their skills as narrowly and precisely
        as possible so that they can be more specific   d
        in their job search;

    c) Accept the fact that joblessness produces
        emotional highs and lows;

    d) Take a realistic look at themselves and their
        financial condition;

    e) All of the above.

APPLIED QUESTIONS

I. Organizational Socialization: The Process of Joining Up.

    1. The ABC Company wanted the whole world to know what
        it is like to work there. They hoped that people
        who did not want to work in their sort of
        environment would simply not apply. This is an
        example of:

a)   Orientation;
b)   The encounter stage;   c
c)   Anticipatory socialization;
d)   All of the above;

2.   The new supervisor had been an outstanding engineer.
     Because of that, he had been promoted to a
     management position. It was the first time he had
     ever been faced with having to lead and motivate
     people. He was trying to learn how to do those
     things. This is an example of:
     a)   Orientation;
     b)   The encounter stage;   b
     c)   Anticipatory socialization;
     d)   All of the above;

3.   A firm has a 2-year management training program.
     At its completion, trainees are placed in
     supervisory jobs. Upon starting these jobs, people
     are entering what stage of socialization:
     a)   Getting in;
     b)   Breaking in;   c
     c)   Settling in.

II.   Careers: Changes Throughout Life.

1.   Which of the following fits the definition of a
     career:
     a)   John Akers' rise to CEO at IBM;
     b)   A young woman's three years' experience as   d
          counter clerk at a car rental agency and her
          unsuccessful attempts to land a more
          lucrative job;
     c)   A 45 year-old man has never been at one job
          more than 3 years, and his moves over time have
          been in unrelated fields, more often than not
          made without accompanying salary increases;
     d)   All of the above.
     e)   None of the above.

2.   Which of the following is <u>not</u> a career component:
     a)   The time a secretary spends each day putting
          her boss' correspondence on the word processor;
     b)   The time this secretary spends at home getting   d
          her family budget on a spread sheet on her own
          PC there;
     c)   The time this secretary spends going to word
          processing workshops;
     d)   All of the above are career components;
     e)   None of the above are career components.

3.   An individual knows that in order to advance to
     the next level of management he would have to show
     evidence of arriving at work an hour earlier than

he has become accustomed to, work until 6:30 or
7:00 p.m. several evenings each week, and be
available for Saturday work at late notice.   In
choosing not to do so, what has he done:
   a)   Made a cost-benefit analysis;
   b)   Made a decision which will result in him   a
        having no career;
   c)   Acted irrationally;
   d)   All of the above.
4.   Which of the following is an example of what an
     organization might do to match organizational and
     individual needs:
   a)   Pre-retirement planning programs in which the
        employee can participate;
   b)   Providing employees feedback regarding the   d
        quality of their performance;
   c)   Offering tuition refund programs to employees
        who wish to pursue either baccalaureate or
        advanced degrees;
   d)   All of the above;
   e)   None of the above.

III. Factors Influencing Career and Occupational Choices.

1.   According to Holland's theory, which of the
     following sets of interests is associated with the
     investigative personality type:
   a)   Science, math;
   b)   Computational skills, business systems;   a
   c)   Manual skills, mechanics;
   d)   All of the above.
2.   According to Holland, which of the following
     personality types is associated with the
     occupations CPA, statistician, administrative
     assistant:
   a)   Conventional;
   b)   Realistic;   a
   c)   Investigative;
   d)   Social.
3.   Emily's mother is a physician. Which of the
     following issues will potentially affect Emily's
     career and occupational choices:
   a)   A wide range of educational possibilities
        exist;
   b)   She will be tightly constrained by sex-role   a
        labelling;
   c)   A lack of information about possible career
        paths;
   d)   All of the above.

4. In deciding whether a certain company is one for which you would want to work, which of the following is <u>imperative</u> for you to know:
   a) The size of the organization;
   b) The size of the industry in which it exists;
   c) Your own career goals and plans;
   d) The jobs that your prospective supervisor has had with the organization.

   c

IV. Career Stages.

1. In which of the following would vertical movement likely be most limited:
   a) U.S. Army;
   b) Ford Motor Company;
   c) Family-owned grocery store;
   d) A city government's Department of Finance and Accounting.

   c

2. An individual in the personnel department at corporate headquarters of a large grocery chain is told that she cannot advance further without some line experience at the company's retail outlets, and so is assigned to one of those outlets as an assistant manager, but without a promotion. Which of the following kind of moves has just occurred:
   a) Vertical;
   b) Horizontal;
   c) Inclusion;
   d) Movement toward the center.

   b

3. Another name for that kind of move (in question 3, above) might be:
   a) Career plateau;
   b) Job rotation;
   c) Inclusion;
   d) None of the above.

   b

4. The president of a university selects 4 faculty members and 3 administrators to meet with him monthly for advice and counsel on policy matters. These individuals thus experience which of the following kinds of movement:
   a) Vertical;
   b) Horizontal;
   c) Inclusion;
   d) Job rotation.

   c

5. Barbara has just been given a stack of purchase orders that no one else has had the time (or patience) to process. She is upset at first, until she is assured that the division chief knows about this and has promised to "take care of her." What career stage does Barbara appear to be in:

   a)   Withdrawal;
   b)   Maintenance;   d
   c)   Advancement;
   d)   Establishment.
6. A manager has a job offer at a sizeable increase
    in pay. One factor that affects his decision is
    his concern that if he doesn't make this move, he
    may become "locked in" to his current employer.
    What career stage does this manager appear to be in:
    a)   Withdrawal;
    b)   Maintenance;   c
    c)   Advancement;
    d)   Establishment.
7. A manager has just been moved out of the office
    area where the bulk of the decision-making goes on.
    He has been put in charge of a special project to
    provide information to the physical facilities and
    space committee (but to date has not been asked for
    any information). What career stage does this
    manager appear to be in:
    a)   Withdrawal;
    b)   Maintenance;   b
    c)   Advancement;
    d)   Establishment.
8. Brad had a reasonably good promotion record until
    about two years ago. He has had no promotions
    since then, and he knows that he will not receive
    any more. Still, he gets good performance reviews
    and at least average increments of merit pay. He
    is convinced that his boss thinks he does a good
    job. What career stage does Brad appear to be in:
    a)   Withdrawal;
    b)   Maintenance;   b
    c)   Advancement;
    d)   Establishment.
9. The withdrawal career stage:
    a)   Begins for most people around age 50;
    b)   Is the time at which individuals no longer are   e
         involved in mentoring younger managers;
    c)   Is the time at which individuals cease their
         involvement in representing the company
         externally;
    d)   All of the above;
    e)   None of the above.
10. Mentors are evaluated upon the results of their
    mentoring. Which of the typical factors that
    offset who mentors choose will be the strongest:
    a)   Pleasantness;   b
    b)   Performance;
    c)   Being sought out by the employee;
    d)   All of the above.

IV. Career Planning Factors.

1. Which of the following is an example of career planning:
   a) An individual considers the relative attractiveness of a sales job vs. a job as a management trainee;
   b) An individual considers the relative attractiveness of working in a "clean" environment such as a bank vs. working in a "smokestack" industry environment;
   c) An individual considers whether the costs of pursuing a master's degree are worth it;
   d) All of the above.

   d

2. Which of the following is an accurate statement regarding career planning outcomes:
   a) Employee anxiety levels increase as they learn more about what is expected of them;
   b) Managing becomes more difficult because of the additional burden which career planning imposes on the manager;
   c) Employees have more and better information, enabling them to make better career decisions;
   d) All of the above.

   d

3. The couple where the wife has decided to work until they can save enough money for a down payment on their first home is termed a:
   a) Traditional couple;
   b) Semi-traditional couple;
   c) Typical couple with dual outside careers;
   d) Egalitarian couple.

   b

4. According to the authors, relocation problems experienced by dual career couples:
   a) Cause employers to do their best to avoid hiring a member of a dual career couple;
   b) Are given some relief when employers provide job assistance to a spouse;
   c) Occur in at least 50-60% of the cases;
   d) All of the above.

   b

5. With respect to the child-care concerns of dual career couples:
   a) 80% or more of employed women will be faced with these concerns;
   b) The vast majority of employers with day-care centers believe it has had a positive impact on recruitment;
   c) Some employers offer financial assistance in the form of salary-reduction programs;
   d) All of the above.

   d

6. Which of the following factors is reported to be the one which the largest percentage of managers see as important for the success of women as managers:
   a) Help from mentors;
   b) Ability to manage subordinates;   a
   c) Willingness to take career risks;
   d) Ability to be tough, demanding, decisive.

7. A top-level manager for a company says, "I'm doing something I never did before. I'm making an effort to keep up with the jobs available out there." This is becoming more common and is in part a reaction to:
   a) Increasing number of mergers and acquisitions;
   b) Increasing employee loyalty;   a
   c) More serious pre-retirement planning;
   d) Job rotation.

PROGRAMMED STUDY SUPPLEMENT

1.	The _____ is the career stage in which performance feedback becomes critical to feelings of success or failure, increased commitment to the organization occurs, and peer relationships take on great importance.	advancement career stage
2.	The sequence of work-related positions occupied by a person over a lifetime is known as a _____.	career
3.	_____ requires an individual to make decisions and engage in activities to attain career goals.	career development
4.	_____ is the process of accepting group beliefs and values before actually becoming	anticipatory socialization
5.	A stage at which one's career has "flattened out" and the likelihood of future promotion is very low is known as a _____.	career plateau

6.   A _____ is a period of time characterized by distinctive and predictable developmental tasks, concerns, needs, values, and activities.   career stage

7.   _____ is the term applied to people that have little chance for promotion and are just hanging on until retirement.   decliners

8.   The first portion of one's career is termed the _____.   establishment career stage

9.   _____ are used by some organizations to tie people into the organization at the advancement stage of their careers.   golden handcuffs

10.   _____ are based on the premise that a relationship exists between personality orientation and career choice.   Holland's personality types

11.   _____ sometimes takes the form of job rotation programs designed to groom people for eventual promotion.   horizontal career movement

12.   _____ brings an individual into the inner circle of the organization.   inclusion career movement

13.   During the _____, a person may take the path of the stars, the solid citizens, or the deadwood.   maintenance career stage

14.   In the establishment stage of one's career it is important to become associated with a _____.   mentor

15.   Failing to live up to one's career hopes and expectations can contribute to experiencing a _____.   mid-life crisis

16. A _____ provides job applicants with an accurate picture of the job they would be doing and the organization in which it exists.

    realistic job preview

17. _____ affects career choice by providing socialization experiences and practical constraints.

    social background

18. _____ are employees at a point in their career where they are reliable and do good work but have little chance for promotion.

    solid citizens

19. _____ are employees in the maintenance stage of their careers who have been picked by top managers to continue to receive promotions.

    stars

20. Opportunities for _____ are partially influenced by the number of hierarchical opportunities available.

    vertical career movement

21. The _____ is the time when managers may begin to play the role of maverick or entrepreneur.

    withdrawal career stage

22. _____ families experience problems of career integration, relocation decisions, and child-care arrangements.

    dual career

23. A _____ is the individual's choice of occupation, organization, and career path.

    career plan

24. _____ is a program that introduces new employees to their new situation.

    orientation

25. A period of time in one's work life characterized by distinctive and fairly predictable developmental tasks, concerns, needs, values, and activities is a _____.

    career stage

26. Organizations that assist laid-off managers   outplacement
     in career planning and job hunting are   firms
     called _____.

CHAPTER 21

NATURE OF PLANNED ORGANIZATIONAL CHANGE

LEARNING OBJECTIVES

When you read and when you review Chapter 21, keep in mind the learning objectives which have been established by the authors. Look them over first as a guide to picking out the most important parts of the chapter, and then think about them as you are going through the chapter. When you have finished the chapter, ask yourself whether you have met the objectives.

The authors intend that when you have finished studying this chapter you should be able to:

* Identify the goals of planned organizational change.
* Discuss the sources of pressures on organizations to change.
* Explain reasons for individual and organizational resistance to change.
* Diagnose the pressures for and resistance to change in a work setting.
* Provide suggestions for overcoming resistance to change.
* Describe some general models or approaches for organizational change.

CHAPTER OUTLINE

After you have read the chapter, complete the following outline.

I.   GOALS OF PLANNED CHANGE.

    A.

    B.

II. PRESSURES FOR CHANGE.

    A.   Globalization resulting from

        1.

        2.

        3.

        4.

    B.   Changing technology.

        1.   Information technology:

        2.   Virtual reality:

        3.   Rationalization:

        4.   Computer-integrated manufacturing:

    C.   Rapid product obsolescence.

        1.   What are the major impacts of rapid product
            obsolescence?

    D.   Changing nature of the workforce.

1. Changes in the U.S. workforce by 2000 will include

    a.

    b.

    c.

    d.

    e.

2. "Quality of work life" refers to

3. Changes in the global workforce by 2000 will include

    a.

    b.

    c.

III. RESISTANCE TO CHANGE.

    A. Individual resistance.

       1.

       2.

       3.

       4.

       5.

B. Organizational resistance.

1.

2.

3.

4.

5.

C. Overcoming resistance to change.

1. Force field analysis is

2. The equilibrium of current forces can be altered by

a.

b.

c.

3. Lewin's approach to changing behaviors consists of three steps.

a.

b.

c.

4. Successful methods for dealing with resistance to change often includes three features:

a.

b.

c.

D. A systems model of change involves affecting one or more
    of five interacting variables.

    1.

    2.

    3.

    4.

    5.

E. Innovation is

    1. Reasons suggested for the low rate of innovation in
        U.S. firms are

        a.

        b.

        c.

        d.

        e.

        f.

F. Action research is

    1. Three steps in action research.

a.

b.

c.

2. Strengths of an action research approach to change.

a.

b.

3. Advantages of employee involvement in change.

a.

b.

G. Organizational development is

1. The basic tenets of organizational development.

a.

b.

c.

d.

e.

DIRECTED QUESTIONS

I. Goals of Planned Change.

1. Which of the following statements regarding change is accurate:

a)   Unless change is properly planned, it does not
     occur;
b)   If change is not planned, organizations will   c
     change but people will not;
c)   Planned change is necessary because management
     cannot control its environment;
d)   Planned change is necessary so that management
     can control the environment.

2.   Planned organizational change occurs:
     a)   To improve organizational adaptability;
     b)   To change patterns of employee behaviors;   d
     c)   Because management cannot control its
          environment;
     d)   All of the above.

3.   Changing individual behaviors:
     a)   May not be important for organizations in the
          long run;
     b)   Is independent of changing an organization's   c
          adaptive strategies;
     c)   Should produce behaviors consistent with the
          demands of the organization's environment;
     d)   All of the above.

II. Pressures for Change.

     1.   Which of the following is <u>not</u> one of the major
          categories of pressures for change identified by
          the authors:
          a)   Individual security and regression;
          b)   Rapid product obsolescence;   a
          c)   Changing technology;
          d)   Globalization.

     2.   The use of robots in American industry is an
          example of:
          a)   The changing nature of the work force;
          b)   Individual resistance to change;   c
          c)   The results of one of the major pressures for
               change facing organizations;
          d)   None of the above.

     3.   Which of the following helps organizations adapt
          to rapid product obsolescence:
          a)   Longer production lead times;
          b)   Greater organizational stability and   c
               continuity;
          c)   Temporary organizational structures;
          d)   All of the above.

     4.   The changing nature of the work force has meant
          that:
          a)   There's likely to be less interorganizational
               mobility;

  b) There's likely to be more occupational
    mobility;
  c) Fewer major career changes will be undertaken
    by workers;
  d) All of the above.   b

5. The quality of an individual's work life involves
 or affects:
  a) The individual's well-being at work;
  b) The individual's productivity at work;   d
  c) The individual's productivity off the job;
  d) All of the above.

6. Managers in the future will need which of the
 following characteristics:
  a) Specialization in either the technical or the
    functional areas of their organizations;
  b) Greater focus on stability and consistency   e
    than on change;
  c) Less focus on interpersonal than on technical
    skills;
  d) All of the above;
  e) None of the above.

7. Which of the following is <u>not</u> one of the primary
 pressures to change that has been brought about by
 increased global competition:
  a) Emergence of newly industrialized countries;   d
  b) Germany and Japan's strong revitalization
    after World War II;
  c) Shift from planned to market economies;
  d) Breaking up of "power blocks" of international
    traders.

8. A display and control technology that surrounds the
 user with an artificial environment that mimics
 real life is:
  a) Virtual reality;
  b) Robotization;   a
  c) Artificial intelligence;
  d) CIM.

9. A system that uses computer networks linking sales,
 production, and shipping is:
  a) Virtual reality;
  b) Robotization;   d
  c) Artificial intelligence;
  d) CIM.

10. Which of the following is true regarding the
 changing nature of the work force:
  a) The labor force will grow at twice the rate to
    which we are accustomed;
  b) A lower percent of the labor force will be   c
    under 35 years of age;

c) A larger proportion of new workers will be
    members of minority groups;
d) All of the above;
e) b and c.

III. Resistance to Change.

1. Resistance to change:
    a) Should not occur if the change has been
        properly planned;
    b) Shows up in a relatively small number of   c
        forms, regardless of its origin;
    c) Can be expected to accompany the introduction
        of change;
    d) None of the above.
2. Which of the following is <u>not</u> a form of individual
    resistance to change:
    a) Habit;
    b) Selective perception;   c
    c) Fixed investment;
    d) Fear of the unknown.
3. Resistance to change which involves established
    organizational stability and altering continuity
    is which source of organizational resistance:
    a) Resource limitations;
    b) Organization structure;   b
    c) Fear of the unknown;
    d) None of the above.
4. Managers should:
    a) Anticipate the sources of resistance;
    b) Be able to identify the types of   d
        resistance;
    c) Learn how to overcome resistance;
    d) All of the above.
5. Any given situation tends to be:
    a) A function of the forces resisting change;
    b) A function of the forces pressuring for   c
        change;
    c) A combination of the above;
    d) None of the above.
6. To initiate change, managers should:
    a) Increase the strength of pressures for change;
    b) Decrease the strength of resistances to   e
        change;
    c) Alter a resistance into a pressure for change;
    d) Any or all of the above;
    e) None of the above.
7. The scheme developed by Kurt Lewin for looking at
    change is:
    a) Field survey method;
    b) Force field analysis;   b

      c)   Field experimentation;
      d)   Environmental field studies.
8. The first step in force field analysis is:
      a)   Taking steps to remove resistances;
      b)   Determining which resistances are most easily
          reduced or removed;
      c)   Identifying the pressures for and resistances
          to change;
      d)   Identifying the results of a change.

                  c

9. Reducing the forces maintaining the organization's
    current behavior is known as:
      a)   Moving;
      b)   Refreezing;
      c)   Unfreezing.

                  c

10. Successful methods for dealing with resistance to
    change often includes:
      a)   Empathy and support;
      b)   Communication;

                  d

      c)   Participation and movement;
      d)   All of the above;
      e)   b and c.

IV. Models and Processes for Organizational Change.

1. Problem-solving methods or techniques are
    considered by the systems model of change under
    the category:
      a)   Technology variables;
      b)   Task variables;
      c)   Structure variables;

                  a

      d)   People variables.

2. Communication, authority, and responsibility are
    considered by the systems model of change under
    the category:
      a)   Technology variables;
      b)   Task variables;
      c)   Structure variables;

                  c

      d)   People variables.

3. The task, technology, people, strategy and
    structure variables in the systems model of change
    usually appear in a change process in which of the
    following ways:
      a)   All five are present;
      b)   At least two are present;

                  a

      c)   At least one is present;
      d)   In some cases, none is present.

4. Which of the following statements is <u>not</u> true
    regarding action research:
      a)   It involves planning and carrying out
          activities to correct problems;

    b)   It is done largely without employee   b
        involvement or participation;
    c)   It involves extensive data gathering;
    d)   It resembles the "scientific method" of study.

5.   Which of the following is <u>not</u> one of the major
     values or advantages of the action research
     approach to change:
     a)   The steps in the action research sequence
        need be taken only once;
     b)   It involves employee participation;   a
     c)   It is based on careful diagnosis;

6.   Which of the following is a basic premise
     underlying organization development:
     a)   Greater objectivity in change direction by
        involving people in changes wherein they have
        no direct concern;
     b)   The need to change one part of the organiza-   e
        tion without changing any other parts of
        the organization;
     c)   Emphasis on long-run rather than short-run
        problems;
     d)   All of the above;
     e)   None of the above.

7.   Organization development:
     a)   Uses action research in most of its programs;
     b)   Generally involves system-wide changes;   d
     c)   Seeks to create self-directed change to which
        organizational members are committed;
     d)   All of the above;
     e)   None of the above.

8.   Reasons cited for inability to generate sufficient
     innovation in U.S. business include:
     a)   Overemphasis on long-run durability;
     b)   Overemphasis on investment;   d
     c)   Lack of rigid organizational structure;
     d)   Reward structures that punish creativity;
     e)   All of the above.

APPLIED QUESTIONS

I.   Goals of Planned Change.

    1.   Which of the following is the type of event for
       which planned organizational change is most
       necessary:
       a)   Import quotas are relaxed, allowing a larger
          volume of product in from foreign competition;
       b)   An employer decides to offer employees an   a
          opportunity to purchase company stock;

    c)   An employer installs in incentive plan in
        hopes raising production and thus profits;
    d)   All are equally related to planned organiza-
        tional change.

2. In which of the following is a rigid hierarchy
    most likely to cause problems:
    a)   Aerospace industry;
    b)   Retail industry;   a
    c)   Military;
    d)   Furniture manufacturing.

3. Which of the following is an organizational
    adaptive mechanism:
    a)   An abrupt swing in the labor market for
        scientists and engineers;
    b)   A new fair employment regulation;   d
    c)   A guideline as to the meaning or intent of a
        new product liability law;
    d)   Organizational culture.

II. Pressure for Change.

1. Increases in educational levels of managers:
    a)   Is necessary to enable them to manage under
        conditions of changing technology;
    b)   Is necessary to manage in light of
        globalization;   d
    c)   Is part of the changing nature of the work
        force;
    d)   All of the above;
    e)   None of the above.

2. Rapidly changing technology creates a set of
    conditions wherein middle managers:
    a)   May be unable to make decisions;
    b)   May have to deal creatively with more and more   b
        "unique" circumstances;
    c)   May become unnecessary;
    d)   May become more like skilled workers than
        managers.

3. Rapid product obsolescence:
    a)   Reduces the possibility for developing future
        managers and leaders;
    b)   Requires managers who are more willing and   b
        able to decentralize decision-making;
    c)   Requires managers who are better able to
        obtain and retain direct personal control over
        decision-making;
    d)   Requires better long-range planning.

4. Which of the following is most likely to become a
    pressure for change:
    a)   An increasing proportion of non-union
        manufacturing firms;

    b)   Uncertainty about whether a new job that has   a
        just been offered will be in existence next
        year;
    c)   Union members' belief that collective action
        is the best way to deal with employees;
    d)   None of the above suggest pressure for change.

5.   Management training of the future should emphasize
    which of the following:
    a)   Ways of helping workers cope with the most   b
        routine tasks;
    b)   Complex reasoning skills;
    c)   Highly specialized tasks;
    d)   All of the above.

III. Resistance to Change.

1.   Examples of overt resistance to change include:
    a)   Strikes;
    b)   Resignation;   a
    c)   Absenteeism;
    d)   All of the above.

2.   Examples of covert resistance to change include:
    a)   Tardiness;
    b)   Industrial sabotage;   a
    c)   Reduced productivity;
    d)   All of the above.

3.   Which source of resistance may be involved when a
    manager confronts a new idea by simply ignoring it:
    a)   Dependence;   b
    b)   Selective perception;
    c)   Economic reasons;
    d)   Interorganizational agreement.

4.   Which source of resistance may be involved when
    employees oppose a new "coffee break policy" which
    would ensure everyone a 20 minute break each half
    day but would require that everyone take breaks
    at the same time:
    a)   Habit;
    b)   Selective perception;   a
    c)   Fear of the unknown;
    d)   Economic reasons.

5.   An organization embarks on a new program to reward
    employees for taking initiative in an attempt to
    reduce employee apathy. Which source of resistance
    would be in effect if employees felt they needed
    their supervisor's approval before actually
    following through on this:
    a)   Economic reasons;
    b)   Habit;   c
    c)   Dependence;
    d)   None of the above.

6. Employee resistance to a new piece rate incentive
    plan may be due to:
    a) Economic reasons;
    b) Dependence;
    c) All of the above;
    d) None of the above.

    a

7. Organizational plans to increase employee
    participation in decision making are frequently
    met with resistance by some managers due to:
    a) Fixed investments;
    b) Interorganizational agreements;
    c) Threats to power and influence;
    d) Resource limitations.

    c

8. Which form of organization structure is most
    likely to contribute to resistance to change:
    a) Organic;
    b) Mechanistic;
    c) No noticeable difference between the two.

    b

9. A university has a group of senior professors
    who do an adequate job of teaching but thwart the
    school's attempts to introduce change. The
    school is faced with the problem of:
    a) Resource limitations;
    b) Organization structure resistance;
    c) Fixed investments;
    d) Interorganizational agreements.

    c

10. In order that the plant meet the quota set for
    it at corporate headquarters, each worker must
    increase productivity by approximately 10%. So
    far no one has responded at all. Management now
    reacts by posting a chart comparing what is
    required to what each individual is actually doing.
    This is an example of an attempt at:
    a) Unfreezing;
    b) Moving;
    c) Refreezing.

    a

11. An announcement has been made that the company is
    going to adopt a "leaner" management approach.
    After eliminating several management positions, a
    new organization chart is distributed, showing a
    "flatter" organization structure. This is an
    example of:
    a) Unfreezing;
    b) Moving;
    c) Refreezing.

    c

IV. Models and Processes for Organizational Change.

1. The employees resist a manager's attempt to change
    production methods at first. Then, the manager
    talks with each of them about the reasons behind

their resistance and assures them their fears are
unfounded. They admit that he has dealt with their
questions and thus support his plan. This manager
has engaged in:
   a)   Action research;
   b)   OD;
   c)   Refreezing;
   d)   Technological innovation.

    a

3. A manager calls her employees together for a
   session in which they are asked to identify the
   problems which they see in their part of the
   organization. They are told that the group's
   project will be to work toward changes which will
   address the problems they identify. They are
   involved in:
   a)   Action research;
   b)   OD;
   c)   Refreezing;
   d)   Technological innovation.

    b

3. An OD program attempts to increase the creative
   level of first-line supervisors and at the same
   time move middle managers to the point where they
   are not threatened by creative first-line
   supervisors. This is an example of the fact that:
   a)   OD is a system-wide change effort;
   b)   OD seeks to create self-directed changes;
   c)   OD emphasizes long-run change;
   d)   OD utilizes action research.

    a

PROGRAMMED STUDY SUPPLEMENT

1. A particularly powerful force for change
    occurs if the _____ comes from within
    the group rather than from outside.

    pressure
for
change

---

2. _____is a data-based, problem-solving
    process of organizational change that
    replicates the steps of the scientific
    method.

    action
research

---

3. _____examines the pressures for change,
    the resistance to change, and the equilibrium
    toward which these factors tend.

    force
field
analysis

4. The creation or adoption of new products,   innovation
    services, processes, or procedures by an
    organization is referred to as _____.

---

5. _____is the term applied to the change   refreezing
    management step which stabilizes an organiza-
    tion at a new state of equilibrium.

---

6. _____refers to a set of activities   planned
    and processes designed to change individuals,   organiza-
    groups, and organization structure and   tional
    processes.   change

---

7. The complex networks of computers, tele-   informa-
    communications systems, and remote-controlled   tion
    devices in today's organizations is known as   systems
    _____.   technology

---

8. _____ comes from both the nature of   resistance
    individuals and the nature of organizations,   to change
    and can never be expected to disappear
    totally.

---

9. In change management, the shifting of behavior   moving
    is called _____.

---

10. In the systems model of change, the _____   task-
    refers to the job, the _____ to the   variable;
    workers, the _____ to the organization,   people
    and the _____ to the problem-solving   variable;
    techniques or methods.   structure
                                                       variable;
                                                       technology
                                                       variable

---

11. The _____ is the degree to which members   quality
    of an organization are able to satisfy   of work
    important personal needs through their work   life
    experiences in the organization.

---

12. The step in change management which involves   unfreezing
    involves reducing the forces maintaining
    the status quo is called _____.

13. Formerly seen in science fiction only, _____ are now being used in the workplace and are impacting employment levels and the nature of managerial work.

robots

14. _____ is planned organizational change based on study of the behavior of individuals and organizations.

organizational development

15. The _____ of a business means that organizations cannot pretend the rest of the world does not exist.

globalization

16. _____ is created by an artificial environment that mimics real life.

virtual reality

17. The _____ describes the organization as comprised of five interacting variables that could serve as the focus of planned change in an organization.

systems model of change

18. The _____ refers to the planning process the organization engages in to determine its its goals and how best to accomplish them.

strategy variable

19. The major goal of _____ is to shorten the lead time for transforming a new idea into a product or service in the hands of the consumer.

computer-integrated manufacturing

CHAPTER 22

APPROACHES TO PLANNED ORGANIZATIONAL CHANGE

LEARNING OBJECTIVES

When you read and when you review Chapter 22, keep in mind the learning objectives which have been established by the authors. Look them over first as a guide to picking out the most important parts of the chapter, and then think about them as you are going through the chapter. When you have finished the chapter, ask yourself whether you have met the objectives.

The authors intend that when you have finished studying this chapter you should be able to:

* Discuss the importance of an accurate diagnosis of organizational problems prior to selecting an approach to organizational change.
* Identify and describe four people-focused approaches to organizational change.
* List and explain five approaches to organizational change that focus on task and technology.
* Describe structure- and strategy-focused approaches to organizational change.
* Discuss ethical issues in organizational change.

CHAPTER OUTLINE

After you have read the chapter, complete the following outline.

I.   OVERVIEW OF CHANGE APPROACHES.

    A.   Organizational diagnosis.

        1.   The key contingency in selecting an approach to organizational change is

        2.   Four basic steps in organizational diagnosis.

           a.

           b.

           c.

           d.

        3.   Factors affecting readiness for change.

           a.

           b.

           c.

           d.

           e.

        4.   Principles of change.

           a.   Facts affecting the interpretation of organizational diagnosis.

              (1)   Interacting forces:

              (2)   Symptoms:

   b.   Practical principles of organizational change.

        (1)

        (2)

        (3)

        (4)

        (5)

        (6)

        (7)

II.   PEOPLE-FOCUSED APPROACHES TO CHANGE.

   A.   Survey feedback,

        1.   Components of survey feedback,

             a.

             b.

             c.

        2.   Alternative methods for feeding back data.

             a.

             b.

             c.

        3.   A major strength of survey feedback is

   B.   Team building is

        1.   Team building actions.

             a.

b.

c.

2. Steps in the team building cycle.

a.

b.

c.

d.

e.

f.

C. Process consultation is

1. Process events are

2. Process consultation programs typically focus on

a.

b.

c.

d.

e.

D. Quality-of-work-life programs are

1. QWL programs focus on conditions such as

2. Major objectives of QWL programs.

a.

b.

3. Examples of QWL components.

    a. Flextime:

    b. Alternative work schedules:

4. Give examples of possible negative outcomes of QWL programs.

III. TASK- AND TECHNOLOGY-FOCUSED APPROACHES TO CHANGE.

A. Job design.

    1. How can it be used to bring about change?

B. Sociotechnical systems.

    1. How can it be used to bring about change?

        a. Autonomous work groups are

C. Quality circles.

    1. How can it be used to bring about change?

D. Characteristics of high performance-high commitment work systems.

1.

2.

3.

4.

5.

E. Continuous improvement programs.

1. Underlying forces.

IV. STRUCTURE- AND STRATEGY-FOCUSED APPROACHES TO CHANGE.

A. Adaptive structures.

1. Collateral organization:

a. Characteristics of a collateral organization.

(1)

(2)

(3)

(4)

(5)

b. Advantages of collateral organization.

(1)

(2)

2. Matrix organization:

    a. Purpose of a matrix organization:

3. Network organization:

    a. How is a network organization different than a collateral or a matrix organization?

B. Strategic change:

1. Open systems planning is

    a. Steps in open systems planning.

        (1)

        (2)

        (3)

        (4)

        (5)

        (6)

2. Visioning is

V. ETHICAL ISSUES IN ORGANIZATIONAL CHANGE.

A. Major areas of ethical issues are

    1.

    2.

3.

4.

DIRECTED QUESTIONS

I.   Overview of Change Approaches.

1.   Which of the following change approaches is
     primarily a task and technology focus:
     a)   Quality of work life;
     b)   Matrix organization;   c
     c)   Quality circles;
     d)   All of the above;
     e)   None of the above.
2.   Which of the following change approaches is
     primarily a people focus:
     a)   Quality of work life;
     b)   Quality circles;   a
     c)   Sociotechnical systems;
     d)   All of the above;
     e)   None of the above.
3.   Which of the following change approaches does not
     have a structure focus:
     a)   Sociotechnical systems;
     b)   Matrix organization;   a
     c)   Strategic change;
     d)   All of the above;
     e)   None of the above.
4.   Which of the following change approaches is
     considered to have the highest direct impact
     on the structure of a system:
     a)   Process consultation;
     b)   Sociotechnical systems;   d
     c)   Job design;
     d)   Collateral organization.
5.   Which of the following change approaches is
     considered to have the highest direct impact
     on the tasks of a system:
     a)   Process consultation;
     b)   Sociotechnical systems;   c
     c)   Job design;
     d) Collateral organization.
6.   Which of the following change approaches is
     considered to have the least direct impact
     on the people within a system:

a)   Survey feedback;
b)   Quality circles;
c)   Sociotechnical systems;
d)   Quality of work life.

b

7.   Which of the following is the key contingency
     that influences the choice of approach(es)
     to be used:
     a)   The nature of the organization;
     b)   The nature of the problem the organization
          is trying to solve;
     c)   The nature of the individual making the
          decision;
     d)   None of the above.

b

8.   The basic issues that must be addressed in
     organizational diagnosis include:
     a)   Recognition and interpretation of the
          problem and assessment of the need for
          change;
     b)   Determination of the organization's
          readiness and capability for change;
     c)   Identification of managers' and employees'
          resources and motivations for change;
     d)   All of the above;
     e)   None of the above.

d

9.   Employee expectations regarding change:
     a)   Is a critical variable with regard to
          individual readiness for change;
     b)   Are typically unrealistically high;
     c)   Are typically unrealistically low;
     d)   Are acceptable regardless of whether they
          are positive or negative, so long as they
          are realistic.

a

10. Which of the following is not accurate
     regarding organizational diagnosis:
     a)   Organizational behavior is the product of
          many interacting forces;
     b)   All organizational information gathered
          during a diagnosis will represent causes
          rather than symptoms of problems;
     c)   That which is observed or diagnosed may have
          multiple causes;
     d)   What is observed or diagnosed will largely
          be employee behaviors, problems, and the
          current state of the organization.

b

11. A high level of satisfaction with the current
     situation and a low perceived personal risk from
     change would create which state of readiness to
     change:
     a)   High readiness;
     b)   Moderate to indeterminant readiness;

b

c) Low readiness;
d) None of the above.

12. A low level of satisfaction with the current situation and high perceived personal risk from change would create which state of readiness to change:
    a) High readiness;
    b) Moderate to indeterminant readiness;
    c) Low readiness;
    d) None of the above.

b

13. Which of the following is <u>not</u> one of the practical principles of organizational change?
    a) You must not change more than one element of a system at one time;
    b) Change always generates some stress;
    c) People resist anything they feel is punishment;
    d) Participation reduces resistance to change.

a

II. People-Focused Approaches to Change.

1. Which of the following statements is accurate with regard to survey-feedback:
    a) It is one of the least frequently used organizational change approaches;
    b) Its primary objective is to introduce specific changes in an organization;
    c) Its primary objective is to improve relationships;
    d) It is used as an action tool rather than as a diagnostic tool.

c

2. Questions about which of the following are typically included in a survey feedback questionnaire:
    a) Communication processes;
    b) Motivational incentives;
    c) Decision-making practices;
    d) All of the above;
    e) None of the above.

d

3. Which of the following is <u>not</u> one of the basic timing methods for feedback in the survey feedback approach:
    a) Simultaneous;
    b) Waterfall;
    c) Lateral;
    d) Bottom-up.

c

4. Survey feedback:
    a) Emphasizes future changes in organizational structures;

b) Usually brings about fundamental changes in structures, task designs, technology or strategy;
c) Identifies problems and clarifies issues;
d) All of the above.

c

5. The survey feedback approach:
   a) Relies on changing the organization's structure;
   b) Usually brings about fundamental changes in task design;
   c) Typically results in changes in the technology of the organization;
   d) All of the above;
   e) None of the above.

e

6. The basic purposes of team building include:
   a) Improving the effectiveness of individual effort;
   b) Resolving problems without having to first gather data;
   c) Examining relationships among the people doing the work;
   d) All of the above.

c

7. The action-research sequence in team building includes:
   a) Perception of problem;
   b) Data sharing;
   c) Diagnosis and action planning;
   d) All of the above.

c

8. Conditions necessary for the success of team building include:
   a) Independence between the group members;
   b) Team goals must be the goals set by higher management;
   c) Problem solving activities must be closely related to interpersonal issues;
   d) All of the above;
   e) None of the above.

e

9. Team building has been <u>least</u> clearly linked to changes in:
   a) Productivity gains;
   b) Problem solving skills;
   c) Group decision-making skills;
   d) Organizational climate.

a

10. Team building:
    a) Has been found to be an effective way to involve employees in an organizational change program;
    b) Assumes that employee involvement is helpful, though not necessary;

a

    c) Has been found to have a strong direct impact on performance;

    d) All of the above.

11. Which of the following is <u>not</u> a process event in the process consultation approach:

    a) Behaviors of people at meetings;

    b) Encounters among employees at work;   c

    c) Facilitative activity by a skilled third party;

    d) None of the above.

12. Process consultation is:

    a) A much more clear-cut specific set of activities than are included in team building or survey feedback;

    b) The human actions which occur within groups   c
to perform work;

    c) To help individuals or groups examine the process by which they are working toward task accomplishment;

    d) A skilled third party consultant or facilitator.

13. Typical areas of concern in process consultation include:

    a) Conflict resolution;

    b) Ways in which employees take on different roles in groups and organizations;   d

    c) Group understanding of leadership styles;

    d) All of the above.

14. QWL programs:

    a) Have more precise definition and focus than survey feedback and team building;

    b) Are solely for the purpose of improving group   e
or organizational productivity;

    c) Are primarily centered around production problems;

    d) All of the above;

    e) b and c.

15. For which of the following changes is the direct linkage with QWL programs <u>least</u> clear:

    a) Employee work attitudes;

    b) Employee involvement in group matters;

    c) Organizational culture;   d

    d) Productivity.

III. Task- and Technology-Focused Approaches to Change.

1. The task-focused approach to change emphasizes:

    a) Changes in individuals' or groups' activities;   a

    b) Changes in the tools used to perform the work;

    c) Both of the above;

    d) None of the above.

2. Which of the following is <u>not</u> a job design
    method of change:
    a) Job engineering;
    b) Job rotation;
    c) Job enlargement;   d
    d) Job analysis.
3. Job design techniques:
    a) Work best if they are used alone, so that
        their effects can be isolated;
    b) Work best in the context of a comprehensive   b
        organizational change program;
    c) Are based on the assumption that all employees
        want enriched work;
    d) None of the above.
4. The sociotechnical systems approach to change:
    a) Regards the organization as a technical system;
    b) Usually includes a major redesign of the way
        work is done;
    c) Focuses first on the social system and then on   b
        the technical system;
    d) Focuses first on the technical system and then
        on the social system.
5. Autonomous groups:
    a) Are part of the job design approach to change;
    b) Redesign work tasks to allow greater autonomy;
    c) Require additional management because of their   d
        relative independence;
    d) Tend to be self-managing.
6. With regard to the effectiveness of the
    sociotechnical systems approach to change:
    a) The linkage to performance is not clear;
    b) Relative to other approaches, it appears to   e
        have less impact on performance;
    c) Tends to lower worker satisfaction because of
        the isolation of the autonomous work groups;
    d) All of the above;
    e) None of the above.
7. Quality circles:
    a) Are examples of autonomous work groups;
    b) Deal with employee development and inter-
        personal problems rather than production
        problems;   d
    c) Have a wider focus than other change
        approaches;
    d) Allows management to retain more control
        over the activities of the participants than
        in other approaches.
8. Evaluations of quality circles:
    a) Are built in to each quality circle design;
    b) Have usually indicated success;   b

   c)   Have usually indicated failure;
   d)   None of the above.
9. High performance/high commitment work systems are
    designed to foster a work culture and structure
    having which of the following characteristics:
    a)   Highly centralized decision making;
    b)   Strict retention of functional and/or
         departmental boundaries;
    c)   The technology controls the organization;
    d)   Empowerment.

         d

10. Continuous improvement programs are:
    a)   Total quality control;
    b)   Total quality management;
    c)   "Quick-fix" solutions;
    d)   a and b;
    e)   b and c.

         d

IV. Structure-and Strategy-Focused Approaches to Change.

1. Which of the following elements is often included
    in structural approaches to change:
    a)   Rules;
    b)   Budgets;
    c)   Selection criteria;
    d)   All of the above;
    e)   None of the above.

         d

2. Matrix organizations:
    a)   Are relatively easy to manage;
    b)   Are relatively inexpensive to implement and
         maintain;
    c)   Are particularly appropriate in the face of
         complex technology and rapid change;
    d)   All of the above.

         c

3. Which of the following is true concerning the
    selection and implementation of a matrix
    structure:
    a)   They are best when the emphasis is on
         independent rather than collaborative
         behavior;
    b)   Group effectiveness is not a primary concern;
    c)   A high degree of cooperation between projects
         or functions is needed;
    d)   None of the above.

         c

4. Collateral organizations have which of the
    following characteristics:
    a)   Managers are restricted to use of their
         formal subordinates;
    b)   Information exchange is relatively slow and
         cumbersome;

         c

     c) All communication channels are open and
       connected;
     d) All of the above.
5. A collateral organization:
     a) Utilizes people outside the normal commun-
       ication and authority channels;   d
     b) Has different norms than the rest of the
       organization;
     c) Is linked to the formal organization and
       coexists with it;
     d) All of the above.
6. Evaluations of the collateral organization
   approach indicate that:
     a) They give managers way to match up problems
       with structures;   a
     b) Improvements stemming from them have been
       well-documented;
     c) They deal best with routine problems;
     d) None of the above.
7. Collateral organizations are believed to be
   particularly good at:
     a) Developing managerial skills;
     b) Fostering organizational innovation;   d
     c) Coping with crises requiring decentralized
       decision-making;
     d) All of the above;
     e) None of the above.
8. Which of the following approaches to change
   involves a re-examination of the organization's
   basic goals as well as the specific plans
   for attaining those goals:
     a) Strategy-focused approaches to change;
     b) Structure-focused approaches to change;   a
     c) Matrix organization approach to change;
     d) Open systems planning.
9. Open systems planning is:
     a) Choosing a desired future state for the
       organization;
     b) Using a parallel organization to supplement
       the existing formal organization;
     c) The blending of technology and teamwork;   d
     d) Designed to help an organization system-
       atically assess its environment and
       develop a strategic response to it.

V. Ethical Issues in Organizational Change.

   1. In which of the following areas may ethical
      issues exist:

 a)   Change approach selection;
 b)   Change target selection;
 c)   Management responsibilities;   d
 d)   All of the above;
 e)   None of the above.
2.   An example of an ethical issue in the area of
 change is:
 a)   The question of whose vision guides a change;
 b)   The degree of openness surrounding a change;
 c)   The question of which behavior will need to
 be changed;
 d)   The selection of a method for making the   e
 change;
 e)   All of the above.

APPLIED QUESTIONS

I.   Overview of Change Approaches.

 1.   A firm is experiencing some organizational problems
 due to the automation of some of the production areas.
 Which of the following change approaches would seem
 most appropriate to adopt to deal with this:
 a)   Survey feedback;   d
 b)   Team building;
 c)   Matrix organization;
 d)   Quality circles.
 2.   It has been determined that the complexity and role
 of the rapid change in the technology with which
 this organization is forced makes it impossible to
 have efficient communication under the many-layered,
 centralized reporting relationships that exist now.
 Which of the following change approaches would seem
 most appropriate to adapt to deal with this:
 a)   Collateral organization;   a
 b)   Job design;
 c)   QWL;
 d)   Process consultation.
 3.   A major concern exists within an organization
 regarding the need to make some changes in how a job
 is done. Which of the following change approaches
 would seem most appropriate to adopt to deal with
 this:
 a)   Process consultation;   b
 b)   Quality circles;
 c)   Matrix organization;
 d)   QWL.

4. In interviewing a firm's middle management staff
    prior to designing a process consultation activity,
    an outside consultant learns that these employees do
    not believe that any real changes will actually
    occur, regardless of how well the activity goes.
    What needs to be done:
    a) Abandon the idea of change for the time being;   c
    b) Select a different change approach;
    c) Organizational diagnosis;
    d) None of the above.

5. An organization has a bad morale problem among its
    workers. Management has tried the survey feedback
    approach, the team building approach, and a QWL
    program. Morale has not improved. Which of the
    following may be the problem:
    a) These methods are not appropriate to deal   c
        with people problems;
    b) Change goals have been improperly set;
    c) Inadequate recognition and interpretation
        of the problem;
    d) None of the above.

6. The employees are fed up with current working
    conditions, but have responded coolly to the union's
    attempts to get them to join. They believe that
    even if they could get the union on, the company
    would still be able to "get them" for having
    brought in a union. Their readiness to change is:
    a) High;   b
    b) Moderate to undetermined;
    c) Low;
    d) Can't tell from this information.

II. People-Focused Approaches to Change.

1. Which of the following conditions is <u>not</u>
    consistent with the use of survey feedback:
    a) Management wants to transmit as well as
        receive information;
    b) Management is primarily interested in   b
        changing the organizational structure;
    c) Management wants to start change from the
        top down;
    d) Management wants to start change from the
        bottom up.

2. Management has the following goals in mind for a
    survey feedback approach being considered. Which
    is consistent with that approach:
    a) The belief is that management's behavior is
        appropriate but that the behavior of
        subordinates needs to be modified;   b

b) Management wants changes to occur within the existing organizational structure;

c) The intent is to swing the balance of influence away from the subordinates and toward the supervisors;

d) All of the above.

3. Which of the following conditions is <u>not</u> consistent with the use of team building as an approach to change:

a) The new design people and the marketing people must work closely together;

b) The major concern is to solve problems directly related to the group's primary tasks;   c

c) The team building must identify a way to deal with the fact that the group is basically powerless to make changes on its own;

d) None (i.e., all <u>are</u> consistent with the use of team building).

4. Which of the following problems is team building most likely to be able to deal with successfully:

a) Statistics for the last quarter indicate that productivity is down by 1.3%;

b) There has been a corporate re-organization and   b the new management board has not yet begun to work well together in problem solving situations;

c) The average performance appraisal score for employees has dropped nearly a full point in the last fiscal year;

d) All are problems that team building is designed to address.

5. Which of the following problems is process consultation most likely to be able to deal with successfully:

a) Statistics for the last quarter indicate that productivity is down by 1.3%;

b) There has been a corporate re-organization and the new management board has not yet begun to   b work well together in problem solving situations;

c) The average performance appraisal score for employees has dropped nearly a full point in the last fiscal year;

d) All are problems that process consultation is designed to address.

6. Which of the following problems are QWL programs likely to be able to deal with successfully:

a) Turnover has increased greatly over the last two quarters;

b)   Both workers and managements have become   d
      concerned about the health and safety
      conditions and practices at the plant;
c)   The latest report shows that the group's
      productivity has dropped by 1.3%;
d)   All are problems upon which the concept of
      QWL programs focuses.

III. Task- and Technology-Focused Approaches to Change.

1.   Which of the following problems is the job design
     approach intended to address:
     a)   The specific technical requirements of
          carrying out the job appear to need change;
     b)   Workers want to be able to do a wider variety
          of things;   d
     c)   Workers want work with greater challenge;
     d)   All are problems which job design is intended
          to address.

2.   Which of the following problems is the socio-
     technical systems approach intended to address:
     a)   The department is getting a new group of
          computers, which has the work force upset about
          potential loss of status and loss of jobs;
     b)   Regional offices need to better understand the
          new computerized operations and to be able to   d
          adapt them to local conditions without lengthy
          delays from corporate headquarters;
     c)   Workers feel that they have no say-so in
          their jobs and as a result turnover rates have
          increased dramatically over the past 4 years;
     d)   All are problems upon which the sociotechnical
          systems approach is intended to focus.

3.   Which of the following concerns is the quality
     circle approach intended to address:
     a)   Employees are apathetic about preparing
          themselves for improved performance and
          progress within the company;
     b)   Rates of defective products have increased   d
          over the past year;
     c)   Upper management has identified 2 major
          problems on which to focus;
     d)   All are concerns upon which quality circles
          are intended to focus.

4.   An organization is in the process of changing its
     manufacturing facility to a state-of-the-art
     advanced technology unit. It hopes to make the
     new system effective through teamwork, delegation,
     and a shared sense of purpose. This would be:

     a) A high performance/high commitment system;
     b) A quality circle;
     c) A sociotechnical system;   a
     d) Process consultation.

5. Which of the following is a true statement with regard to Continuous Improvement Programs?
     a) They work best for the short run issues;
     b) They are the same thing as quality circles;   c
     c) They focus on quality;
     d) All of the above.

IV. Structure- and Strategy-Focused Approaches to Change.

1. An organization has entered into the dynamic hi-tech industry group as a result of one recent acquisition and a merger. One result that may accompany these events is:
     a) A matrix form of organization may be called for;   a
     b) A more mechanistic form of organization may be called for;
     c) A collateral form of organization may be called for.

2. A strategic planning committee comprised of top level managers in a variety of functional areas within an organization is an example of:
     a) A matrix organization;   c
     b) A mechanistic organization;
     c) A collateral organization.

3. A crisis involving the number of grievances in the clerical operations at an organization's offices across the country was developed. A permanent committee consisting of office managers and labor relations specialists from each major location has been formed. That committee is an example of:
     a) A matrix organization;   c
     b) A mechanistic organization;
     c) A collateral organization.

4. The Board of Directors of an organization experiencing some decline decides to hold a retreat for its top management to discuss whether the primary mission of the organization still makes sense in today's market. This is:
     a) Strategy-focused approach to change;
     b) Structure-focused approach to change;   a
     c) Matrix organization approach to change;
     d) Open systems planning.

5. A business school considers whether it should change from a strictly undergraduate institution to one that also offers graduate degrees. One process that is involved in the deliberation is:

a)   Team building;
b)   Visioning;
c)   Process consultation;   **b**
d)   Sociotechnical systems.

V.   Ethical Issues in Organizational Change.

1.   The organization plans to make a two-phase change, but to get employees' cooperation in Phase I it does not tell them about the second phase that is coming. The ethical issue here is:
a)   Change approach selection;
b)   Change target selection;
c)   Managerial responsibilities;   **d**
d)   Manipulation.

PROGRAMMED STUDY SUPPLEMENT

1.	Work groups that are self-managing are called _____.	autonomous groups
2.	_____ is an organizational change process whereby members of a work group diagnose how they work together and plan changes that will improve their effectiveness.	team building
3.	A _____ is a parallel, co-existing organization that a management can use to supplement the existing formal organization.	collateral organiza-tion
4.	_____ is an organizational change process consisting of data gathering, data organiza-tion, and communication of those data to the people who provided the data.	survey feedback
5.	_____ is a typical component in QWL programs and gives employees some control over their own work schedules.	flextime

6. An approach that restructures the way work is performed in order to improve performance is known as _____ .

    job design

---

7. An approach that focuses simultaneously on social and technical variables is the _____ approach.

    sociotechnical system

---

8. An approach used when an organization grows more complex and requires a more flexible adaptive organizational structure is the _____ .

    matrix organization

---

9. _____ must be done well because of the great importance of proper identification of the nature of the problem the organization is trying to solve.

    organizational diagnosis

---

10. _____ consist of activities undertaken to improve conditions affecting an employee's experience with an organization.

    QWL programs

---

11. _____ is guidance provided by a third party to help members of an organization perceive, understand, and act on certain events (such as communication, leadership, etc.) that occur in their work environment.

    process consultation

---

12. Small, semi-autonomous groups that meet to solve and monitor job-related production problems are called _____ .

    quality circles

---

13. The blending of technology and teamwork creates a _____ .

    high performance/ high commitment work system

---

14. _____ is designed to help an organization systematically assess its environment and develop a strategic response to it.

    open systems planning

15. _____ is planned organizational change designed to alter the organization's intended courses of action to attain their goals.

strategic change

---

16. Choosing a desired future state or condition for the organization is called _____.

visioning

---

17. Part-time employment, job-sharing, and work at home are examples of _____.

alternative work schedules

---

18. _____ is another name for autonomous work groups.

self-managing teams

---

19. _____ are based on the philosophy that one-time programs and "quick-fix" solutions are not in the best interest of an organization.

continuous improvement programs

---

20. _____ share some features of matrix and collateral organizations but emphasize sophisticated information technologies.

network organization